Born in 1941, Paddy Ashdown served in the Royal
Marines from 1959–1972, including with the Com-
mandos and the Special Boat Service. After a period in
the Diplomatic Service, he entered politics representing
Yeovil as a Liberal Democrat Member of Parliament.
After his time as Leader of the Liberal Democrats,
he was Knighted and then raised to the peerage as
Lord Ashdown of Norton-sub-Hamdon. From May
2002–January 2006, Lord Ashdown was the High Rep-
resentative for Bosnia and Herzegovina. In recognition
of his service he was awarded the highest Diplomatic
Service honour, the GCMG, by HM The Queen in 2006.
Swords and Ploughshares was shortlisted for the 2007
RUSI Medal for Military Literature and the 2008 British
Army Military Book of the Year Award.

Swords and Ploughshares

Bringing Peace to the 21st Century

PADDY ASHDOWN

PHOENIX

A PHOENIX PAPERBACK

First published in Great Britain in 2007
by Weidenfeld & Nicolson
This paperback edition published in 2008
by Phoenix,
an imprint of Orion Books Ltd,
Orion House, 5 Upper St Martin's Lane,
London WC2H 9EA

An Hachette Livre UK company

1 3 5 7 9 10 8 6 4 2

Copyright © Paddy & Jane Ashdown Partnership 2007

The right of Paddy Ashdown to be identified as the author
of this work has been asserted by him in accordance with
the Copyright, Designs and Patents Act 1988.

A CIP catalogue record for this book
is available from the British Library.

ISBN: 978-0-7538-2331-6

Typeset at The Spartan Press Ltd,
Lymington, Hants

Printed in Great Britain by Clays Ltd,
St Ives plc

The Orion Publishing Group's policy is to use papers
that are natural, renewable and recyclable products and
made from wood grown in sustainable forests. The logging
and manufacturing processes are expected to conform to
the environmental regulations of the country of origin.

www.orionbooks.co.uk

To Ahmet Sitkić and millions like him,
who have paid the price for our mistakes

Contents

Acknowledgements

I emerged blinking from the trenches of the Office of the High Representative (OHR) in Bosnia and Herzegovina at the end of my mandate on 31 January 2006. The first thing I did was to take two wonderful weeks skiing with my children and grandchildren. And the second was to start to write this book. I quickly realised how little I knew and how much I had to learn if I was to write something which would make sense beyond the borders of Bosnia. Finding out what worked elsewhere, listening to others' experiences and reviewing and ordering my own, completely reshaped the way I have come to look at this whole area and contributed to many of the ideas which lie at the heart of this book, most of which I either did not know, or did not realise I knew when I started.

None of this would have happened without the assistance of many people, some of whom were complete strangers when I started, but all of whom have given unstintingly and generously of their views and suggestions. Without them this book could never have been completed.

I am especially grateful to the team in my office (the OHR) in Sarajevo: Julian Astle, Julian Braithwaite, Gisbert Bruns, Lawrence (Larry) Butler, Catherine Colloms, Edouard D'Aoust, Don Hays, Helene Holme Pedersen, Daniel Korski, Edward Llewellyn, Ian Patrick, Archie Tuta, Mark Wheeler and Susan Wright. I am also indebted to Mathew Rycroft, Britain's outstanding ambassador to Bosnia and Herzegovina, who was a constant source of wise advice during my mandate and gave me much practical help in writing this book (though he is in no way responsible for its contents).

I have also had most generous help from a number of academics chiefly but not exclusively connected with St Anthony's College, Oxford. These have included Richard Caplin, Toby Dodge, Kalypso

Nicolaides, Anke Hoeffler, Dominik Zaum, Adam Roberts and Timothy Radcliffe.

Then there has been a wide range of people who have been kind enough to look at the text and provide their corrections and suggestions. These have included Jim Dobbins, who masterminded the seminal Rand publications on post-Second World War interventions from which I have drawn inspiration and borrowed facts in equal measure; my wife Jane; my next door neighbours, Steph Bailey and Steve Radley; some old friends such as Robert Cooper, Helen Dahrendorf, Miranda Green, Harriett Hentges, Emyr Jones Parry, Richard Holme, Jo Ingram, Greg Jefferies, Margaret Karns, Carol Ross, Dan Serwer, Rupert Smith and some I have never met before, such as Sir Roderick Braithwaite, William Patey and Dr Sarah Percy.

Adele Brown, who works in the House of Commons, deserves a very special mention for she not only patiently put up with my ignorance on legal matters, but also contributed directly and heftily to Chapter 3 on international law.

My wonderful assistant Sarah Frapple once again showed the patience of angels in much of the typing and all of the cataloguing and storing of my diaries, as well as an uncanny ability in finding bits in them when I needed them. My thanks also to Deana Brynildsen who typed and looked after my diaries in Sarajevo and to Daisy Leitch for her encouragement and help with crucial research in the early stages of this book.

Finally I want to thank Michael Sissons, Jim Daly and Fiona Petheram of PFD, my literary agents, for their confidence, patience and advice to me in the tortuous process of preparing the book, and to Ian Drury of Orion and Barry Holmes for their help with the editing.

Needless to say, although all of these and more have contributed immeasurably to make this book possible in its present form, any mistakes, errors or infelicities are mine and mine alone.

Preface

Nine-tenths of tactics are certain and taught in the books; but, the irrational tenth is like the kingfisher flashing across the pool. This is the test of generals. Success can only be ensured by instinct sharpened by thought. At the crisis, it is as natural as a reflex.   T. E. LAWRENCE, *The Evolution of a Revolt*

This book is not 'teach yourself state-building'. You cannot stabilise the last peace, any more than you can fight the last war. It may be possible to win our modern short sharp digital conflicts in days and by numbers. But constructing the peace that follows cannot be done by formula or according to some rigid template. Nor can it be done by slavishly following what you did elsewhere. Each country is different. What worked in the nine peace stabilisation missions will fail in the tenth.

Building – or sometimes even more difficult, rebuilding – a state is a deeply complex enterprise with an infinite number of variables which should be viewed, in the words of Francis Fukuyama, as *'more of an art than a science'.*[1] It requires the application of intelligence, a high degree of political skill, vast resources and a sustained political will on the part of those who attempt it. It is not for the faint-hearted or the easily distracted. And the best that can be achieved is most probably only partial success. State-building with the aim of recreating your own, in a foreign place, will nearly always end in failure, or frustration, or a broken heart – and most often all three. Immanuel Kant said, *'out of the crooked timber of humanity, no straight thing can ever be made.'* For states, being made up of quarrelling humanity, this is especially true. The task therefore is not to seek perfection, but to achieve the most acceptable form of imperfection possible and then hand over to the people of the state to complete the process of building the nation they want, rather than the one you dreamt of for them. So this book is not intended as an encyclopaedia of actions whose implementation will guarantee success, but rather as a practitioner's compendium of things that may work because they have worked in the past and others that may fail because they have led to failure in the past; with a few more prescriptive suggestions thrown in at the end.

Real life is never as clear cut as it is when described on the pages of a book – and this work is no exception to that rule. If, in making some of the proposals here, I have strayed into making recommendations of perfection which will only apply when conditions are optimal, it is simply because there is no other way to describe what we should be aiming for. But I realise that conditions are never optimal and the options are never perfect. In peacemaking, as in so much else, the important thing is to make the right trade-offs between what is best and what is possible. In the end it is the judgement of the person on the ground that matters and nothing in this book is intended to distract from that central imperative. I have tried, as far as possible, to relate issues to on the ground experience, drawn from a wide range of peacemaking and peacekeeping missions. Inevitably, given my personal history these frequently come from my time in Bosnia and Herzegovina.[*] I apologise in advance for the large number of Bosnian examples. But it is, I suppose, inevitable that a practitioner's guide will depend heavily on the personal experience of the practitioner who wrote it.

The book is organised in three self-standing parts. Part I, 'The story so far' provides a broad overview of the theory and practise of peacemaking and state-building as it has developed since the Second World War. It includes a summary of recent developments in the field of international law in this area and a brief outline review of fifteen international interventions, ten under UN leadership and five under international community leadership (chiefly by the United States). Part II, 'Post-conflict reconstruction', discusses how our

---

[*] I have referred to Bosnia and Herzegovina throughout this book by its shorthand term 'Bosnia'. Similarly, although Bosnian Muslims are often referred to these days as 'Bosniaks' to distinguish them from Croats and Serbs, the term 'Bosniak' originally means simply someone, of whatever ethnic origin, who comes from Bosnia. I have therefore referred to Bosnian Muslims with their full title rather than as 'Bosniaks'.

current practice of peacemaking could be improved, and includes an analysis in detail of the two phases of post-conflict reconstruction: stabilisation and state-building. Part III 'How can we do it better?' describes in detail what we have to do to avoid burning our fingers so frequently. A word of warning here. In order to divide this subject into manageable chunks, I have chosen to arrange the various component pieces of peacemaking and peacekeeping into 'phases', both before and after post-conflict reconstruction has started. But the essence of successful peacemaking and reconstruction is that it is not a linear exercise which advances logically and in an orderly fashion from one phase to the next. It is rather a holistic process in which the phases overlap messily and progress almost always has to be made across a number of fronts at the same time.

Similarly, in the final chapter, where I look at the new structures and practices being developed and make some proposals as to how these could be strengthened, I have, again for presentational purposes, described the actions and inputs of individual nations. It is important to realise, however, that successful peacemaking and keeping is a multilateral, rather than unilateral activity. What individual nations do in this field is important. But it is their ability or otherwise to work together which is critical.

Since this is a book based on practice, I have included in Appendix B, for those who wish to know what actually happens on the ground, a personal narrative drawn from my own diaries, describing in detail a one-year slice of the decade-long project to rebuild the state of Bosnia and Herzegovina.

Introduction

Helping to make peace and rebuild states seems to have been the leitmotif of my life. In 1960, as a nineteen-year-old officer in the Royal Marines, I was deployed with my unit, 42 Commando, to Kenya to prevent the spread of instability from the Congo. A year afterwards, in 1961, we found ourselves in scorching July heat on the Mutla Ridge above Kuwait city, almost exactly where, thirty years later, the terrible 'turkey shoot' took place as US aircraft destroyed the last remnants of the Iraqi army fleeing Kuwait. In 1961, our 500 Royal Marines were supposed to dissuade the then Iraqi dictator, Abdul Qassim, from launching four armoured divisions into Kuwait. Mercifully it worked.

Borneo

But these had been mere dress rehearsals. Practical peacekeeping began in earnest for me on a Singapore beach, on the balmy night of 8 December 1962. It was the early hours of the morning and my wife, Jane and I – married only eight months – were energetically enjoying a pre-Christmas party. Suddenly, the music stopped and there was a brief announcement that rebels had earlier that day captured the little oil-rich country of Brunei and taken British hostages. We were ordered to return immediately, draw live ammunition and be ready to fly out at dawn to recapture Brunei City, the capital. Two hours later, I kissed my wife goodbye and an hour after that, along with the sixty Marines in my Troop, was bumping across the South China Sea in a Hastings aircraft. We nursed our rifles between our knees, a strong sense of apprehension about the action ahead and, in most cases (including mine), a rather nasty hangover. Next to me was a cadaverous and uncomfortable looking figure in a lounge suit, carrying a briefcase. He looked completely out of place among sixty sweating Marines. To while away the ninety-minute journey to our forward base on the island of Labuan in Brunei bay, I tried to wheedle out of him who he was and what he was doing there. He gave me nothing.

When we arrived at Labuan airfield we were met on the tarmac by the coffins of six Gurkhas killed the night before. They were loaded on to our aircraft for the journey back to Singapore. At the sight of these, my taciturn flying companion leapt magically to life, declaring in a loud voice that he was from the Commonwealth War Graves Commission and promptly taking charge. All this, as you may imagine, did little to raise morale among my fellow Marines going into battle for the first time. It remains a mystery to me why someone, somewhere decided that this ghoulish creature should go in with the first wave of assault troops on what turned out to be quite a nasty little engagement to retake Brunei City that night.

The following day the Commando carried out two simultaneous dawn assaults – one airborne and one by sea. The airborne one, in which I took part, was on the little town and port of Lawas, and was happily unopposed, the rebels having fled. We were able to 'rescue' the British hostages and restore order without difficulty. One of the hostages turned out to be a young medic from the United States Peace Corps, who had distinguished himself by tipping every one of the sharpened bamboo stakes (or *panjis*) protecting the British District Officer's house, in which the internationals were holed up, with a lethal dose of strychnine. Our colleagues in the seaborne assault on the neighbouring town of Limbang were not so lucky. In this attack, five of my fellow Marines were killed and five wounded. So began the jungle war between Britain and Indonesia, known as 'Confrontation', which dominated the next four years of my life.

My first task after driving the rebels out was to try to find their leader, Yassin Effendi. We chased him through the mangrove swamps of Brunei bay for three months – but never caught him. Forty-five years later, hunting Radovan Karadžić in Bosnia, I was to learn again how difficult it is to catch a single person moving in difficult country among a population who still regard him as a hero. My next task was to command a border outpost known as Stass, five hours' tough walk from the nearest road head. With thirty men, my mission was to dominate and patrol about 200 square miles of mountainous jungle, control the border crossing with Indonesia and fight any insurgents who tried to come across. I ran my own intelligence operations, trained up my own small local guerrilla army and oversaw, in as much as it was possible, the civilian administration of the area. Later, when, in high secrecy, our political masters in Britain gave us the go-ahead, we crossed over the border into Indonesia and actively took the fight to our enemy. Later still, in command of a special forces unit, No 2 Special Boat Section, we developed new techniques for infiltrating enemy territory from a submerged submarine, carrying out our operations and then swimming back out to sea to rendezvous with the submarine – still submerged – several nights later. 'Confrontation' ended before we were able to put these particular techniques into practice – but I got to understand the high importance of special forces operations in this kind of conflict.

I learnt many other lessons in this period, too. The importance of clear political direction from the top – in this case from Denis Healey, the then Labour Defence Minister, who I later joined in the House of Commons and who I have admired ever since. The importance of knowing the language (I was the only person in the whole Commando Brigade, at the start, who could speak Malay and, later, the local dialect, Dyak). The fact that soldiers in this situation do not win the peace – they simply hold the ring while a political solution is found. But soldiers can wreck the peace, if they behave in ways that lose either local or international political support. I had a very early lesson in this. The local Borneo people among whom we lived, Dyaks and Ibans, and on whom we depended for our safety and our ability to win in the jungle, had been until recently – probably still were in many cases – headhunters. This was daily evident to us in the collections of shrunken human heads on the rafters of the long houses in which we lived. In the early days of our operation I made much use of local irregulars to help us dominate the huge tract of jungle under my command. After their first successful engagement my happy irregulars, flushed with victory, returned to our base and proudly rolled out for my inspection four human heads taken from the dead bodies of their enemy. They were much offended when I told them that whatever their customs and however much they wanted new trophies for their longhouses, in the twentieth century taking other people's heads was wrong. They protested that, if they couldn't take heads, how were they to prove to me how successful they had been in battle? I seem to remember that we settled in the end on a right ear from every body as sufficient proof. It seemed a reasonable compromise at the time. But I doubt if this distinction would have saved me from scandalised opprobrium if today's saturation media coverage had been focused on our operations then.

I also learnt, crucially, that in order to win this kind of war you have to have local opinion with you. In retrospect, I think we won our little war probably as much because we brought modern medicine to the isolated, cut off mountain villages we operated in, as we did because we defeated our enemy from a military point of view.

Northern Ireland

After Borneo, came Belfast (with a three-year interregnum, learning Chinese). This was my home city and a very different kind of jungle. But the lessons remained the same. As a young Northern Irish boy of mixed Catholic/Protestant parentage, walking the streets of Belfast I had known that the troubles were coming. The denial of rights to the Catholic minority in Northern Ireland made that a certainty. The problem, in other words, was a political not a military one. The military could not solve it: they could, once again, only hold the ring, waiting for a political solution. Only now, thirty-six years later, are we perhaps seeing the gradual emergence of a lasting political solution to end Northern Ireland's long and bloody misery. I suspect history will say that in the first twenty-five years of our engagement in Northern Ireland we did no more than contain the problem, waiting for the ingredients of a long-term peace to emerge.

Another abiding lesson here: it takes a long time to build peace. You can fight a war quite quickly nowadays – but building the peace that follows is more often measured in decades.

Cyprus

I left the Royal Marines in 1972 and joined the Foreign Office. Two years later, as a First Secretary in the UK Mission to the UN in Geneva, I was co-opted on to British Foreign Secretary Jim Callaghan's negotiating team at the Cyprus Peace Conferences of 1974. Here I saw at first hand, peacemaking from the other end of the telescope. And learnt two key lessons. Firstly that it is vital for the international community to speak with one voice, if it is to have any hope of persuading nations to step back from conflict. I shall never forget the very close contact between Jim Callaghan and Henry Kissinger – even to the extent that Kissinger was prepared to reposition the whole US Seventh Fleet in order to persuade Greece and Turkey that America was behind what Britain was trying to do. And therein lies the second lesson. That the diplomacy of conflict prevention works best where it is reinforced by a credible military threat. Later I was to watch David Owen and Cyrus Vance constantly frustrated in their attempts to find peace in the Bosnian war, because the international community refused to back their diplomatic efforts with military options – and the Serbs knew it.

The next two conflicts I observed from a distance. During the Falklands War I was an aspiring Liberal Parliamentary candidate in Somerset. And during the first Gulf War, as the Leader of the Liberal Democrats in Britain, I was a commentator from the safety of the green benches of the House of Commons and London's television studios.

Bosnia and Herzegovina

Then came Bosnia and Herzegovina. Like all the most important things that have happened to me in my life, Bosnia came completely by accident. I was walking through the House of Commons shortly after the 1992 General Election, complaining to one of my closest advisers[1] that, for opposition politicians, the period after elections was the very worst. There was nothing to do. The Government was entitled to its honeymoon and all we could do was stand on the sidelines and wait till politics returned to normal. My friend said: 'You are fascinated by wars – why don't you go out and have a look at the latest one which has just started in ex-Yugoslavia?' At that time I couldn't have found Sarajevo on a map.

But I was bored. So it seemed a good adventure. I scrounged a lift on a special forces RAF Hercules and flew into Sarajevo in the first few weeks of the siege. Thus began a decade and a half of involvement with this remarkable little country that has now become so much part of my bloodstream. During the war I visited Bosnia and spent time in Sarajevo twice a year throughout the siege. I became convinced at the time, as did so many other ordinary citizens, that this conflict was, in some strange way, our generation's Spanish Civil War – a terrible human tragedy, a scandalous act of appeasement by our leaders in the face of aggression and a predictor of the kinds of wars we would have to learn to cope with in the future.

Kosovo

After Bosnia came Kosovo. I visited the province twice before the war. On the second visit, I was present in the Albanian villages as Milošević started to drive out the inhabitants by artillery bombardments in what the world later discovered he called 'Operation Horseshoe'. Next day I met Milošević and warned him that he could be indicted under the Geneva Convention for this gross violation of the rules of war in respect of the treatment of unarmed civilians. And three years later I was able to remind him of this conversation when I gave evidence against him at his trial in the Hague in 2002.

Later in the Kosovo campaign, after the bombing started, I visited the refugee camps in Albania and Macedonia and met General Jackson, the British commander of KFOR – the NATO ground force designated for Kosovo – as he was planning his invasion. In my report to the Prime Minister of 22 April 1999, written just after seeing Jackson in his Kumanovo camp outside the Macedonian capital, Skopje, I warned Mr Blair that, unless we were able to persuade the United States (he was just about to go and see President Clinton) that they had to be prepared to commit troops on the ground, we would never be able to persuade Milošević to stand down. At that time, NATO was within an ace of losing to Milošević. To his great credit, Mr Blair did persuade President Clinton, against the overwhelming weight of the President's own advisers. This was a remarkable feat for a British Prime Minister and, in my view, entitles Mr Blair to be credited with playing the key role in the liberation of Kosovo and in saving NATO from a catastrophe.

High Representative

Finally, for nearly four years I served as the International Community's High Representative in Bosnia and Herzegovina. I made many mistakes in this job, learnt many hard lessons and made many good friends. It is an unbelievable privilege to be involved in helping to rebuild a state ravaged by war. I owe a huge debt to the remarkable and courageous people of Bosnia. They were generous with my mistakes, unfailing in their courtesy and gently taught me what should be done and how it should be done. It is to one of them; one among too many hundreds of thousands driven in blood and terror from their homes because we failed, that this book is dedicated. Ahmet Sitkić was 77 years old when my wife and I spent a night with him in his rotting tent a thousand feet above the beautiful Drina valley. I asked him why he had come back. He told me that this was the third time in his life that his house had been burnt and he had been driven out. The first was the Germans in 1941. The second was the Partisans a few years later. And then in 1992 came 'Arkan'.[2] He was the worst. He killed everything – men, women, children, chickens, sheep, dogs, cats – everything. But Ahmet had returned and like so many other refugees around the world, patiently rebuilt his house and cleared his land again. As he said to me, that is the lot of the refugee – they have no other option.

We have shown we are not very good at rebuilding states after conflict. The aim of this book is to try to ensure that, for the millions of Ahmet Sitkićs of this world, we learn to do this better.

Part I

The story so far

I

Why intervene?

On the idle hill of summer,
Sleepy with the flow of streams,
Far I hear the steady drummer
Drumming like a noise in dreams.

Far and near and low and louder
On the roads of earth go by,
Dear to friends and food for powder,
Soldiers marching, all to die.

A. E. HOUSMAN, *A Shropshire Lad*

In April 1999, at the height of the Kosovo war, I visited the small
northern Albanian town of Kukes, just a kilometre or so from the
Kosovan border. In normal times, Kukes is a bleak market town of a
thousand or so, positioned high up on the mountainous ramparts
which divide Albania from Kosovo and southern Serbia. But on this
day it was a great heaving mass of humanity as some 40,000
refugees, driven out of Kosovo by Milošević's guns, had washed up
here in tractors, carts and on foot to take shelter in the rain and mud
around the town. In amongst them were the television cameras of
the world, more aid agencies than you could count and the tattered
remnants of the Kosovo Liberation Army. They were all gathered
round a hastily constructed heliport, run by a Genoese fireman
called Alessandro who was organising, as though his whole life had
been dedicated to it, a constant stream of helicopters carrying aid,
VIPs and all the colourful paraphernalia of the international intervention circus.

I wandered among the refugees, listening to their stories and
trying to absorb the scale of their personal disaster. In among the

stories of misery and killing and brutality, I remember one conversation especially vividly. It was with a twenty-year-old Kosovar Albanian girl who said: 'I was always told that the West only went to war for land or oil. Yet here is NATO and the international community, fighting for me – fighting for one purpose – to get me home.' In one sense at least, she was right.

In most international conflicts refugees are the by-product of war – its forgotten leftovers. Kosovo was the first war in which getting the refugees home became the purpose of the war and the single measure of victory or defeat. Yet this simple fact – that the international community was going to war not for territorial rights but for human rights – has far-reaching consequences for the international community, its institutions and its laws. Kosovo may have been the first time that refugees became, ostensibly at least, the central aim of an international intervention in the domestic jurisdiction of a sovereign state. But it was very far from being the first time refugees had been one of the causes of such an intervention. In the Congo, in Somalia, in Haiti, in El Salvador, in Bosnia and in many other previous conflicts, refugees leaving a country because of internal repression, chaos or civil war, have been one of the reasons for international intervention to suppress conflict and rebuild peace and stability.

Because peace intervention failures have attracted more attention, we tend to forget sometimes just how common such interventions are in today's world, how much the practice of international intervention has accelerated since the end of the cold war, and what has been the overall record of success and failure. In fact, international interventions in failed states or to suppress conflict have now become very much part of the ordinary routine of international relations – though you wouldn't think so sometimes when you consider our capacity to make and remake the same old mistakes again and again. These interventions can be divided into two groups – those conducted by coalitions of the willing, usually led by the United States, and those led by the UN.

US-Led Interventions

Between 1945 and the end of the cold war in 1989, US-led international coalitions have launched a new military intervention on average once in every decade. Since the end of the cold war, this rate of intervention has increased to once every other year. As early as his first Presidential election campaign, George W. Bush started off resolutely declaring that all this would end; henceforth the United States would not do 'nation-building' (sic). The policy of George Bush junior was summed up most colourfully by his present Secretary of State Condoleezza Rice, then his campaign security adviser, when she famously said: *'Carrying out civil administration and police functions is simply going to degrade the American capability to do the things America has to do. We don't need to have the 82nd Airborne escorting kids to kindergarten.'*[1] By 2002, however, world events, and especially 9/11, had forced a more realistic approach, summed up in the United States National Security Strategy as follows: *'expand[ing] the circle of development by opening societies and building the infrastructure of democracy'* would be a key part of America's response to the destruction of the Twin Towers. Henceforth the United States would: *'help build police forces, court systems, and legal codes, local and provincial government institutions, and electoral systems'*. The stated aim of this policy was to: *'make the world not just safer, but better'*.[2] As both Iraq and Afghanistan show, there has been no slacking off in the pace of US-led interventions under the George Bush Presidency, though regrettably, little evidence of a capacity to learn how to do this better either.

UN-Led Interventions

Interventions led by the United Nations have been even more numerous – and accelerated even faster. During the cold war the UN mounted an intervention mission every four years. In 1992 the then Secretary General Boutros Boutros-Ghali laid the foundation for a new UN concept of intervention when he said: *'The time of absolute and exclusive sovereignty . . . has passed; its theory was never matched by its reality. It is the task of leaders of States today to understand this and to find a balance between the needs of good internal governance and the requirements of an ever more interdependent world.'*[3] Today, on average the Security Council decides on a new intervention mission once in every six months, with the duration of each mission also rising – most UN missions now last between five and ten years.[4]

The effect of this has been, on the face of it at least, beneficial to an increasingly turbulent and instable world. A recent academic study[5] found that military intervention by the international community turns out to be the best way of stabilising peace and reconstructing nations after conflict. The number of armed conflicts in the world has declined by more than 40 per cent and the deadliest of these (defined as those where the battle deaths exceed 1,000) by 80 per cent, since the end of the cold war in 1992, with the greatest number of conflicts now concentrated in Africa.[6] A similar study by the University of British Columbia[7] confirms the trend with findings showing that, since the end of the cold war, the effect of the accelerated pace of international intervention has contributed to halving the number of wars in the world, with an even greater reduction in the number of dead, wounded and displaced. In short there is good reason to argue that intervention is not only becoming much more commonplace than we think – but is also making the world a somewhat safer place in turbulent times.

The mystery, therefore, is – why aren't we doing it better? Why do we still make such painful and costly mistakes, a tendency revealed in stark relief by the situation in Iraq, where we seem to have produced a copybook example of how post-conflict state-building should not be done? High profile failures like Iraq should not, however, blind us to the fact that, overall, the success stories outnumber the failures by a wide margin. What all this shows is that we do intervene, that we are doing it more and that we can be successful. But just because you can do something does not mean that you should do it. Liberals like me have to justify that international intervention in the domestic jurisdiction of sovereign states is not only possible, but necessary and consistent with our Western democratic values. Here I want to return to the example of Kosovo.

On my second visit to Kosovo, in December 1998, I was present as the main battle units of Milošević's army began the second phase of his campaign to drive out the Kosovar Albanians, 'Operation Horseshoe'. The scene was one of terror and tragedy as the inhabitants fled on tractors, on foot and in carts from the guns on the hills above them. My mind was on intervention to stop this horror. But among the mayhem and misery of that day, one unconnected image, almost overlooked at the time, has come back to me powerfully ever since. It was this; every Albanian village, however small, had a graveyard, and every Albanian house, however poor, had a satellite dish. But while the graveyards, according to Islamic tradition, pointed toward Mecca, the satellite dishes pointed at Murdoch. And I wondered which of these two facts would affect the lives of these people more. The way that their religion required them to bury their dead? Or the way that the living got their news and their entertainment and their window on the world? The answer is obvious. Despite the rise of radical Islam, in this area of the world at least, Murdoch will be more influential in most of these lives than Mecca – with all that that potentially means in terms of threat to their culture, their religion and even their individual identities.

Globalisation of Power

What I saw that day was, in tiny microcosm, the phenomenon of our age and one which I believe now poses one of the greatest challenges that we face: the globalisation of power and the need to construct some system of global governance to control it.

Here is a test. List all those institutions which are growing in power, size and influence; currency speculators, commodity traders, satellite broadcasters, transnational corporations, drug traffickers, internet operators, global terrorists, international criminals. First note the size of this growing transnational society; then note how all of them operate in ways which pay no attention to the rules of states or their borders and frontiers. Now list those institutions which are under threat or challenge. Monarchies, police forces, the political classes, the establishments of power – perhaps even democracy itself. And note how all of these depend for their existence on the notion of the nation state.

This migration of power from the nation state to the global arena, where the structures of regulation are few or ineffective, is one of the most destabilising factors of our age. History teaches us that where power is uncontrolled, chaos and conflict almost always follow. That is why governance has to follow power. If power now increasingly lies on the global stage, then we have to find the means to create governance on the global stage too. And that will require constructing, albeit slowly, stumblingly and painfully an effective system of international law to combat the threat of global lawlessness.

We have understood for some time that lawlessness in one state can affect the peace of states and peoples, not just in the region, but across the globe. Our failure to finish the job and establish stability in Afghanistan after the Soviets left was paid for in blood and terror on the streets of New York just over a decade later. Indeed one of the chief reasons why Osama bin Laden moved his operations from Sudan to Afghanistan was precisely to take advantage of the chaos and lawlessness there after the Soviets left. What we have not so far fully realised is that the challenge of lawlessness does not just apply to states, but to the global space, too.

We may not yet understand this – but Al Qaeda do. They use the global space as their space. Satellite broadcasting, the internet, international financial institutions, the networks of international travel – these are their chosen logistical networks. As one respected commentator in the USA has put it, *'if Bin Laden didn't have access to global media, satellite communications and the internet, he'd just be a cranky guy in a cave.'*[8] Similarly, it has been calculated that nearly 60 per cent of the estimated $4 million required to fund 9/11 actually passed at one time or another through the financial institutions housed in the Twin Towers. What makes Al Qaeda so difficult to counter is that it barely has physical bases any longer, in the military sense of the word. It has little or no structure, and only a tiny tangible physical presence. It has deliberately given up most of the attributes of physical form. Its most powerful weapon is its ability to remain an idea, an ethereal concept, floating in the global space, where it can morph, draw recruits, plan operations and execute preparations without any of the cumbersome and vulnerable paraphernalia of a conventional military structure. It is, rather, a viral network that materialises in the moment of the attack and vanishes again into the global space the moment after. And we cannot follow it there, because this space is almost as trackless and as lacking in effective governance by the rule of law as any desert in Iraq or mountain fastness in Afghanistan.

We need to recognise that, while many aspects of global power are benign and beneficial (global free access to information, global trade, global travel etc), some, such as international crime, global terrorism, global drugs networks, the global effect of the actions of rogue states (through environmental damage, destabilisation of regions, proliferation of WMDs, refugee movements etc) are not. Malign global forces now have the power to destabilise and capture weak states (like Afghanistan) and deal heavy blows to strong ones (like the United States on 9/11). We have learnt to our painful cost that we cannot leave these lawless spaces without risking our own stability and security – and that applies to the global spaces, too.

Paradoxically, our failure to bring justice and lawful order to the global space also presents us with an equal and opposite threat – the possibility that the globalisation of trade will fail, leading to a plunge back into protectionism and regional competition. The collapse of the Doha trade liberalisation talks, the fact that the international rules governing intellectual property rights and currency relationships are increasingly contested and the rise in protectionist sentiment in Europe and Latin America are all indicators that, for some at least, the struggle for the future has become not how to liberalise global relationships for the benefit of all but how to raise walls high enough to protect yourself.

Interdependent World

What makes this even more dangerous is that we now live in a world which is not just increasingly global, but also increasingly interdependent. We cannot ignore the actions which one state takes, if the result is to threaten the stability of its neighbours or the wider peace of the international community. Most wars are no longer between states but instead within them or across their borders. As the Bush administration's October 2005 National Intelligence Strategy puts it: '*the lack of freedom in one state endangers the peace and freedom of others, and . . . failed states are a refuge and breeding ground of extremism.*'[9] Meanwhile, a recent study by the CIA identified 114 cases of state failure between 1955 and 1998.[10]

And so, finally, we are being forced to confront the fact that, though the end of the cold war may have ushered in a more stable world in terms of major conflicts and superpower confrontation, it has brought us a more instable one when it comes to the changing nature of conflict, the rise of terrorism and the effects on world peace of the actions of failed and rogue states. Far from being the End of History as described by Francis Fukuyama, history is alive and kicking – and kicking rather hard at the moment. Far from being more tranquil, our global village is looking increasingly troubled. Among the issues that have come to haunt us, or come

back to haunt us, are some very old geo-strategic cultural antagon-
isms, like the ancient struggle between Christianity and Islam, and
some very new challenges such as globalisation and resource competition. These were either completely invisible or on the very
margins of debate a decade ago. Today they are full-blooded, front
and centre and demand our attention.

A Perfect Storm

There are huge and powerful forces stirring in our world. We have
very difficult decisions to take if we are to preserve our fragile living
space, share our diminishing resources and cope with rising as-
pirations in the developing world. These decisions would be difficult
enough in stable times, but we are going to have to take them
against the backdrop of strenuous resource competition, a massive
shift of global power away from the nations and economies of the
West to the nations of the Pacific rim and against the background of
rising radicalism in the world of faith.

Meanwhile we in the West are facing a crisis of confidence in our
own institutions and a lack of belief in the mores and creeds which
used to act as a reliable and understood framework for the way we
live our lives. Our leaders, sometimes so frighteningly full of con-
viction about their own country's immediate short-term interest,
seem to lack a wider long-term vision for the increasingly interdependent world of which they are a part. There is, in short, a
perfect storm gathering out there.

We should not allow ourselves to be deluded into believing that,
because most of our recent conflicts have been intra-state, therefore
inter-state conflicts are a thing of the past. Indeed one way to look at
the recent spate of 'little wars' is that they are the pre-shocks which
always take place before a major change in the established order.
I am very pessimistic about our ability to avoid large-scale war involving the use of weapons of mass destruction in the Middle East in the
next five years and in the Far East in the next twenty. But our chances
of avoiding such a major conflict will be much improved if we are can
find better ways to control the minor conflicts which are likely to be its
precursor; if we can assemble a structure of international law able to
bring order and the rule of law to the global space and if we can learn
better how to tackle the ingredients of instability.

Wars, especially civil wars, have been a major contributory factor in the five great global scourges of our day: AIDS, poverty, famine, illegal drugs and international terrorism. At a time when we understand that third world development and poverty alleviation are key strategic goals for global stabilisation, we simply cannot ignore the fact that war is the world's greatest impoverisher and destroyer of life chances. According to a recent study,[11] the annual cost of civil wars worldwide is some $100 billion. They tend to last around ten times longer than inter-state conflicts, are longest where low income and inequality are greatest, shorten average life expectancy in the country concerned by three years and cost the country and the region in which they take place an average of some $65 billion over the course of their duration.

If we are to maximise the chances of a peaceful transition through what are likely to be highly instable decades, we have to accept the challenge of beginning to create a broad framework of international law to govern the global space. Crucial to this will be the theory and practice of legal intervention on behalf of the international community in the domestic jurisdiction of states where that is possible and necessary, in order to suppress conflict and rebuild peace. Holocaust survivor Ursula Franklin once wrote that peace is not the absence of war, but the presence of justice. As a liberal I agree with that and find no difficulty in applying it to international as much as national space.

Liberalism and Intervention

As the international community's High Representative in Bosnia I was often asked how I could square liberal principles with the exercise of power which could and did make decisions undemocratically (though hopefully, as I shall explore later, not contrary to the people's wishes). My answer was always the same. Bosnia was not an exception. There have been many cases in recent times when it has been necessary to assist a country to transition from war, especially a terrible war like that in Bosnia, to full democracy. In these circumstances and for a limited period of time, it is sometimes necessary to put democracy second to the imperative of ending the conflict and establishing the institutions of justice and good governance upon which democracy depends. Germany after the Second

World War was one example where the international community, using other than democratic means, did just that. Japan is another. In more modern times, Bosnia, Eastern Slavonia, El Salvador, Mozambique, perhaps East Timor and others are further examples. None of these countries are less democratic as a result of having passed through this period of 'tutelage' – indeed, they are often more developed democratically than most others in their region.

My second answer was that standing aside and doing nothing would be likely to result in more damage to the people of the country concerned and to the wider peace than doing our imperfect best to carry out this difficult and contentious exercise. Most governments realise this and increasingly accept that intervention and post-conflict state-building is now part of the everyday business of global politics and diplomacy. Even the United States Department of Defense has recently acknowledged that stability operations are a core mission for the US military.[12] The British, US and Canadian governments have all recently formed new units in an attempt to do this better. In Chapter 9 I shall describe my doubts about whether the approach they have chosen to follow is the right one. But the implicit acknowledgement that this has to be done and that we have to learn to do it better is a welcome one.

Summary

We live in a world increasingly characterised by the growth of global power and the interdependence of nations. The lesson of history is that, where power goes, governance must follow. So the challenge for our age is to create better systems for global governance based on a structure of international law and improved mechanisms for preventing the spread of instability. The best means to do this is through spreading wealth and socio-economic development. But that does not absolve us from taking action when the wider peace is threatened by state failure or the actions of rogue states. The only way to do this is through intervention when all other avenues have been exhausted. The question therefore should not be 'should we intervene?' but rather, 'when is it right and wrong to do so?', 'when is it legal and illegal?' And, above all, since we have wasted so much time and so many lives forgetting what we ought to have remembered, 'how can we do it better?'

2

A short history of peacemaking –
a tale of hubris, nemesis and amnesia

As it will be in the future, it was at the birth of man –
There are only [three] things certain since Social Progress
   began.
That the dog returns to his Vomit and the sow returns to her
   Mire,
And the burnt fool's bandaged finger, goes wabbling back to
   the fire
   RUDYARD KIPLING, 'The Gods of the Copybook Headings'

It was all Woodrow Wilson's fault. Of course he and the 1919 Versailles Peace Conference[1] in Paris had the very best of intentions. But the world has, nevertheless, been coping with the bomb they placed under the international system ever since. For it was US President Woodrow Wilson at Versailles who introduced the concept of self-determination as the foundation for recognised statehood. Before that the world had been run exclusively on the basis of the Westphalian principle. According to the Westphalian standard, establishing statehood was an entirely empirical matter. A state was said to exist when it had the attributes of a state, behaved like a state at home and fulfilled the duties of a state abroad. Not before. To obtain a legal personality recognised by other states, it had therefore to do what other states could do: have effective control over a territory delineated by stable borders, provide its citizens with the services – especially security – which citizenship was entitled to, and interact with other states on a basis of equality and reciprocity.

Wilson, at the head of a United States which had yet to flip back into one of its periodic bouts of isolationism, saw it as his mission to rework the Westphalian model into something which could be applied worldwide, based on the concept of self-determination. It was a perfectly reasonable response to a Europe whose global imperialist ambitions had been a primary cause of the bloodbath which had just ended. He believed that the principle of self-determination would create politically unaligned states existing within open markets and that this would lead on naturally to a grand concourse of independent nations in the world that would assure peace through the League of Nations.

Although the full effect of a change from an empirical standard to one depending chiefly on self-determination[2] was not felt for half a century after Versailles, the Wilsonian model ran into difficulty quite early on. There were some areas of the world for which the architects of Versailles could not find neat solutions, based either on a Westphalian model or on the principle of self-determination. These were either the untidy leftovers of empire, or the places where the ancient tectonic plates of religion, race and ethnicity met. At Versailles, they drew the borders on three 'new' states as 'gap fillers': Czechoslovakia, Yugoslavia and Iraq. The break-up of Yugoslavia and Czechoslovakia would come much later. But Iraq created problems almost from the start. In 1932, Iraq became the first 'mandated' state to gain independence as a fully self-determining member of the League of Nations. But this, duly accompanied by solemn commitments to the creation of a liberal democracy, did not prevent the internal divisions in the country from very quickly making themselves felt. A series of bloody coups took place almost immediately and culminated thirty years later with the Ba'ath Party's seizure of power in 1968 and the dictatorships, first of Abdul Qassim and then of Saddam Hussein. Our present day difficulties in Iraq are, in part at least, the consequences of trying to hold together what some might argue shouldn't have been put together in the first place.

But our problems in finding a model which makes sense of the world today are not just confined to three uncomfortable agglomerations which emerged from the First World War. When Wilson and the Versailles order established self-determination as the key measure of statehood, they altered the way we were required to think about the world, without altering the framework within which we had to take the world's decisions. Whatever the Wilsonian revolution and its effects, the world is still based on a purely binary model, whose origins were created in the Westphalian era; that is, if you are a state you are everything and if you are not, you are nothing. The world system formally only recognises states. Between recognition as a state and 'nothingness', there is nothing. No gradations, no interim structures corresponding to reality in our increasingly complex world – nothing.

The End of the Binary World

This is, at least, the theory. But we have been forced to adapt this model by the uncomfortable fact that most of the world's problems today occur in entities which are not states, but are not nothing either. Palestine, Kashmir, Chechnya, Kosovo, Northern Ireland are just some examples. We have had to acknowledge that our present world is rather more complex than the purely binary model with which we are required to work.

In a boring moment of a Balkan conference in the late 1990s a British ambassador and I amused ourselves by trying, rather flippantly I have to confess, to design an international model which would more closely accord to the international realities we actually find in the world. We decided that, between full statehood and 'nothingness' there were in fact three other categories of international 'thing' to take into account. Below full Westphalian statehood, there were entities that we defined as Non-Internationally Recognised State-Like Entities (or NIRSLEs), which had form and demanded recognition and often could cause greater problems for the rest of us than many states, but were themselves not states (for example, Kosovo, Palestine, Chechnya, Northern Ireland and, at the time, East Timor etc). Then there were Internationally Recognised Non-State-Like Entities (IRNSLEs). These were the entities that the world regards as states, but in reality are not, because they cannot perform the functions attributable to statehood as defined in the Westphalian model. Bosnia and Herzegovina was, at the time, one example. Others are Somalia, the Democratic Republic of Congo and the Iraq of today.

The third category covered other entities which are not states, but supranational structures into which some states in a region have pooled some of their sovereignty, because that gave them greater power in the world. These institutions did not claim to be states, but they could have huge influence on the world and on individual states within it. NATO is one example, the EU is another. The problem with these institutions is that, formally at least, the world is not structured to take account of them. The UN Security Council works largely on the basis of the old binary system, in which only states have rights of recognition and voting. So, for that matter, do the rest of the world's international institutions.

Our conference doodling with all this was not, of course, intended to be taken seriously. But it did illuminate a problem we have in trying sensibly to manage world affairs. We can muddle through with these unacknowledged complexities and we do. But our international structures are locked into the old shape of the world and not the new one and we are thus denied a model which properly corresponds to the way we find things on the ground. Perhaps we are beginning to stumble towards some ad hoc solutions to these problems of structure. In some cases the supranational institutions of more modern times seem to provide a framework in which to cope with the pressures of a world whose formal structure does not accord with reality.

I was sometimes asked how Bosnia and Herzegovina could ever become a state in the classic model. I used to reply that I wasn't sure. What I was certain of was that Bosnia could become a state with a very light-level state structure dealing with only those things a state must deal with (foreign affairs, macroeconomics, justice etc) but leaving most power to be exercised at the local level in a highly decentralised system. Was this a state in the classic model? Probably not. But perhaps it didn't matter. Perhaps, in our modern world, where the old structures are disaggregating under the pressures of tribalism, ethnicity and religion, we will have increasingly to accept a certain degree of dysfunctionality at the state level in order to cope with these pressures at the local level.

Nationalism and Supranationalism

The beauty of the EU is that such 'states' can exist within the overarching supranational structure of the Union. Belgium, the very headquarters of the Union, is arguably one of them. I used to joke that, if Belgium were to apply to join the EU today, I suspected it might be refused on the grounds that it no longer possessed sufficient attributes of statehood!

Although the initial disintegration of Yugoslavia into its component republics began in tides of blood, it has continued rather peacefully in recent years. I doubt this would have been possible, except within the structure of the European Union. Belgrade and Zagreb have finally understood that the best way to be united with their fellow Serbs and Croats in Bosnia is no longer to fight wars to change borders, but to join them on the way to the EU. Without the prospect of membership of the Union one day, this would never have happened. Montenegro would similarly never have waited until a safe moment to break with Serbia had it not been for pressure from the Union. It remains to be seen if we are, in an ad hoc way, creating structures which at last make sense of the post-Westphalian world initiated, albeit by accident, at Versailles. Meanwhile we have to live in an untidy world in which we have discovered that, if we are to have peace, then we have from time to time to intervene in the jurisdiction of sovereign states.

The Non-Intervention Principle

This, too, was not at all as it was supposed to be. One of the aspects of the Wilson doctrine of 1919 was the concept of the inviolability of the sovereignty of states. This doctrine was subsequently codified in Article 2 paragraph 7 of the United Nations Charter of 1945, which explicitly rules out UN intervention in the internal affairs of any member state.[3] This concept was reinforced as late as 1960, in the UN Assembly Declaration on Colonialism which explicitly stated that all newly independent states were also entitled to enjoy the principle of sovereign non-interference.[4] While there are in the UN Charter some exceptions to this principle (which will be touched on in the next chapter), the clear expectation of the world at the time the UN was set up was that interventions within the jurisdiction of its member states would be rare and exceptional. Instead of which, they have become common and are now an accepted part of international affairs.

Indeed, at the very time that the United Nations was asserting the non-intervention principle, the same nations who were its architects were busily creating the Bretton Woods institutions, whose mandate was based on the principle of intervention in the economies of failing and impoverished states. The two Bretton Woods institutions, the International Monetary Fund (IMF) and the World Bank (WB), were specifically mandated to re-shape, if necessary through highly intrusive measures, the economies of states whose internal practices, in their view, threatened the economic well-being of their citizens or the stability of the global economy. By the 1980s the so-called 'Washington Consensus' energetically embarked on a process of using the IMF and WB to intrude into the economic sovereignty of post-colonial states, by offering credit facilities tightly linked to economic reform. The aim was to create an economic world order which paralleled the political world order that the UN was seeking to establish. By the mid 1980s structural adjustment loans (basically loans given to poor or failing states in return for economic and governance reform) amounted to a quarter of all World Bank lending. Conformity to the conditions set by the IMF is also increasingly a pre-condition for lending by the other International Financial Institutions (IFIs) – such as the EU.

I make these points, not because I subscribe to the view of some that this is all a bad thing and imperialist in intention. I don't. I happen to believe that in the main the approach of the Bretton Woods institutions has produced results which have proved both beneficial to the citizens of the countries concerned and helpful in reducing instabilities in the world economic system. Rather, my point is that even while the world was piously saying that we would not intervene, the world was, in fact, intervening like mad because it realised it had to. So what has happened on the ground? What follows is a brief description of post-war international peace stabilisation and state-building missions. It is by no means comprehensive. I have chosen what I think are the most important post-Second World War intervention missions and those which best illustrate some of the lessons to be learnt. I deliberately have *not* included places where the international community arguably *should* have intervened but didn't (such as Rwanda) because, self-evidently, there are no lessons to be learnt about an intervention which never took place. If, incidentally, what you think you detect in the following pages is a common thread of hubris, nemesis and amnesia, you would be correct.

Inevitably, in assessing these examples I have had to decide how to define success and failure. This is, of course, a purely subjective judgement, but it would be as well to state on what I have based this judgement in the analyses which follow. The first criterion I have used for success is whether a country in which an intervention has taken place has returned to violence. This is not, as it might first appear, to set the bar too low. A recent series of academic studies have pointed out that countries emerging from conflict face a 50 per cent chance of returning to hostilities within a five-year period.[5] My second criterion is whether, at the end of the intervention, the country concerned has state structures, an element of the rule of law and effective systems of governance which broadly conform to the standards prevailing in the region. It is also necessary to decide on a definition of the term 'intervention'. All the examples which follow in this chapter involve military force because they are the most contentious, the best known and the best documented. But elsewhere in this book I have adopted a broader definition of intervention as: any action undertaken by the international community, either together or singly, which uses diplomacy, development, assistance, or military means, in order to prevent a state failing, alter its behaviour, or assist it to rebuild after conflict.

Congo

In 1960, the very same year as the General Assembly was asserting the rights of newly independent states to enjoy the principle of sovereign non-interference, the UN found itself intervening in the Congo.

The UN didn't burst in to the Congo unannounced. It was invited by the government to ensure the removal of Belgian forces, which had been parachuted in, in contravention of the Treaty of Friendship between Belgium and the newly decolonised Congo, under the pretext of protecting Belgian citizens in the chaos which followed independence. A more seductive case for intervention could hardly be imagined. Here was the UN acting on invitation to assist in the process of decolonisation and removal of the troops of a previous colonial master from the territory of a newly independent UN member. None of this, however, saved the UN from the unique difficulties of the Congo, a failed state from the moment of its inception, or from the pains that accompany any attempt to use force to end a vicious civil war and rebuild (or in this case, build for the first time) the institutions of a peaceful state. In fact the UN's initial response to the crisis in the Congo was swift, heavyweight and comprehensive. A UN army was installed and fully equipped with its own air force, capable of taking on and defeating opposing forces, which it did. It was backed by what was effectively a full parallel government structure, able not just to shadow the Congo government but also to create the institutions which the Belgians should have created before they left, and to train the Congolese to man it. In the end, however, although the UN could be said to have achieved its short-term security and decolonisation aims, the exercise failed to fulfil its ambitious aim of creating a sustainable, functioning and stable state.

Even in this first UN intervention, the difficulties which were later to dog successive interventions, both by the UN and the international community, were already plainly evident: lack of unity of UN command, especially between the UN's military and civilian arms; over-ambitious aims; attempts to establish democratic structures too early; a failure to grasp the true nature of the state in which the intervention was taking place, and, critically, a misappreciation of the amount of time and resources it takes to rebuild a state after conflict. The UN felt it got its fingers badly burnt in the Congo and for the next quarter of a century and more, limited its military operations to purely permissive environments, into which it was invited by both sides – and even in these the UN insisted that the use of force by its troops should be confined to their own self-defence. I remember witnessing the fatally debilitating effect of this doctrine at first hand thirty years later in Bosnia, where UN insistence that its forces should not intervene in what was happening on the ground made it an accomplice at one remove to genocidal aggression and, in the process, reduced its standing with the combatants to a level almost beneath contempt.

Namibia

Although there were other UN actions in the intervening years (such as Cyprus) the UN's next major challenge came in Namibia in 1988, when it was brought in to police the peace agreement signed in New York between the governments of South Africa, Angola and Cuba, ending twenty-three years of warfare and opening the way for Namibian independence. The task of the UN in Namibia was to supervise elections and manage the transition process to independence.

The cold war was ending around this time, and with it the period of proxy wars fought as extensions of the confrontation between the superpowers and usually with their active assistance in the supply of arms and the training of combatants. During this extremely bloody period for the developing world, the UN had been essentially powerless as the superpowers, blocked by nuclear stalemate at home, had fought out their conflict on other people's territories and at the price of other people's blood. Namibia therefore benefited from a new international consensus in favour of intervention and opened the way to a period in which the pace of interventions by the UN and the international community accelerated sharply. The successful UN operation in Namibia also benefited from having the active assistance of the neighbouring states (something which, as we shall discover later, turns out to be very important in state-building after war), a competent indigenous government, disciplined professional security forces and an ultimate destination for the country which was agreed by all parties.

El Salvador

1992 was a bumper year for intervention operations, both by the UN and by the wider international community, in this case principally the United States. First came El Salvador, with the peace agreement of January 1992 which ended, after twelve years of fighting, one of the cold war's 'proxy' conflicts in the United States' backyard. Like the UN's operations in Namibia, El Salvador was broadly successful and set positive benchmarks for subsequent UN operations, including for the first time tackling issues such as disarmament, demobilisation and re-integration of the opposing side's military forces. One crucial lesson learnt here, and then promptly forgotten elsewhere, was the importance of the early establishment of the rule of law and an understanding that this could only be done effectively by addressing all components of the justice system. Not just police, but judges and prosecutors, criminal codes, economic law and detention facilities. Indeed El Salvador could have taught us, too, that this lesson of the holistic approach did not only apply to the establishment of the rule of law – it applies across the whole area of state-building. Sustainable peacemaking and state-building has to be done in an interlocking way and not just by picking on one or two sectors. Unfortunately, however, these lessons were forgotten almost as soon as they were learnt in El Salvador.

Success in the relatively benign conditions of El Salvador may have seduced the UN into the hubris of underestimating the difficulties elsewhere.

Cambodia

A month later, in February 1992 the UN established the United Nations Transitional Authority in Cambodia (UNTAC). This was a much more ambitious operation, more akin in size and complexity to the Congo mission a quarter of a century earlier. It was, in effect, the UN's first post-cold war, full-scale attempt at state-building and was conducted in circumstances much more challenging than those of El Salvador.

Although the UN did achieve many of its primary goals in Cambodia (civil war and foreign forces have not returned to the country), it did not achieve the creation of a stable democracy and an effective government that was its overall objective. Once again the UN found itself a victim of over-ambitious aims which were not matched by resources and soon discovered that it was ill-prepared actually to govern until such time as the indigenous state institutions were capable of taking over. It also discovered that, though the liberal democracies who run the world believe in the magical powers of elections – as many as possible and as early as possible – too early elections, especially if held before the rule of law is properly established, can actually impede the process of state-building.

Somalia

Two months after launching into Cambodia, in April 1992, the UN agreed to monitor the ceasefire in Somalia, deploying 50 unarmed military observers and 500 lightly armed infantry. In a Somalia swimming in heavily armed militia, many of whom were supported from neighbouring states, they ran into trouble almost immediately. By November the UN's Pakistani soldiers were holed up in Mogadishu airport, fighting for their lives. The Security Council responded by authorising the deployment of a heavyweight American-led task force with the aim of regaining control of the country. 28,000 US troops were sent in, authorised to use decisive force, and order was quickly restored. Fatally, however, this force was withdrawn too early and the, by then combined, US/UN mission was given an expanded mandate but massively reduced troop numbers and resources to finish the job. No attempt was made to engage the neighbouring countries, many of whom were actively stoking up the Somali conflict. Meanwhile, the US cut their troop numbers to only 1,200 and placed them under the command of the US, not the local UN mission head. Worse still, some of the US special forces, despite operating from the same base and in the same areas as US conventional forces, were not even under local US command, but took their orders directly from Washington.

It was not long before the whole operation – and the US troops in particular – paid the price for reducing troop numbers too early and for the fatally muddled command structures on the ground. The events which followed, immortalised in the film *Black Hawk Down*, led to the deaths of eighteen US servicemen in front of the television cameras of the world and the decision by the Clinton administration to pull out, amid downward spiralling chaos in Somalia.

One of the key lessons of Somalia is that it is best to go in with overwhelming force; best to remember that the troops you need in the early stages of state-building may be as many, or even more, than you require to win the war; and best to stay longer, rather than pull out early. The early hopes of El Salvador were being quickly crushed in the harsher realities of more difficult parts of the world.

Yugoslavia

And now the pressure of that meat grinder was just about to get even more intense, as the UN found itself, in the early months of 1992, being drawn into the maelstrom of the collapse of Yugoslavia. First came the war between Serbia and Croatia and the creation of UNPROFOR (United Nations Protection Force). UNPROFOR's mandate was muddled and unworkable from the start. It was neither a peace enforcement, nor a state-building mission. It was founded on the rather naive notion that if it existed, and put itself between the warring parties, they would politely stop warring and start living peacefully together. These deficiencies did not show themselves too dramatically in the early stages of UNPROFOR's deployment in Croatia, where things between the warring parties quickly moved to a three-year stalemate, providing Croatian President Tudjman and Serbia's Milošević the space to turn to the more immediate business of carving up Bosnia and Herzegovina, as they had secretly agreed to do some years earlier.*

Bosnia

The more bitter crucible of Bosnia quickly and cruelly showed up the weaknesses of UNPROFOR. London and Paris, the main troop contributors to UNPROFOR in Bosnia, demanded and got a robust enforcement mandate, but then failed to send adequate forces to carry it out. The US, meanwhile, refused to get involved, beyond helping with the enforcement of the Bosnian no-fly zone. This failure to back good intentions with adequate military force on the ground led swiftly to UNPROFOR being treated as a standing joke by all sides. On 28 May 1995, following an attack on British troops in the besieged town of Gorazde and the capture of UK and Ukrainian soldiers as hostages by the Bosnian Serb army, Western leaders met secretly with UNPROFOR's commander, General Janvier, and agreed that, in the final event, they would not defend the Bosnian safe havens.[6] It was inevitable that this would, in time, become known to the Serb commander General Ratko Mladić, who was a past master at probing the limits of his enemy.

On 11 July 1995, Srebrenica fell and more than 7,000 Muslim men and boys were slaughtered by Mladić's army. This was the UN's blackest hour for which it, and its troop-contributing nations in Bosnia, still carry an indelible mark of shame.

As the Bosnian war rumbled on, another intervention was taking place on the other side of the world.

---

*President Tudjman of Croatia indiscreetly revealed this plan to me after too much wine at a dinner at the Guildhall in London on 6 May 1995 when he drew for me, on the back of a menu, a map of how the war would end, showing Bosnia divided neatly in two between Croatia and Serbia. When I asked him 'Where was Bosnia?' he replied 'No Bosnia'. I subsequently gave evidence against one of his generals at the Hague on the basis of this piece of gastronomic cartography.

Haiti

The United States had had its fingers severely burnt in Somalia. But it could not afford to ignore events in its own backyard. In 1994, under an agreement brokered by then ex-President Carter, US troops entered Haiti in overwhelming force, armed with a tough UN Security Council mandate permitting them to use 'all means necessary' to stabilise the country and return democratically elected President Aristide to office. In short order, the Haitian military was abolished, a new civilian police force was created, local and national elections were held, new mayors, members of parliament and a new prime minister were elected and Aristide was restored to office. The mission proceeded smoothly and ended on the appointed schedule: but too early to create the deep-seated democratic change, or the long-term economic reforms which Haiti needed in order to become a self-sustaining and successful state.

Not for the first time, the Haiti intervention, though successful in the short term, proved that though winning wars can be quick, building peace takes time and patience. These are not easy commodities to come by in democratic countries, whose time frames are driven by domestic elections, whose politicians need quick results and whose public will always demand that the troops should be brought home at the earliest date possible.

Bosnia II

Between 1992 and 1995 the international community tried desperately and repeatedly to halt the Bosnian war through negotiations. But since they had already made it publicly clear that they were not going to intervene to stop the conflict they had no leverage and whichever side was winning at the time (mostly the Serbs) had no incentive to negotiate when they felt they could still win on the battlefield. Since the international community was prepared to do nothing on the ground, it achieved nothing at the negotiating table.[*]

---

[*] I shall discuss this event and the lessons which spring from it in more detail in Chapter 7.

Eventually, however, four years and perhaps as much as 250,000* deaths later, as the horrors of the Bosnian war became increasingly intolerable to Western public opinion, the international community was forced to intervene. The Bosnian Muslim/Croat coalition finally gained ascendancy on the battlefield, NATO bombed the Serbs, who quickly capitulated, and Bosnia's long and bloody tragedy ended in exhausted stalemate. The protagonists on all sides and their patrons in Zagreb and Belgrade, under extreme US and international pressure, signed the Dayton/Paris Peace Agreement† and the process of rebuilding Bosnia after Europe's worst war for fifty years could begin. The task now was to build the peace.

Eastern Slavonia

While in Bosnia and Herzegovina the war ended inconclusively, in Croatia, the US-trained Croatian army swept the rebel Serb forces from their territory, in Operation Storm, in 1995.‡

Under pressure from the world's most powerful nations, an agreement was signed in 1995 between the Croats and the Serbs that Eastern Slavonia, originally part of Croatia but occupied during the war by the Serbs, should be re-integrated back under the rule of Zagreb. The UN's role was to oversee this process and it established the United Nations Transitional Administration in Eastern Slavonia (UNTAES), under the command of an ex-US Air Force general, Jacques Klein, to carry out the task. The UN's aims were ambitious: to demilitarise the area within thirty days, establish a temporary police force, facilitate the return of refugees, run the transitional civil administration, ensure the delivery of public services, organise

---

* This figure is disputed – some say the figure of war deaths in Bosnia did not exceed 120,000.
† Referred to elsewhere in this book by its shortened title, 'Dayton'.
‡ As Tudjman had predicted they would at that bibulous dinner party in the Guildhall in London, three months earlier. I had treated his boast with incredulity and bet him a bottle of the best Croatian white wine that his forces couldn't do it, a bet which was duly paid after Operation Storm. But not before, at the height of the Croat advance I deliberately leaked Tudjman's 'map on the menu', revealing that the ultimate aim of the operation was the division of Bosnia. As I hoped, this helped generate huge international pressure on Tudjman to halt 'Storm' prematurely before its aims were fulfilled.

elections and launch a programme of reconstruction and development.

UNTAES was probably the most successful of all the post-cold war UN or international community-led state-building exercises. It had a robust mandate and the resources and forces to carry it out. It had a unified military and civilian command structure (something we immediately forgot to remember was important, in neighbouring Bosnia). It had the support of the neighbouring states and it had an agreed final destination to which all subscribed and toward which all, including, broadly, the population of the country, were willing to work. It also had, in Jacques Klein, a head of mission prepared to be robust, with a splendidly Nelsonian capacity for placing a blind eye to his telescope when it came to reading signals from headquarters in New York which attempted to interfere from 4,500 miles away in things he knew better about on the ground. As a result the UN mission in Eastern Slavonia fulfilled all its mandated tasks and closed down in January 1998, two years to the day after it started.

Bosnia III

Stabilising the peace in Bosnia was a much more difficult nut to crack. The war had been inconclusive. The country had been devastated. Perhaps as much as a sixteenth of its population had been killed (a bigger proportion of war deaths than in France during the First World War) and half had been driven from their homes in blood and terror. To add to this, Bosnia was nationally and religiously divided in three and had a history of occasional ethnic conflict stretching back well over a hundred years.

Here the international community took a different route. Instead of a UN mission, it created the Office of the High Representative (OHR), charged with overseeing the civilian aspects of peace implementation. OHR was responsible, not directly to the UN, but to the Peace Implementation Council (PIC), a self-defining body made up of a coalition of the willing – basically, those nations who were prepared to contribute, either financially or in other ways, to building a sustained peace in Bosnia. However, ignoring the lessons of Eastern Slavonia and El Salvador, the international community created a completely separate structure for the security aspects of peace implementation. A separate military arm (originally IFOR, or the Implementation Force), was created and deployed under the command of NATO in Brussels, entering Bosnia in overwhelming force, with 60,000 troops, in 1995. Worse still, a whole host of UN and other agencies was brought in to deal with specific tasks, such as democratisation, education, economic reform, refugee return, human rights, police restructuring etc. Most of these had muddled and overlapping mandates.* Although the Dayton Agreement gave the High Representative the task of coordination within the international community, he had no powers to enforce this. The result was duplication of the international effort, confusion amongst the Bosnians and the severe dissipation of the energies of the overall international effort.

A UN police mission was brought in to reform the police. But the rest of Bosnia's war-corrupted judicial sector, from judges to basic framework laws, was largely ignored. Amazingly, we once again failed to learn the lessons of previous missions and decided that elections – and lots of them – were more important than establishing the rule of law. The effect was that, though elections were free and fair, those who were elected were those who had prosecuted the war and/or gained from it through corruption. Bosnia came very close to becoming a criminally captured state before we could start reversing this, and suffers still from the after effects.

Nevertheless, ten years and some $17 billion later, the work of the OHR is now drawing to a close, the basic structures of a highly decentralised state are in place, the economy is growing and Bosnia stands at the beginning of the long road that, over time, will hopefully lead to full membership of the European Union. From this point of view the stabilisation process in Bosnia and Herzegovina could be regarded as a success. But we have wasted much time, a lot of money and many opportunities in the process. Readers who are interested in further details of what happened on the ground can find them in Appendices A and B.

---

* The exception to this was the highly successful reconstruction programme in Bosnia, which took place between 1995 and 1999 and was led by the World Bank.

Kosovo

There were those who hoped that the bloody war in Bosnia would mark the end of the process of the disintegration of ex-Yugoslavia. But Slobodan Milošević, then president of the remaining Serb rump of Yugoslavia, had other ideas and it soon became evident that this time he had Kosovo in his sights. Once again, NATO had to bomb, only this time not just in Kosovo, but also in Belgrade and throughout Serbia. It was touch and go.

Milošević eventually capitulated to NATO bombing. If he had held on a few weeks longer there was a real probability that NATO would have backed down and he would have won.[*] Nevertheless, when he threw in the towel in Kosovo, he left the UN with one of its most difficult tasks of reconstruction. In designing the mission, the UN took care to try to learn the lessons of Bosnia. It created a single unified command to implement the civilian aspects of post-conflict reconstruction (though there was still a separate command for military aspects). A structure was created in which there was efficient burden sharing between the agencies involved, through a pillar system reporting directly to the SRSG (the Special Representative of the Secretary General), a single mission head equipped with huge powers – essentially those of a full-scale protectorate. This was a model that we subsequently tried to copy in Bosnia. Clear mandates were drawn up for the different agencies involved and adequate resources were provided to fulfil the task, including initially some 60,000 troops for a 'country' the size of Devon.

There were mistakes, to be sure. Although the UN deployed 100 police within two weeks of the mission commencing, the bulk of the 5,000-strong UN civilian police (CIVPOL) force was far too late in arriving, a very common deficiency in peacemaking operations. Meanwhile, NATO did not or could not fulfil the terms of UN Security Council (UNSC) Resolution 1244, which required it to take responsibility for public security in the intervening period before UN CIVPOL arrived and did not send the thousand-strong contingent of military police until a year later.[†] Since the start of the mission, the SRSG has suffered from having his decisions constantly

---

[*] See p. 6 for my conversation with Jackson at Kumanovo camp.
[†] See Chapter 4 for more details.

second-guessed by UN headquarters in New York, resulting in a certain lack of muscularity in some of the things that the mission has done (or more frequently, not done). But these are relatively small matters.

Two more fundamental issues have proved more enduringly damaging to the UN mission in Kosovo. The first is a very common problem in peacemaking missions – an insufficient ability to 'see through' the war phase and to make an accurate assessment of the kinds of problem that would be encountered when building the peace. This has been compounded, as always, by that ever present demon of the law of unintended consequences. No one predicted (though they could have done) that the biggest problem the Kosovo mission would face was not getting the Albanian Kosovars back to their homes (I remember seeing the miffed faces of the UN's refugee agencies when the Kosovar Albanians did this without their help), but protecting the Serbs in theirs. The second was the complete inability of the international community to answer the one question which everyone in Kosovo wanted answered – what will be the status of Kosovo in the future?[*]

Sierra Leone

Meanwhile, in 1999, a year and a half after the mission in Slavonia closed, the UN found itself back in the peacemaking business in Sierra Leone. Once again the task was to police a peace agreement which – it was hoped – had brought to an end an African conflict that had started even before the Balkan wars had begun.

The task was very similar to that in Namibia, but with two crucial differences. The first was that there was no 'buy-in' from the neighbouring states, one of which, Liberia, had its own civil war and provided sanctuary and refuge to one of the warring parties. The second was the quality of the UN troops sent in. Militarily capable Western nations declined to provide the leadership of the UN force in Sierra Leone or to contribute to it, as they had done in neighbouring Liberia. So the UN force was led and manned by forces from less militarily capable nations. The command of the UN's troops on the ground was also badly divided. The mission

[*] See Chapter 7 for more details.

started to lose control, as contributing nations (chiefly India and Nigeria) began unilaterally to withdraw their forces. Only decisive action by the United Kingdom, which sent in troops, saved the day. The UK mission in Sierra Leone went on to achieve partial success, showing that, with decisive action, even a badly compromised effort can be turned round.

It is speculative to suggest that, if the militarily capable Western nations who had authorised this intervention through the Security Council had themselves also made a contribution to it, then the UK might not have had to carry out its rescue mission. But it is worth noting that in neighbouring Liberia, where Western nations did eventually provide a tough and capable quick reaction force at the heart of the UN mission, no such 'rescue mission' was needed. The near failure in Sierra Leone can be put down to a determination in the planning phase to depend on best case scenarios, the dangers of divided or internally incompatible elements in the command structure and poor quality troops on the ground. It is important to remember that peacekeeping is the most difficult kind of soldiering, requiring high levels of discipline, good communications and strong leadership qualities, especially in the junior command echelons.

East Timor

Only a matter of months after Sierra Leone came East Timor. Here the UN's task was, first to restore order and then to supervise the creation of a state in the newly independent nation of East Timor. A heavyweight, fully capable international military operation, much like that in Bosnia – but this time led by Australia – was sent in. Order was quickly established and the task of maintaining it was then handed over to a conventional UN peacekeeping force – the first time such a two-stage process has been attempted in these kinds of operation.

The East Timor mission, under the leadership of one of the UN's most able peacemakers, Sergio Viera de Mello (later tragically killed in the suicide bomb attack on the UN headquarters in Iraq), ranks as one of the UN's most successful, with the effective administration of the country being handed over to domestic structures in a little over two years (though in the light of present events in East Timor this may have proved too early, as I shall discuss later). It suffered nevertheless, and again, from one of the UN's most persistent state-building deficiencies, the slow deployment of civilian administrators and civilian police after the fighting ended.

Iraq and Afghanistan

Since the events of 9/11 two more state-building exercises have been launched, this time not by the UN (though the UN plays a part in both), but by US-led international coalitions. It is too early to reach definitive conclusions about the success or failure of the operations in Iraq and Afghanistan, though, at the time of writing, the situation looks increasingly difficult. What is now very clear however, is that, when it comes to peacemaking after the conflict, we have failed in Iraq. This is not to say that nothing positive can emerge; or that ignominious retreat is the only outcome. It is merely to state the obvious – that the Coalition cannot now achieve the ambitious aims it set for itself four years ago. Iraq is a particularly painful example of the hubris which attends over-ambitious aims, when it comes to post-conflict reconstruction.

There are lessons worth learning from both these conflicts. The US, famous in all its peacemaking operations for the use of over-whelming force, seems to have decided to follow the route more usually associated with the UN and use instead minimalist forces in Iran and Afghanistan. This was not an incorrect judgement when it came to winning the wars in these countries. But the lesson that it often requires more forces to stabilise the peace, especially in the initial phase, than it requires to fight the war that preceded it, seems to have been lost. Secondly, it is clear there has been a planning problem in both cases.

There was planning for the post-war phase in Iraq. But the original work, carried out by the US State Department, was ditched wholesale when the US Department of Defense (DoD) took over responsibility for the state-building phase in Iraq only seven weeks before the war started. DoD's planning for post-war Iraq was based, fatally, on best, rather than worst case scenarios and be-trayed an inability to 'think through' the war phase and to formu-late actions based on an accurate appreciation of the nature of the country in which the US-led Coalition were getting involved.[*] This was exacerbated by the fact that the US disbanded the entire Iraqi army without having a plan for demobilisation and, especially, for the employment of demobilised soldiers.

The consequence was a security vacuum that the US did not have the troop strength on the ground or the local partners in Iraq to fill. The very first lesson of state-building is to dominate and control the security envelope, from the very moment the war ends, and transition this as fast as possible into the rule of law. The United States' inability to do either of these in Iraq has I believe been the crucial difficulty from which the US-led operation has still not been able to recover. I shall return to this in greater detail later.

A second crucial impediment to success in Iraq (less so in Afghanistan) was that we forgot to remember that it is difficult – almost impossible – to build a state broken by war, without the active and constructive engagement of its neighbours. The US has taken on itself the almost impossible task of stabilising a peace and building a state in a region which is itself deeply instable and where most of the immediate neighbours are, at the least, unwilling to help and at the worst actively trying to disrupt.

There will, I suspect, be many acres of print written about Iraq and Afghanistan, especially the former. It is not the purpose of this book to provide a definitive analysis – not the least because it is still too early in the case of Afghanistan to do so. One thing, however, can be said with some confidence. That, although for dash, speed and courage the US Army's defeat of Saddam Hussein's forces may have been a near copybook example of how these kinds of war can be won, the way they have stabilised the peace in Iraq provides a near copybook example of how they should not be.

Summary

There is a mismatch between the realities in our world and the model we use to solve its problems. This is particularly acute when it comes to dealing with intra-state conflicts, because they very frequently take place in the 'no man's land' which lies beyond the margins of statehood. We cannot ignore these instabilities because

---

[*] See Chapter 7 for a further discussion of this failure of planning.

they can threaten the wider peace. Which is one of the reasons why the pace of intervention has quickened since the end of the cold war. The UN has managed a lot of these interventions, and international coalitions, almost invariably led by the US, have managed others. About half of the post-Second World War interventions could be regarded as successful in creating a sustained peace, even if they have only rarely resulted in building efficient states. The overall record, therefore, could be regarded as a mixed one. But two features remain constant: our amnesia when it comes to learning lessons and our ability to go on repeating our mistakes.

3

What is legal?

In the very heat of war the greatest security . . . must be in the unabated desire, and invariable prospect of peace, as the only end for which hostilities can be lawfully begun. So that in the prosecution of war we must never carry the rage of it so far, as to unlearn the nature and dispositions of men.

These and these alone would be sufficient motives for the termination of war, and the cultivation of peace . . . In the first place it is dangerous to prolong a contest with a more powerful enemy. In such a case some sacrifices should be made for the sake of peace, as in a storm goods are sometimes thrown overboard to prevent a greater calamity, and to save the vessel and the crew.

Even for the stronger party, when flushed with victory, peace is a safer expedient, than the most extensive successes. For there is the boldness of despair to be apprehended from a vanquished enemy, dangerous as the bite of a ferocious animal in the pangs of death.

If indeed both parties are upon an equal footing . . . (this) is the most favourable moment for making peace, when each party has confidence in itself.

And may God, to whom alone it belongs to dispose the affections and desires of sovereign princes and kings, inscribe these principles upon their hearts and minds, that they may always remember that the noblest office, in which man can be engaged, is the government of men.

HUGO GROTIUS 1583–1645, *On the Law of War and Peace*
(De Jure Belli ac Pacis)

In the long, uncertain days that preceded the invasion of Iraq in 2003, British diplomats at UN headquarters in New York wrestled with a seemingly impossible task: how to push a second resolution authorising the use of force through a heavily divided Security Council. A resolution expressing concern at Saddam's Weapons of Mass Destruction (WMD) capabilities and non-cooperation with weapons inspectors had already been agreed, but nowhere did it specifically authorise military intervention as a way of dealing with Iraq's wayward dictator. The British government, facing widespread domestic scepticism over the call to war, pushed forcefully for a new resolution hoping that it would provide enough legitimacy to ward off critics and reassure an uneasy public. But in the end it was not to be. Unable to secure agreement among the Permanent Five (P5) members of the Security Council for a second resolution, the hawks in the White House went ahead and intervened anyway, with the UK following closely behind.

In the months that followed, the UN went into meltdown, with its detractors lambasting it for comprehensively failing to rise to the challenge. They may have had a point, but in making it they chose to ignore a number of important facts. For all its inadequacies, procedural and substantive, a majority of states would have been more content, and crucially perhaps more willing to help, had the Security Council authorised the invasion of Iraq. This desire for a stamp of approval reveals important truths, not least that states continue to believe that intervention in another state is unlawful and perhaps immoral, unless a legal justification can be found for it; and that most states continue to believe that the UN has a relevant role to play in granting this approval.

*   *   *

The question of the legitimacy and morality of war has long occu-pied the minds of philosophers and lawyers down the centuries, from St Augustine of Hippo, to St Thomas Aquinas, to Hugo Grotius, quoted above. Most of this chapter will be about the legalities of armed intervention. But there is a moral dimension to this question, too, which deserves mention. Firstly because, as we shall discover in a later chapter, success in these ventures depends crucially on winning the support of public opinion and this will often be as much influenced by perspectives of morality as by issues of legality. And secondly because wherever morality points today, the law very often follows tomorrow.

All religions have at one time or another addressed the issue of the 'just war'. Here is one example, drawn from the United States Catholic Bishops' Conference in November 1993, shortly after the end of the Cold War:

> Since the just-war tradition is often misunderstood or selectively applied, we summarise its major components.
>
> First, whether lethal force may be used is governed by the following criteria:
>
> - **Just Cause:** force may be used only to correct a grave, public evil, i.e., aggression or massive violation of the basic rights of whole populations;
> - **Comparative Justice:** while there may be rights and wrongs on all sides of a conflict, to override the presumption against the use of force the injustice suffered by one party must significantly outweigh that suffered by the other;
> - **Legitimate Authority:** only duly constituted public authorities may use deadly force or wage war;
> - **Right Intention:** force may be used only in a truly just cause and solely for that purpose;
> - **Probability of Success:** arms may not be used in a futile cause or in a case where disproportionate measures are required to achieve success;
> - **Proportionality:** the overall destruction expected from the use of force must be outweighed by the good to be achieved;
> - **Last Resort:** force may be used only after all peaceful alternatives have been seriously tried and exhausted.
>
> These criteria (jus ad bellum), taken as a whole, must be satisfied in order to override the strong presumption against the use of force.
>
> Second, the just-war tradition seeks also to curb the violence of war through restraint on armed combat between the contending parties by imposing the following moral standards (jus in bello) for the conduct of armed conflict:
>
> - **Noncombatant Immunity:** civilians may not be the object of

direct attack, and military personnel must take due care to avoid and minimise indirect harm to civilians;

- **Proportionality**: *in the conduct of hostilities, efforts must be made to attain military objectives with no more force than is militarily necessary and to avoid disproportionate collateral damage to civilian life and property;*
- **Right Intention**: *even in the midst of conflict, the aim of political and military leaders must be peace with justice, so that acts of vengeance and indiscriminate violence, whether by individuals, military units or governments, are forbidden.*[1]

What is fascinating to note, as we shall find later, is just how many of these 'moral' principles either draw from or have contributed to the law on international intervention, as it has developed since the cold war, including arguably the most contentious of the criteria: '**Probability of Success**: *arms may not be used in a futile cause . . .*' Some may find it shocking to find that a list of moral principles contains such a fundamentally utilitarian one. However, the inclusion of the 'probability of success' criterion as one of the principles of the just war goes right back, at least implicitly, to Francisco de Vitoria[2] at the beginning of the sixteenth century. This is the answer to the often asked question: 'If you say we should intervene in country X to stop the conflict, then why are we not intervening in Chechnya and Tibet?', to which the moral answer is: 'Because, if there isn't a prospect of success, it would be sacrificing lives needlessly' and the practical answer is: 'Which prime minister or president would commit the young men and women of their country to an enterprise which has no chance of succeeding?'

Whatever the importance of morality, it is usually legalities that play a larger part in influencing the actions of nations – or should do. It would be easy to set the issue of the legality of intervention aside, and argue that it is little more than a sterile, academic debate, removed from the practicalities of realpolitik. But that would be short-sighted. In fact, international law is an integral part of state-building and it is vital to have an understanding of its nature and parameters. A robust yet impartial legal framework for intervention is crucial if we are to guard against illegitimate, self-serving interventions. There are practical considerations and implications too. History is replete with examples demonstrating that unlawful interventions, or those that are perceived to be illegitimate, rarely have a positive impact in the short, medium and even the long term. Add to this mix the fact that the public, the military and our politicians crave legality, and the importance of international law becomes clear.

Yet determining whether intervention is legal or not is fraught with pitfalls. The first reason for this is that this is not yet law which has evolved to a near stable state – it is very much law in the process of evolution – 'work in progress' if you like. Like any other system of laws which have evolved over time, international law does not spring fully formed from a single pen or a single source. It is developed from custom, practice and precedent in a frequently uncomfortable and sometimes haphazard manner. This means that when it comes to deciding what is legal and what is not, we are almost always aiming at a moving target. The second pitfall could be described as the consequence of this 'untidiness': when it comes to the devilish detail of international legal rules on intervention, caveats, exceptions and exceptions to exceptions are the norm and navigating round or through them is the challenge.

Ascertaining what is and is not legal is made even more complex by the fact that the original legal system envisaged by the framers of the UN Charter has not stood the test of time. Rather, it has been battered and bruised by decades of political conflict and shifting political ideologies and allegiances that few could have predicted when the first rules on intervention were detailed in the 1945 UN Charter.

The Charter's vision of a collectively focused, centralised security apparatus, supported by a standing military force at the UN's disposal, was logical and visionary for its age. But all too quickly, the start of the cold war stymied hopes that such a system could exist, let alone flourish and be internationally embraced. Instead, the UN found itself hamstrung from the outset, wounded by super-power manipulation and burdened by a Security Council that was to remain almost wholly impotent for four decades. And consequently, modern rules on intervention are often the product of historical experience and geopolitical compromise, occasionally between the UN's member states (who currently number 192), but more frequently by a coterie of countries with the military might to enforce what they believe to be right. This has made ascertaining the legal baseline a somewhat complex task. What follows, therefore, is far from a comprehensive legal analysis. Rather, it is a quick canter through some sixty years of legal and illegal interventions and some of the factors that moulded them, with the aim of showing how and why the rules we have today are framed as they are, and to prompt thinking on where we might go from here.

The Charter Regime and the Cold War

As far as international law is concerned, we still live exclusively in a state-centric world where state sovereignty, theoretically at least, reigns supreme. This is problematic for those trying to pin down legal justifications for legitimate international interventions that intrude into the domestic jurisdictions of states. How does one square a state's right to conduct its own affairs as it sees fit, essentially to live and let live, with the moral duty, say, to help people in a failing state suffering from widespread and egregious human rights abuses meted out by the state itself?

It was a question that the founders of the UN Charter, the basis for much of modern international law, tried to grapple with. Their response was thus: state sovereignty is paramount but not absolute. It should be guarded, prized and viewed as a fundamental tenet of international law. It follows that intervention is prohibited except in very limited circumstances. The cornerstone of this doctrine can be found in Article 2(4) of the UN Charter which *'prohibits the threat or use of force against the territorial integrity or political independence of any state, or in any other manner inconsistent with the purposes of the United Nations.'* The norm prohibiting intervention doesn't apply just to states, but to the UN as well, as Article 2(7) states: *'Nothing contained in the present Charter shall authorise the **United Nations** [emphasis added] to intervene in matters which are essentially within the domestic jurisdiction of any state or shall require the Members to submit such matters to settlement under the present Charter; but this principle shall not prejudice the application of enforcement measures under Chapter VII.'*

There are two key exceptions to the prohibition on the use of force contained in Article 2(4) and that of non-intervention in Article 2(7). The first is a right to self-defence, individual or collective, under Article 51. The second is the right to take enforcement action under Chapter VII of the UN Charter, through the Security Council, in response to '*a threat to the peace, a breach of the peace or an act of aggression*'.

The ink on the Charter was barely dry when the cold war began. And with it, states began to test the limits of the new prohibition on intervention according to their strategic interests and in so doing simultaneously contributed to the rather unsteady development of rules in this area. In international law, what states do, say and think (known as state practice and opinio juris) can contribute to the development of customary law, in the way that precedent can influence common law. Essentially, the law on interventions develops by taking its cue from what states claim to be their legal reasons for intervening.

Although some of the legal justifications for many of the interventions which took place in the early years of the cold war were genuine, many more were little more than spurious covers for the politically motivated use of force. For instance, there was Egypt's intervention into Palestine/Israel in 1948, which used the thin pretext of the prevention of massacres. The Soviet invasion of Hungary (1956) and Czechoslovakia (1968), were justified by the USSR on the basis that the Soviets were invited in to help restore order enjoyed by ordinary people and that it therefore had consent to intervene. Few countries accepted these legal justifications at face value, and instead rightly saw them as little more than an extension of the cold war, which amounted to forcibly exporting Communism. However, with a veto on the Security Council, the USSR ensured that official international condemnation was limited, and predictably polarised.

There were many other interventions that also cited humanitarian concerns. For example, the USA's early involvement in Vietnam, legal justifications for which included protecting Vietnamese nationals from Communist insurgents; South Africa's intervention in the Angolan civil war (1975–6), ostensibly to assist with displaced people; and Indonesia's invasion and annexation of East Timor, allegedly to protect the Timorese people who favoured integration with Indonesia. In truth, however, behind the mask of diplomatic and legal pretexts it was clear that humanitarian concerns were very limited.[3] One case where such concerns were arguably stronger and more genuine was India's intervention in East Bengal in 1971, where there were reportedly ten million refugees languishing in India who had to be enabled to return. This intervention led to the creation of Bangladesh.

Others, such as the interventions that took place in the Congo in 1960 (by the Belgians), in 1964 (US/Belgian) and in 1978 (Belgian/ French), and the 1976 raid on Entebbe in Uganda used, in part, the legal justification of the protection of nationals, a variation of the right to self-defence. However, hindsight has confirmed what to many seemed obvious at the time, that most of these interventions were (with the exception of Entebbe) little more than colonial adventures aimed at securing access to mineral resources in the newly independent states.[4] Understandably, these newly independent states were not about to take assaults on their hard won independence lightly, and the process of decolonisation and increased claims to self-determination were to have a profound effect, not only on international relations, but also on the rules on intervention.

With the Security Council in almost perpetual paralysis during the cold war, newly independent states in the General Assembly made their voices heard when it came to what they considered to be illegal interventions, in a bid to ensure that they would be free from interference from more powerful states in the future.[5] These prohibitions on the right to intervene came largely in the form of a series of 'soft law' declarations. Although these are not binding in the way that certain resolutions of the Security Council are, they were important in helping to identify what states believed the rule on non-intervention covered at that point in time. They gave insight into what was considered legal and what was not. Take, for instance, the Declaration on the Inadmissibility of Intervention of 21 December 1965 (five years after the UN itself had intervened in the Congo) which stated:

> No state has the right to intervene, directly, or indirectly, for any reason, whatsoever, in the internal or external affairs of any other state. Consequently, armed intervention and all other forms of interference or attempted threats against the personality of the state or against its political, economic, and cultural elements, are condemned.[6]

Then in 1970 came the Friendly Relations Declaration,[7] which prohibited any interference by a state against the political, economic, social and cultural elements of another state. It also referred to intervention in the instance of a civil war, stating that:

> every state has a duty to refrain from organising, instigating, assisting or participating in acts of civil strife or terrorist acts in another state, or acquiescing in organised activities within its territory which are directed towards the commission of such acts.

In later years, these declarations came to be relied upon as authoritative interpretations of international law and were given an important stamp of approval by the International Court of Justice in, perhaps, the most important case to examine the limits of permissible intervention – that of Nicaragua v USA in 1986.[8] The case itself confirmed that the principle of non-intervention is part of customary international law, despite the fact that breaches of this rule may be frequent.

The Security Council's impotence was to have another unforeseen effect that would lay the foundations for future UN interventions and help to redefine the limits of state sovereignty – the emergence of UN peacekeeping forces. Although the 'blue helmets' of the UN are now one of the most widely recognisable facets of UN activity, they were in fact an innovation born of pragmatism in response to the failings of the collective system, rather than a carefully thought-out idea included in the UN Charter. Between 1948 and 1988 peacekeeping forces continued to be established despite the fact that there is no specific legal provision for them in the Charter. As with so many areas of international law their existence, and the rules that governed their activities, gradually evolved through state practice to the point where peacekeeping and the deployment of peacekeeping forces are now a widely accepted and much valued practice. During the 'proxy wars' of the cold war period, the role of the UN's 'blue helmets' was far more limited than it is today. But over the years, the UN's involvement in states has increased as more challenges to state sovereignty have emerged. Since the end of the cold war there has been a six-fold increase in UN preventive diplomacy missions, a four-fold increase in UN peacemaking missions (to end war), a similar increase in UN peace operations (to reconstruct peace and stop war restarting) and an eleven-fold increase in the countries subject to UN sanctions.[9] Key to this trend has been the rapid rise of the international human rights movement.

This movement had already gained a toehold in both the 1945 UN Charter and later the 1948 Universal Declaration of Human Rights. But by the 1960s new treaties such as the International Covenant on Civil and Political Rights and the International Covenant on Social, Economic and Cultural Rights gave expression to emerging claims that state sovereignty involved rights, as well as responsibilities. Challenges also came in the form of various events in the 1980s which stretched the limits of intervention to breaking point and sometimes beyond. Notable was the USA's invasion of Grenada in 1983, ostensibly in response to a request from the Organisation of Eastern Caribbean States for assistance. In reality, there was international consensus that this pretext, too, was little more than an unconvincing fig leaf for intervention suited to US geopolitical ends. But, using a tactic favoured by all of the Permanent Five members, the US managed to avoid formal international opprobrium by vetoing a Security Council resolution that would otherwise have strongly condemned the intervention as a violation of international law.

Six years later the US argued that it had intervened in Panama in self-defence to protect nationals abroad. The fact that the United States made a clear distinction between its legal justification (the protection of nationals) and the actual political goals that it sought (regime change and the restoration of democracy) is something that has happened with other interventions, making it all the more difficult to determine what is and isn't legal.

Had the Berlin Wall not been torn down, the pattern that had emerged during the cold war of states sporadically intervening, allegedly for humanitarian reasons but often fuelled by purely political motives, might have continued unchecked. But the sudden end of the cold war was radically to alter the nature and arguably the permissible limits of intervention. For forty years, states had watched the UN play only a restricted role in interventions. All that was about to change.

Post-Cold War Interventionism

The post-cold war environment revealed myriad challenges for international law. Although the total number of all wars worldwide sharply diminished, the predominance of inter-state conflict was quickly replaced by a predominance of intra-state ones. For every newly emergent state intent on pursuing multi-party democracy there was another that was failing or had failed. Inter-ethnic tensions and historical disputes found space to grow in the numerous political vacuums that materialised when the superpowers pulled out or switched their attention elsewhere. As state authority collapsed, claims for self-determination rose and the international community, buoyed by a new era of cooperation and a new spirit of optimism, grew ever more eager to intervene and resolve conflicts.

The fact that state-centred international law was not constructed to cope with the many complex intra-state conflicts that emerged, failed to dull international enthusiasm. Rather than wait for the law to come up with answers to their questions about interventions, more interventions were planned and executed at breakneck pace and the law was expected to keep up.

Nothing exemplifies this pattern quite like the practice of the Security Council in the period after the cold war. With veto use considerably diminished, the Security Council set about authorising a massive increase in the number and range of interventions carried out by the UN, groups of states and regional bodies. The legal bases for these operations were to flow mainly from Chapter VII of the UN Charter which allows the Council to exercise its most formidable coercive powers under the heading of '*action with respect to threats to the peace, breaches of peace, and acts of aggression.*' There are three key articles in Chapter VII: under Article 39 the Security Council '*shall determine the existence of any threat to the peace, breach of the peace or act of aggression and shall make recommendations or decide what measures shall be taken in accordance with Article 41 and 42, to maintain or restore international peace and security*'.

Interestingly, the Security Council chose largely to avoid making specific reference to these articles when it authorised interventions. Instead, through various authorisations, it gradually widened and interpreted the definition of what constituted a threat to international peace and security, in order to justify a range of different types of intervention. And so, during the 1990s a whole plethora of circumstances came to be regarded as '*threats to international peace and security*' justifying interventions to deal with situations ranging from internal armed conflicts (as with Yugoslavia), recalcitrant states (Iraq) and even (and exceptionally) disruptions to democracy (for example Haiti).

In Somalia and then, more contentiously, in Kosovo, the justification used was humanitarian, a development which was to have, in time, far-reaching consequences.

In September 1997, I returned from my first trip to Kosovo and briefed Prime Minister Blair that we would have to intervene to stop Milošević using the full force of his army to attack the Kosovar Albanian civilians in a manner which was clearly excessive and thus breached both international law and specific provisions of the Geneva Convention. Prime Minister Blair's response was that his officials were already studying the situation but had concluded that the humanitarian situation was not yet 'sufficiently bad' to justify intervention under these provisions. However, the UN Security Council Resolution which was in the end used by NATO member states in an attempt to justify the use of force in Kosovo (UNSC 1199) specifically mentioned the need to avert a humanitarian crisis, which was by then presumably judged to have deteriorated to the point where it could be argued that the provisions of Chapter VII, as interpreted by recent state practice, could be said to apply.

The New UN Peacemakers

One of the biggest beneficiaries of the Security Council's new-found vigour and activism was the UN itself. Previously confined to traditional peacekeeping roles, it found itself authorised to carry out more and more complex roles. This tallied well with UN thinking at the time. In 1992 the then Secretary General, Boutros Boutros-Ghali, published an Agenda for Peace[10] which made the case for peacemaking, where UN forces, operating under Article 40, would enforce rather than simply monitor ceasefires.

In practice, UN missions were often plunged in at the deep end in unfamiliar situations, dealing with unfamiliar actors and forced to adopt new rules of engagement on the hoof. The Security Council, departing from established practice after the Congo, began routinely authorising troops to use force other than in self-defence. While this blurring of the division between peacekeeping and peace enforcement appeared sensible on paper, it became rather messy in practice. Although there were some success stories, those which failed had devastating consequences as Yugoslavia, Somalia and Sierra Leone tragically demonstrated. The UN's fingers had been burnt but the precedent had been set. By 1999 peace enforcement missions had developed to the extent that the UN found itself in charge of running nation-building programmes in post-conflict states from East Timor to Kosovo.

By the time the new millennium was ushered in, enforcement missions were at an all time high and the effect on the legal doctrine of state sovereignty could already be seen. Writing in *The Economist* in 1999, UN Secretary General Kofi Annan noted: '*We need to adapt our international system better to a world with new actors, new responsibilities, and new possibilities for peace and progress.*'[11] Herein lay a legal and practical conundrum: it was impossible to ignore the problems that UN peace enforcement missions had encountered, and in some instances precipitated. Yet never was there a time when enforcement was needed more. The Security Council's answer was to delegate some of the more complex enforcement actions to states and regional bodies, thereby helping to counter UN overstretch resulting from the increasing number of interventions.

Express and Implied Authorisations to Intervene

On some occasions, the Security Council gave authorisation to states to use force under Chapter VII. For example, Security Council Resolution 678 of 1990 took the important step of expressly authorising member states to use '*all necessary means*' to eject Iraqi forces from Kuwait. The fact that there was a general consensus on the appropriateness of the course of action amongst member states meant that express authorisation was possible. But there were other instances, even allowing for the new spirit of international co-operation, when the Security Council was unwilling or unable to sanction interventions. Rather than sit back, states simply became more creative with their legal justifications.

And so the idea of 'implicit' authorisation was born. For example, concern over the internal repression of Iraqi Kurds and Shi'as in 1991, following the expulsion of Saddam Hussein's forces from Kuwait, led to the adoption of Security Council Resolution 688. Although the resolution expressed concern at the situation, it stopped short of authorising force under Chapter VII, or of authorising a joint operation by the US, UK and French[12] air forces to intervene in order to secure no-fly zones in north and south Iraq. Despite the lack of express authorisation to use force, the allied forces went ahead anyway. While the UK was keen to promote the idea that a customary right of intervention existed in circumstances of extreme humanitarian need, the USA's legal justification was based, in part, on its claim to be acting in support of Resolution 688 (which had called on Iraq to end internal repression and stated that its acts threatened international peace and security in the region) and that in turn, Resolution 688 had made reference to Resolution 678 which had authorised *'all necessary means'*. The idea that there was some sort of implied authorisation at one remove, based on a loose connection between the two resolutions, caused some international lawyers sleepless nights. But with three of the interveners holding permanent seats on the Security Council it was only a matter of time before this rather woolly legal basis was used again. Kosovo would be one of these controversial legal instances, when both the implied authorisations and the idea of customary right of humanitarian intervention, existing alongside the Charter, were advocated.

Of the three resolutions passed by the Security Council in 1998 in response to the situation in Kosovo, none expressly authorised states or NATO to use force. While some states claimed that relevant resolutions[13] provided implied authorisation, others, including the UK, claimed that it was an internationally legal response designed to avert a humanitarian catastrophe and was therefore justified under customary international law. The result was a political and legal division between states and lawyers. Few doubted the moral case for action, but the fundamental split which emerged between states over legal justifications showed just how difficult it was to establish a single and solid legal basis for action.

The involvement of NATO in Kosovo was controversial. There was a trend towards the delegation of enforcement action by the Security Council to regional bodies that was to become the norm by the end of the millennium. Article 53 of the UN Charter allows the Security Council to use *regional arrangements or agencies'* for enforcement action, but goes on to add that these have to be authorised by the Council. In the absence of any Security Council authorisation for NATO to use force in Kosovo, it is hard to claim that the NATO military action was justified under this article. Whether NATO's action was lawful under international law – or for that matter under the NATO Treaty – remains contested, even today, among lawyers and politicians.

States have used other controversial legal justifications for action, not least the argument that the Security Council can retrospectively authorise interventions. This has happened on a number of occasions when stalemate in the Security Council meant that authorisations to use force could not be obtained. The ECOWAS operations in Liberia (1990–92) and action in Sierra Leone (1997–8) were, some would argue, both implicitly endorsed after the respective interventions had taken place.[14] Although some contend that this shows how innovative, flexible and non-formalistic the Security Council can be when the need arises, critics counter that it leaves the law open to abuse and encourages its inconsistent application.

In spite of these concerns, there are few signs that this trend will be reversed. In 2003, the USA and the UK relied heavily on the 'implied authorisation' argument for the launch of offensive action against Iraq. In its brief search for political legitimacy the USA proclaimed that it was acting with the support of a coalition of at least forty states and with the implicit backing that was to be found in a range of Security Council Resolutions.

Security Council Resolution 1441, as is well documented, did not expressly authorise force against Iraq. Instead it called upon Iraq to end material breaches of previous resolutions and indicated that otherwise, severe consequences could follow. When the weapons inspectors returned to Iraq but failed to find evidence of the WMD programme, part of the USA and UK's argument was that Iraq's lack of full cooperation placed it in material breach of a number of resolutions, including Resolution 678. Although the resolution was some twelve years old by that point, they nevertheless argued that Iraq's failure to comply with subsequent resolutions which had referred to 678 meant that the authority to use force contained in Resolution 678 had been revived.

If nothing else this just showed how brilliantly creative lawyers can be when their backs are against the wall and legal cover is needed for political action. The problem was that the very creativity of their arguments seriously diminished their capacity to convince most states. From a legal perspective, all this raised serious questions about who should have the power to determine whether and when a material breach occurred (the Security Council?) and if so what should be done about it.

'Pro-Democratic' Interventions

Unilateral declarations by superpowers that they have the right to intervene in the affairs of other states for the general peace tend to raise hackles across the international community, as the 2003 intervention in Iraq clearly demonstrated. States, especially those which are less powerful, are predictably uneasy about the precedent that, say, intervening to install democracy would set and the extent to which such a provision would invite abuse by the powerful. But even the powerful can be queasy about this justification, as the USA showed when it chose not to use restoration of democracy as a legal justification for intervention in Panama (although it acknowledged that this was one of its political motives), relying instead on the right of self-defence to protect its nationals.

The Security Council's record of authorising military interventions to promote or uphold democracy is mixed. A high watermark arguably emerged in 1994 when the overthrow of Haiti's democratically elected government led the Council to declare that the situation constituted a threat to international peace and security.[15] It was later to authorise member states (in effect the US) to create a multinational force to expel the junta and ensure the restoration of the legitimate government.[16] What made this intervention unusual was that it took place at the specific request of the ousted, recognised government of Haiti. The Security Council went to great lengths, however, to stress that the situation was unique and exceptional, in an attempt to avoid the restoration of democracy being used as a precedent for further unilateral intervention. Legal commentators point out that the fact that numerous other cases throughout the 1990s and early 2000s where democratic rule was overthrown[17] did not result in similar UN authorisations to use force, strengthens the argument that Haiti cannot be seen as a precedent for pro-democratic intervention.[18]

Overall, however, recent history has shown that there is far less hostility and a wider scope for the interpretation of the rules if the intervention is multilateral rather than unilateral, particularly if the former commands broad support within the international community, as in the case of Kosovo.

Other International Law

Inevitably, this chapter has concentrated mostly on the United Nations and especially its Charter and the Resolutions of the UN Security Council. It is important to note, however, that international law does not reside only in the UN. It has derived through custom and practice over many centuries, not just in the UN but also in other conventions and treaties, many of which long pre-date the founding of the United Nations in 1948.

Perhaps the most famous of these are the Geneva Conventions governing the conduct of war. As part of the debate on the legality or otherwise of the detention of prisoners in Guantanamo Bay, there have recently been some suggestions from the United States and from the British home secretary, John Reid, that the Geneva Conventions were somehow out of date since they did not take account of issues such as global terrorism. This, however, is based on a misunderstanding of what the Conventions, the most recent of which was signed in 1949, with updating protocols in 1977, actually say. In 2003, the Venice Commission[19] looked at the Conventions precisely in order to determine whether they needed updating in the post-9/11 world and concluded that they did not, since they catered for a much wider set of eventualities than was commonly recognised, including for operations such as those carried out by Al Qaeda.[20]

Meanwhile, the operation of the Geneva Conventions has been significantly enhanced by the rapid extension and invigoration of international criminal law and international justice, through the creation of Ad Hoc Tribunals for the former Yugoslavia and Rwanda under Chapter VII of the Charter and by the foundation, in 1998, of the International Criminal Court. Already case law, especially from the Ad Hoc Tribunals, has helped to clarify and strengthen international criminal law. These conventions and new institutions could be much more imaginatively used for prevention of conflict before the event, as well as for justice after it.

When I returned from my second visit to Kosovo in 1998, I briefed British Prime Minister Tony Blair that both Milošević and the artillery commanders who had bombarded the Kosovar villages which I had visited, seemed more frightened by the threat of indictment by the International Criminal Tribunal for the Former Yugoslavia (ICTY) for breaches of the Geneva Convention than they were of NATO bombing. I suggested that an early indictment of Milošević and his army commanders might cause them to stop their military operations to drive the Kosovar Albanians out of the country, in clear contravention both of the Geneva Conventions and of human rights law. Milošević was indeed later indicted, but not until after the war started. I remain convinced that, if he and his generals had been indicted earlier we might have avoided, not only a lot of suffering in Kosovo, but the need to mount an armed international intervention by NATO later.

The same technique could be used today against those perpetrating the horrors in Darfur where, it is interesting to note, those prosecuting the war are reportedly more concerned about indictment by the International Criminal Court than they are about international intervention. If more states can be persuaded to sign up to the International Criminal Court, then through its judgments it may be possible to apply and enforce individual criminal responsibility.[*] In turn, this could become a means, not just for states and individuals to seek redress after wars, but for international law to be used to limit the savagery of wars, or even prevent them occurring in the

[*] The 2006 Lebanon crisis threw up some interesting new developments in this sphere. Louise Arbour, the High Commissioner for Human Rights, made references during the conflict to violations of international humanitarian law committed in Lebanon by both Hezbollah and Israel. The problem is that Israel, Syria and Iran have not ratified the ICC's Rome Statute. This would have made it difficult to find a legal basis for possible ICC prosecution along the lines hinted at by both Louise Arbour and Kofi Annan. But the possibility has now been aired that personal responsibility could flow in these circumstances.

first place. In other words, these new courts and tribunals which the world has established in recent years and the international law they pronounce upon, have the potential to become instruments, not only for justice, but also for prevention, since they can represent a minatory warning to belligerent or tyrannical leaders.

Responsibility to Protect – An Emerging Legal Base for Legitimate Action?

As I indicated earlier, international law doesn't follow a master plan. It stumbles along, usually clarifying itself only when absolutely necessary. But this weakness can also be seen as a strength and an asset upon which those seeking to strengthen international law can draw. This inherent flexibility in international law means that it can be changed to reflect new circumstances, without losing sight of the fundamental principles that remain crucial in our community of states today.

Perhaps the best example of this is the emergence of a new legal doctrine – the so-called 'responsibility to protect'. Whilst a customary right to protect people from human rights abuse and humanitarian catastrophe had been claimed to exist (for example in the Somalia and, later Kosovo interventions) this has remained disputed territory legally.

However, the world may now be moving to confirm and provide clarification of this right from a legal point of view. Nestled in paragraph 139 of the World Summit Outcome Document, which was agreed by world leaders in September 2005, there was a pledge that may point to the way ahead for international law and interventions. According to the World Summit text: *'each individual State has the responsibility to protect its populations from genocide, war crimes, ethnic cleansing and crimes against humanity. This responsibility entails the prevention of such crimes, including their incitement, through appropriate and necessary means. We accept that responsibility and will act in accordance with it.'*

The World Summit declaration goes on to explain that member states are: *'prepared to take collective action, in a timely and decisive manner, through the Security Council, in accordance with the UN Charter, including Chapter VII, on a case by case basis and in cooperation with relevant regional organisations as appropriate, should peaceful means be inadequate and national authorities are manifestly failing to protect their populations from genocide, war crimes, ethnic cleansing, and crimes against humanity and its implications, bearing in mind the principles of the Charter and international law'.*

The international political endorsement of this principle, which has been some years in the making, is a major achievement.[21] Of course, abstract political declarations are easy to endorse. The real test will be whether the Security Council is prepared to back its words[22] with action, with Darfur arguably the first practical indication of their willingness or otherwise to do so. The concept of 'the responsibility to protect' may also represent a big (and so far rather depressing) legal step forward, because, for the first time, it does not limit action to situations in which trouble has spilled over from one state to another. Therefore, in theory at least, states may have committed themselves to tackling violence which is purely interior to one state. Although it is too early to know this definitively, some academic scholars have suggested that this amounts to an important interpretation of the legitimate scope of Security Council authority in situations of mass violence within a single state.

As you might expect, the 'responsibility to protect' asserted in this paragraph of the World Summit Outcome Document throws up as many questions as it appears to answer. One of the key issues which will have to be determined at some point in the future is whether, in the absence of Security Council authorisation, individual states may invoke the 'Kosovo' doctrine of humanitarian intervention to protect people who face genocide, ethnic cleansing and other egregious breaches of international law. Only through time and by examining the practice of the Security Council will an answer emerge. There are also those who question just how effective the 'responsibility to protect' can be as long as it is forced to work within the currently constituted Security Council.

But on balance, if the World Summit declaration means what it says, it represents a substantial step forward. Especially if it helps to clarify the norms in what has become a thoroughly confused legal tangle and enhances consistency in the application of a system of hastily constructed law, whose inconsistencies at the moment are undermining the importance of legitimacy in international actions and leaving far too wide a scope for abuse by the powerful.

Summary

Definitions of sovereignty and the legal limits on non-intervention have evolved over many years and continue to do so. But, despite the fact that interventions have been common, the norm of non-intervention remains the dominant presumption of customary international law. Although in the early years of the cold war, both scholars and some states argued that the failure of the UN's collective security apparatus meant that intervention could be justified, this was roundly rejected in case law and in state practice.[23] Nowadays, interventions focus less heavily on apparent institutional failings – even though these arguably still exist – and far more on promoting human rights and basic, fundamental freedoms.

With the end of the cold war a new political reality dawned and with it came a growing belief that there is a right to just governance, although state practice suggests that this does not extend to widespread support for unilateral interventions to impose it which are not authorised by the Security Council. Indeed, the Security Council has been instrumental in moulding the law in order to permit interventions that would not have seemed possible during the height of superpower confrontation. It did so by radically widening the definition of what constituted a threat to international peace and security.

For the UN this meant new missions with new complexities. Traditional peacekeeping continued, but peace enforcement was also encouraged, although it met with mixed success. In a development typical of international law more generally, these operations started off without any formal legal basis, but through repetition and state practice came to be accepted, because it suited the states themselves. Later missions would fall under the executive direction of the UN Secretary General with overall authority deriving from the Security Council.

Even though the number and range of interventions authorised explicitly, implicitly and/or retrospectively by the Security Council increased dramatically in the 1990s, the importance of the norm of non-intervention stayed largely intact. In contrast, the concept of state sovereignty changed. If there are lessons to be learnt from Iraq, Bosnia, Somalia, Rwanda, Haiti and Kosovo, they are that the concept of state sovereignty should not prevent states, regional bodies, or even the UN from intervening when genocide and ethnic cleansing are evident. The fact that the Security Council chose to use Chapter VII as a basis for authorisations, as opposed to specific articles within the Chapter, demonstrates just how flexible and non-formalistic Chapter VII can be.

On the relatively few occasions when states or regional bodies did not find Council authorisation forthcoming, they nevertheless continued to try to find a legal basis to support their actions. Although some governments told their parliaments and public their actions amounted to humanitarian intervention, they were far more reticent to use 'humanitarian intervention' as a legal justification, which seems to indicate that they did not believe that such a unilateral right existed. Both states, and the law, appear to be less supportive of unilateral pro-democratic interventions. This has not, however, stopped a handful of states claiming that they have a customary international legal right to use this as a reason for action. But there is no enthusiasm by the majority of states to rely on this as legal justification. However desirable democracy may be, it has not yet displaced peace as the Charter's primary concern.

What all this amounts to is that international law and practice has evolved to the point where international intervention in the domestic jurisdiction of another state has the best chance of conforming to international law and receiving the wider support of the international community when *all* the following conditions are apparent:

1 There has been a gross breach of international law or standards, especially in respect of human rights, or a humanitarian crisis, which demands an urgent but limited response. *And*
2 This threatens the wider peace of the region or the world (for example in the case of weapons of mass destruction). *And*
3 Peaceful and diplomatic efforts have been exhausted. *And*
4 The action proposed is deemed to be proportionate. *And*
5 It is mandated by the 'lawful authority' – that is, UN Security Council authorisation has been sought and received. *And*
6 There is a reasonable prospect of success.

These criteria, it will be observed, bear a remarkably close resemblance to the 'moral' precepts underpinning the modern concept of the just war, articulated by the United States Catholic Bishops at the start of this chapter.

Part II

Post-conflict reconstruction

4

Stabilisation

The first 6 to 12 weeks following a ceasefire or peace accord is often the most critical period for establishing both a stable peace and the credibility of the peacekeepers. Credibility and political momentum lost during this period can often be difficult to regain.

Report of the Panel on United Nations Peace Operations (the Brahimi Report), Para 87

BAGHDAD, April 13, 2003 – The failure of American troops to prevent wholesale looting and burning of public buildings in Baghdad – including even hospitals and the priceless collection of the Iraqi Museum – is breeding anger and frustration among Iraqis already deeply suspicious of US motives for occupying their country.

Iraqi police will start patrolling again on Monday and US forces with Humvees and armoured vehicles now guard Baghdad's main hospitals. But the damage has been done: public services which could have been resumed almost immediately will now take weeks or months to restore. Hospitals have no equipment and civil servants have lost vital files and computer records. The only important public building the Americans protected was the Oil Ministry.

A small group of people were so angry that they protested on Sunday outside the Palestine hotel, where US officers in charge of civil administration have been meeting non-government organisations to plan electricity, water and medical services, and Iraqi police generals to discuss restoring law and order.

But everywhere we go in Baghdad, the resentment and frustration are the same. In most areas, order started to return over the last three days only when local people – on instructions from the Shi'ite

Muslim religious leader Ayatollah Ali Sistani – went out with Kalashnikov assault rifles and set up roadblocks to stop looters and seize back stolen goods.

Safa al-Din Hamza Sultan, who leads a neighbourhood com-mittee in the inner suburb of East Karrada, made his feelings clear when he went to liaise with US forces: 'I told the American major, you've caused this. The state and the security organisations were there. Then they collapsed and you knew that very well. You stood by and let all this happen. You wanted to overthrow the govern-ment, so you should have taken responsibility for security. If you'd put just one soldier on each government building, this wouldn't have happened.'

Around him, the courtyard of the East Karrada mosque was piled with recovered loot: chairs, bookshelves, mattresses, a green velvet armchair. There was more in a meeting room: tractor tyres, packets of drugs, computerised heart monitors . . .

Many people in Baghdad are convinced that US troops actively encouraged the looting, an impression which a US officer in charge of one compound being ransacked did nothing to dispel.*

Lieutenant-Colonel JR Sanderson of the 3rd Infantry Division told journalists at Saddam Hussein's Military Intelligence head-quarters that his men had let the crowds in once they had searched and secured the site: 'The local people here wanted to go back in here quickly and I don't think anyone could have stopped them.'

Kerbala, an hour's drive south of Baghdad, poignantly illustrates that the disaster in Baghdad was completely unnecessary. People who arrived from the Shi'ite holy city on Sunday said that religious leaders had organised community groups to prevent any looting, electricity generators at a grain silo had been hooked up to provide power for the city, and schools were due to open again on Monday.

OUT THERE NEWS Posted on Sunday, 13 April 2003 – 03.03 pm;
by Paul Eedle

---

* The same thing happened after the US operation in Panama City when, accord-ing to Robert Perito in remarks made to the Carnegie Council of 10 March 2004, $1 billion damage was done to Panama City by looting in the presence of US troops, more than was done in the combat operations conducted by them. In Bosnia and Kosovo, too, major destruction, burning, looting and displacement of people was allowed to take place after combat operations.

* * *

In the history of post-conflict reconstruction, there are no mistakes more regularly made or more dearly paid for than failing to dominate the security space immediately after the fighting has stopped and failing to transition this into the rule of law in the months which follow.

Dominate the Security Space

If there was just one golden principle for this phase it would be that the rule of law must be item one, priority one, from day one.

For without the rule of law, there can be no proper democracy, no trust in the institutions of government, no efficient distribution of international aid, no chance of re-growing the economy and no peace for the people.

When it came to planning the war phase of the Iraq operation, Donald Rumsfeld was right to insist to his generals that in this kind of warfare speed could substitute for mass and they did not need to follow the 'Powell doctrine' of overwhelming force to defeat Saddam's forces – it could be done with a much lighter force, combining all arms in close cooperation and moving very fast. But Rumsfeld and the civilian leadership of the Pentagon were entirely wrong to reject outright the notion that creating and maintaining the peace in Iraq might require more troops than winning the war phase there. When US Army Chief of Staff General Shinseki testified to Congress that the reconstruction of Iraq would require '*something of the order of several hundred thousand soldiers*'[1] Deputy Secretary of Defence Paul Wolfowitz rejected this as '*wildly off the mark*', adding that '*it's hard to conceive that it would take more forces to provide stability in post-Saddam Iraq than it would take to conduct the war itself and to secure the surrender of Saddam's security forces and his army.*'

Following the Rumsfeld plan, the United States-led Coalition army seemed initially to prove Rumsfeld and Wolfowitz right by winning an astonishingly rapid victory over Saddam Hussein's forces. But these light coalition forces, so successful in the conflict phase, proved completely inadequate when it came to the crucial first task of providing security in the post-conflict reconstruction phase which immediately followed. The original US plan envisaged the inclusion of twenty companies of Military Police (around 4,500) in the invasion force. But this was reduced to just three companies, which proved totally inadequate to secure Baghdad in the spring and summer of 2003.[2] (The number of US Military Police was subsequently raised to the original twenty companies later in the occupation phase, but by then it was too late for them to regain the initiative.) Overall there were just not enough Coalition troops on the ground after the war ended to dominate the security space, and even if there had been, they were not trained to do that kind of soldiering; the Rumsfeld doctrine also stipulated that the US did war, not 'nation-building'.

To make bad matters worse, the US then completely disbanded the Iraqi army and the security and intelligence services, thus abolishing the only organisations powerful enough to maintain the internal security of the state. Simultaneously, most of the police left their posts and went home. So the new US administration in Iraq was left with a huge security problem and no-one to deal with it. Within days of their stunning victory, the US was already losing the confidence and support of the local population for the failure to make their lives safe. Meanwhile, with the US having lost control of security, the infrastructure rebuilding teams who, it was intended, would reconnect broken electricity lines and shattered water pipes, could not start to do their work.

The story of the US and Coalition occupation of Iraq since has been about only one thing – trying to regain control of the security space which they lost in their first days and weeks. There must be a real question as to whether the same will not also prove to be the case in Afghanistan.

The 'Powell doctrine' of overwhelming force may not have been relevant for the conflict phase – but it is for the stabilisation phase which follows. There are varying estimates as to how many troops are required per head of population, in order to fulfil this stabilisation task. The Coalition force levels in Iraq have averaged around five per 1,000 head of population since the invasion. But according to one US study, if the intervener's goals are ambitious, as in Iraq, it may need as many as twenty troops per 1,000 population, which is almost exactly the ratio NATO deployed in Bosnia.[3] This level of deployment would have produced a force three times larger than was deployed in Iraq, totalling some 500,000 troops who would then need to stay in the country for a period of between five and eight years.[4] There is, however no precise linear correlation between inputs and outputs in peacemaking. But the general, if empirical, rule here is this: the greater the number of troops deployed, the smaller the number of deaths suffered. The problem recently has been that, while the number of interventions has risen, the number of troops nations are prepared to deploy has remained static. The result is severe overstretch as increasing requirements outrun available means. It is merely a matter of record that 1/25th the amount of troops and 1/50th the amount of aid, per head of population, has been deployed in Afghanistan as were initially deployed in Kosovo. The early days' failure of the US-led coalition in Iraq to dominate the security space may be particularly glaring – but it is by no means the only example of this fault.

Then the Rule of Law

On 19 July 1999 I visited General Mike Jackson's Pristina headquarters in Kosovo, just a few days after his triumphant entry into Kosovo at the head of his 30,000-strong NATO army.[5] I asked him about the law and order issue. He replied that he hoped the UN civil police would arrive soon, because putting contingents of KFOR on the streets to do law and order was risky. I know why he said this. With the exception of his British troops, who were trained to do this kind of thing in Northern Ireland, the remainder of his army had neither training nor experience in acting as part soldier, part policeman on the streets of an occupied city. That evening I watched General Jackson's British paratroopers, in berets not battle helmets, quietly patrolling on foot the narrow alleyways of the capital Pristina, just as they would have done in Belfast. And next day I saw the contrast when I visited the German and Italian troops in nearby Prizren and Peć, to find them patrolling these small market towns in their battle tanks – whose guns were so long they could not even go round the narrow street corners and whose huge bulk made mincemeat of the stalls selling produce in the local market.

General Jackson's wish was not to be fulfilled. The first elements of the UN police did not arrive until August and the force was not up to full strength until nearly two years later in 2001.

The corrupt forces and criminal elements which had run the Kosovo war swiftly used the few short weeks after NATO's occupation to move into the gap where the rule of law should have been but wasn't. And there they have remained, more or less, ever since.

In Bosnia the situation was little different and the results little better. NATO arrived in overwhelming force, with the result that the kind of insurgency which has been the curse of success in Iraq never happened. But, again, the soldiers could not and did not fill the rule of law vacuum at the start. The international community in Bosnia did not make the establishment of the rule of law priority number one until 2002, seven years after the war there ended. The result has been that the corrupt forces who ran the war on all sides have now, assisted by early elections, infiltrated the whole structure of the state from top to bottom.

It is not necessary to go to Bosnia, or Kosovo or Iraq to find this phenomenon. Corruption and organised crime are the natural by-products of war and stalk after it like a black shadow. The same phenomenon could be seen in European countries like Italy, France, Germany and even Britain in the years immediately after the Second World War.

Once again, the crucial hours in the battle for the rule of law are the early hours, for it is then that support of the local population and the battle to establish the rule of law can be won or lost. A failure by the interveners to provide security in this period will almost always result in the local population turning to local militia – or even criminal networks, as happened in Iraq.[6] As one US commentator on the Iraq war has said, '*Security cannot be purchased at the expense of justice.*'[7] And it is only the actions of the soldier which can fill these hours until the civil authorities and police arrive. If the soldier won't, or can't as in Kosovo and Iraq, then nobody will.

The trouble is that it requires a special kind of soldier to do this job, for this is the most difficult soldiering of all and only the best quality troops can do it. This is especially true where the situation is toughest. It may be possible to get away with poorer quality troops in uncontested peace maintenance operations. But not if the task is peacemaking against a determined opposition – 'post-conflict stabilisation' (Bosnia after the first month) is much easier than 'in-conflict stabilisation' (as in Iraq and Afghanistan).

There will be cases where, in an 'in-conflict' situation, it is impossible to create a secure space across the whole country at first. The temptation then will be for the army to go to where the enemy is and take them on across the whole country. It is a temptation which, in most cases, should be resisted. The soldier's job in this phase is not to seek out and destroy the enemy, but to win secure space. So, in these circumstances it will usually be better, even if less exciting for the army, to establish islands of security safe for the administrators, infrastructure rebuilders and development workers to get to work. Then the army can begin to 'ink blot' out to create larger and larger areas of security in which life can return to normal, the so-called 'take, hold and build' strategy successfully tried first in the British campaign of the 1950s to counter the Communist insurgency in Malaya.

It is important to realise that the key here is once again security. The purpose of rebuilding the infrastucture and re-establishing governance is not to generate gratitude, but *influence*. Gratitude for reconnecting a village's water supply will only last until sunset, if by night the insurgents are able to return and threaten to kill and maim. In the battle for influence, lethal threat will always win out over bodily comfort. The key therefore is to create security, establish the interveners, not the insurgents, as the prevailing presence and then, through re-construction, the rule of law, economic re-generation and the return of governance, give people a greater stake in preserving peace than they have in returning to conflict.

This was the strategy originally pursued in Afghanistan, where ISAF (International Security Assistance Force) initially secured Kabul and then moved gradually out. However, when the British moved into Helmand province to 'take on' the Taliban, they changed the approach in favour of a 'forward base' strategy under which small units were deployed in isolated 'Beau Geste' fortified positions scattered across the region. I suspect that politics and especially the need to show President Karzai[*] that we were prepared to 'take the fight to the enemy' played a large part in the decision to change the policy. It was a mistake which left troops exposed, soaked up a large amount of troop resources in self-protection that

---

[*] President Karzai's relatives lived in the villages in the north of Helmand province.

should have been used to project governance and brought a halt to the civilian reconstruction effort. According to one US source,[8] President Bush and his advisers wanted to adopt the 'take, hold and build' strategy to counter the rising insurgency in Iraq in 2003/4, but this was overruled by Donald Rumsfeld.

The task of the soldier in this phase, therefore, is not to hunker down in tanks or stay holed up in their bases, but to be out on the street in touch with the local situation and talking to the local people. In these first days a soldier is likely to be called on to switch instantaneously from war fighter, to rudimentary policeman, to caring social worker and back again, sometimes all in the space of a single hour. For these are two very different kinds of warfare. Success in the hot war phase often depends on the maximum concentration of force and firepower. But having to use maximum force and firepower almost always leads to failure in the stabilisation and counter-insurgency phase. As one of the earliest and most prescient of commentators on counter-insurgency warfare, David Galula, puts it, *'a soldier fired upon in conventional war who does not fire back with every available weapon would be guilty of a dereliction of duty; the reverse would be the case in counter-insurgency warfare, where the rule is to apply the minimum of fire ... The population ... becomes the objective for the counter-insurgent, as it was for his enemy'.*[9]

There will be early pressure to bring home the first troops who initially stabilised the peace as soon as possible. It is very important that these troops are rotated out on a 'trickle' basis (i.e. gradually and unit by unit), rather than in one massive rotation in which all are replaced at the same time. The reasons for this are obvious. The 'tribal knowledge' gained by the first troops as to the culture and traditions of the country, and what works and what doesn't, cannot effectively be learnt in a classroom. It is best passed on, on the ground. If all troops are rotated out at the same time, much of this crucial tribal knowledge will be lost and with it the momentum of the early stages of the peace stabilisation process as the new forces gain on the ground knowledge and experience. This is exactly what happened in Iraq when, in one of the biggest troop rotations in history, the entire initial US invasion force left the country and handed over to incomers at the same time. The result was a severe check in the momentum gained in the early days of the occupation, giving a fatal breathing space for the insurgent forces to regroup and press forward their attack on new and inexperienced forces.[10] Even after the police have arrived and the domestic instruments for establishing the rule of law have been created, soldiers of the intervening force will need to be prepared to work with them on some rule of law tasks. In Afghanistan, this has included the battle to bring poppy production under control. In Bosnia it meant helping to tackle smuggling and organised crime. But military commanders are often very reluctant to get their troops involved in these tasks. The local (British) European Union Force (EUFOR) commander[11] in Bosnia in 2004/5 was willing, indeed eager, to have his troops engaged with domestic law enforcement bodies to tackle smuggling and organised crime, because he correctly assessed these as among the major threats to the stability of the state. EUFOR's troop-contributing governments were, however, at best luke warm about these activities, variously believing them to be 'not suitable for the military because of lack of training', outside the 'warrior role' of soldiers, contrary to their national caveats, or likely to lead to an extension in the duration of EUFOR's engagement in Bosnia at a time when troops were desperately needed for more 'strenuous' operational duties elsewhere (Iraq and Afghanistan).

Most soldiers are not trained to do these tasks. But if we are to be serious about international intervention in the future, they need to be as skilled at establishing the rule of law in the early stages of stabilisation and helping domestic law enforcement bodies in the later ones, as they are now at the business of hot war fighting.

There are some 'soldiers' who are used to working in this *demi monde* between hot war and a stable peace. Some because they have had the experience – like the British Army who have been doing this for well over half a century round the world, and the police service of Northern Ireland because they have been doing it for thirty years in that troubled province. And some because this is what they were created and designed to do – these are forces like the French gendarmerie and the Italian carabinieri.[12] These units, trained precisely to fill the gap between conventional armies and conventional police, are the most valuable forces of all in the early days of the stabilisation phase. And, in making up an army for intervention, military commanders would be well advised to include as many of them as they can get hold of.

Once the soldiers have established the secure space their task is to hold that ring while the politicians find a political settlement. You cannot win the peace with soldiers – you can only win wars with them. Making peace is the politicians' job. And sometimes we may have to accept that the ingredients for peace just don't exist – the best we can do is containment, until circumstances change. Though we did not realise it at the time, history may well say that the first twenty-five years in Northern Ireland were spent not in making peace, but in simply containing the conflict until the ingredients for a political solution began to emerge. Only then could we start actually building the peace.

After a secure space, the next priority is to get the administration working and the civil police operating on the ground as fast as possible, either by deploying international civil police – CIVPOL – (as in Kosovo and East Timor) or by training up a local police force (as in Bosnia, El Salvador and Haiti). Our failure on almost every occasion to do this with the necessary speed has been a feature and a flaw of almost every intervention in recent years.

There is a choice to be made here between bringing in international police and training local ones. International CIVPOL can be put on the ground quicker, since it takes time to train up a local force. But they are very expensive (around $150,000 per international policeman per year)[13] and, whether their duties include the exercise of executive powers of law enforcement or just monitoring and mentoring the local police force, they can frequently find it very difficult to do their job in an alien country whose customs they do not understand and whose language they do not speak.

The quality of some international police can also be a problem. Governments by and large, with some notable exceptions, do not send their best policemen and women on these missions. Most have a tendency to send the people who they don't mind losing for a few months. In Kosovo, the CIVPOL were famous for being overbearing, overweight and over fond of sitting in bars and coffee shops. And in Bosnia, especially under the UN mission, there was a real problem with corruption. The Bosnians strongly objected to being told what to do by policemen from third world countries. And far too many of those policemen (and not just from the third world) seemed far too at home in a corrupt society and far too willing to join in. The fact that a very small number of 'bad' international police were involved with trafficked women did terrible damage to the trust and confidence of the local population in the whole international operation in Bosnia.

Even where we have got this right and brought in or trained a competent police force quickly, we have all too often failed to understand that the police, while essential, are not by themselves the rule of law. In Bosnia the UN spent almost $150 million every year for seven years, creating a modern, well-trained international standard police force. And a good job they did of it – by Balkan standards anyway. What they forgot, however, was that the police only enforce the law. They depend on good laws to catch criminals, good prosecutors to prosecute them, good judges to sentence them and sufficient prisons in which to lock them up. Exactly the same mistake was made in the US intervention in Haiti and by the UN in El Salvador, among others.

In Bosnia these other elements of the justice system were either totally corrupt or woefully inadequate. As a result when good, freshly trained policemen arrested a criminal, corrupt judges let them off – and guess who was knocking at the policeman's door next night? The international community in Bosnia recognised the problem of a corrupt judiciary rather early on, but instead of solving it by reforming the judges, they decided to do so by paying them more. This did not have the effect of 'lifting the judge out of the corruption bracket' as had been hoped for, but instead simply raised the price for which judges could be bought.

It was only in 2002, seven years after the war ended, that the international community finally decided to make the establishment of the rule of law its first priority. By this time, however, corruption had seeped into the very marrow and bone of Bosnian society from the lowest to the highest level. The Bosnian state in many of its aspects had become little more than an organised conspiracy to rob from its citizens. And not just its citizens – from the international community, too. International aid to Bosnia was some seven times greater per head of population than the Marshall Plan put into Europe.[14] But vast amounts (it is claimed by some, up to 30 per cent) of the $17 billion of international aid did not benefit the Bosnian citizens for whom it was intended, but simply passed straight through the system into criminal pockets.

So when we made the rule of law our first priority in 2002, we discovered that we had not only to clean up the judiciary, and the prosecutorial service, but also rewrite the criminal and economic codes so as to make it easier for the forces of the law to do their jobs,[*] establish new courts, in part staffed by international judges and prosecutors prepared to take on the highest in the land, and consider a whole new programme for improving Bosnia's penal institutions. Only when we had done this could we begin, as we did three years later, the long, long process of decapitating the networks of organised crime and cleaning out the corrupt structures of the state, starting from the top. Thanks to a lot of hard work, including from the domestic authorities, considerable progress has now been made towards creating a society in Bosnia based on the rule of law. It would have been far better if all this had started earlier.

A Holistic Approach

Establishing the rule of law is a huge task. But it must be done, and it must be done early. And it cannot be done in just one sector – it has to be done holistically across the whole spectrum of the judicial structure of a country.

But this is not the only place where a holistic approach matters. Building peace is not a linear exercise. A state cannot be built sequentially, sector by sector – and it cannot be rebuilt like that either. It must be done on a broad front with the key actions being taken coincidentally not sequentially. This is especially true in the stabilisation phase of post-conflict reconstruction, when the temptation will be to concentrate on the problems which are most immediately visible. Infrastructure reconstruction and refugee return, together with its vital precursor, property repossession, will always be key priorities in this period, as will the provision of humanitarian aid, the connection of basic services, the protection of human rights. These early priorities are natural and right. But it is also important to begin to look long term, even from the first moments.

If the intervening international force is acting, even temporarily, as a government then it has to take on the full responsibilities of a government – from the rule of law, to the economy, to transport

---

[*] The 'Brahimi Report', which also stresses the importance of placing early priority on the rule of law, recommends that, until local laws can be drawn up, the legal gap could be filled by a model interim legal code.

infrastructure, to the defence and intelligence services, to protecting human rights, to local government, to the customs and the police, to health and education, to the operation of the utilities and the setting up and managing of political and governmental institutions. When General MacArthur was instructed, under the 'United States Initial Post-Surrender Policy Relating to Japan' to carry out an ambitious and far-reaching programme of democratic and state-building reform, he decided to abandon his original plan to simply add a civil affairs section to his military headquarters and instead set up a whole new civil structure alongside his military HQ, which in effect shadowed the structure and competencies of the Japanese cabinet. This was staffed chiefly by US civil servants and at its peak in 1948 employed some 3,500 people.

Nowadays the competencies of government cannot be shadowed in such a cohesive way by a single organisation, on a single location. This has to be done, instead, through a multiplicity of agencies such as UNHCR (United Nations High Commission for Refugees), NATO, the OSCE (Organization for Security and Cooperation in Europe), the IMF, the World Bank and others. But the overall effect needs to be the same – underlining once again the crucial need for coordination between the international and non-governmental agencies involved.

However, a holistic approach does not remove the need to make difficult choices about sequencing. Deciding on the first priorities is crucial. And then deciding what comes next – and after that what and when. The range of tasks that need to be done in the post-conflict reconstruction phase will always outrun the resources of time, money and political capital available to do them. There are, after all, only so many crises you can deal with at any one time. So programming the crises and getting the priorities right is key. To do the right thing at the wrong time, is to do the wrong thing because it involves an opportunity cost which diverts resources away from resolving what should have been your priority at that moment. Reuniting the divided city of Mostar was one of our chosen priorities during my mandate in Bosnia. I wanted to tackle this early, but in the event found that there were too many crises to overcome in my first year and I could not afford the expenditure of the extra political capital necessary to do this until we had overcome the other challenges we faced – so there was no option but to delay this until later, when the situation was quieter.

The early establishment of a Mission Implementation Plan, outlining the key tasks and the order in which they will be tackled, is important here – for it is this plan which will help the international mission to stay focused on the things that matter and not be distracted by those that do not. It will also be valuable to think laterally as well as holistically. One of the earliest problems the international community had to face in Bosnia was smuggling on a grand scale (a well-known Balkan tradition stretching back for centuries). Then, as now, smuggling was at the heart of organised crime and corruption. With the benefit of hindsight we now know that arguably the best way to have tackled this might have been to abolish all border tariffs and then use international aid to reimburse the Bosnian state for the lost revenue, until an efficient customs service could be established. If the international community had done this it would probably have wasted far less money and Bosnia would be a far less corrupt society today.

The Economy

Similarly, everyone wants to get the troops out and back home as early as possible. But very few realise that the best way to get troops out quickly is to get the economy going quickly. Indeed, after the rule of law, economic reform[15] should be the next key priority. It most often isn't.

The Allied reconstruction programmes in Germany and Japan after the Second World War once again offer instructive lessons in this area. In Japan, President Truman's first orders to MacArthur in 1945 were to exact reparations from the country and break up the old *Zaibatsu* commercial giants who ran Japan's military industrial machinery during the war. But by 1948, at the same time that Congress was debating the Marshall Plan for Europe, the US had realised that the task of reconstructing Japan would be better served by a policy which encouraged Japan's economic regeneration, even investing US funds to make this happen. Similar initial orders were given to General Lucius Clay, the military governor of the US zone in Germany. He was originally instructed to get involved in economic regeneration only to the extent required to: '*meet the needs of the occupying forces and to ensure the production and maintenance of goods and services required to prevent disorder and unrest*.[16] Clay studiously ignored this directive, and set about actively reviving the German economy as quickly as possible in order to provide the means of survival for the refugees and the homeless. This enlightened policy, later strengthened by the Erhard currency and fiscal reforms of the first post-war German government, is regarded by many as the reason why Germany's economic recovery was faster than any other European country's despite receiving less aid per capita under the Marshall Plan than its European neighbours ($12 per capita, compared with Holland's $45 in 1948).[17] The Marshall Plan itself was an outstandingly imaginative and successful example of using economic means to speed up the process of post-conflict reconstruction, which had far-reaching consequences for Europe, both East and West.

Despite the Bosnian Central Bank's remarkable early successes in stabilising the Bosnian currency and bringing inflation under control, economic reform to liberalise the supply side of the economy did not become a key priority until 2002. Huge international subventions, amounting to perhaps $800 per capita, had kept the Bosnian economy afloat in the late 1990s, during which period the economy grew very fast, but only as the direct result of international aid and reconstruction. Because the fundamentals of the supply side of the economy remained unreformed, domestically generated economic activity was still in deep stagnation seven years after the war had ended. By this time, international aid was dropping and many international humanitarian relief and security agencies were leaving, taking with them the spending power which their employees and organisations put into the local economy. After the huge United Nations Police Mission left Bosnia at the end of 2002, prices for rented accommodation in Sarajevo dropped some 20 to 25 per cent. The consequences of this withdrawal of international support left the underlying weaknesses of the country's economy dangerously exposed, causing the IMF to worry about the need for a devaluation to prevent economic collapse. We decided that we needed to launch an immediate broad-based programme of economic regeneration.

Our first instinct was to think big. What large-scale investment can we put in? This kind of thinking is not always wrong; there are some countries where large-scale investment into indigenous resources may be the answer, or part of the answer – think of the need to invest in rebuilding the oil industry in Iraq for example. But many post-conflict countries do not have the wealth or natural resources that can immediately attract large-scale investment. For these countries the answer is not to try to get large-scale industry going, but to launch a long-term and sustained programme to liberate and stimulate the small enterprise sector. It is from there, in most cases, that the regeneration of the economy will take place. It follows that liberalising the economy, stripping away business-destroying laws and lowering taxes is often the best route to take. In Bosnia in 2002 it took on average six months to set up a legal new business (but only the time for the ink to dry to set up an illegal one). New businesses being set up had to cope with a fractured tax system and an impossible labyrinth of regulatory requirements whose sole purpose seemed to be to provide opportunities for graft and corruption such as, for instance, contributing to the building of a local nuclear shelter. The proprietors of new restaurants opening in Sarajevo had to submit a urine test to the Ministry of Defence – and so on. We launched an aggressive programme of reform, led by the international financial institutions in mid 2002, the first stage of which aimed to get rid of 150 laws in 150 days. This programme enabled us, among other things, to reduce the business registration period by 2005 to between two and four weeks, one of the shortest in the Balkans.

We also had to create a whole new structure of economic laws to regulate public corporations, improve the overall management of the public utility sector and enable efficient business formation, bankruptcy, contracting and the settlement of disputes. The effect of the economic reform programme we introduced continues to be diminished by the inadequacy of Bosnia's business courts which still have, in some instances, a ten-year backlog of outstanding cases to resolve, pointing up yet again the necessity to reform judicial structures and court procedures early in the reconstruction phase.

Nevertheless, thanks to these supply side reforms, matched by a determined attack on some of the residual macroeconomic burdens on the country's finances (especially war debt), the predicted collapse did not happen. Three years later the Bosnian economy was again growing at 5 per cent annually, but this time on a self-sustaining basis, making it one of the fastest growing economies in the Western Balkans, with inward investment, exports and manu-facturing output all growing strongly, albeit from a very low base.

In Hungary, it took some seven years for growth to take off after a similar programme of post-Communist reforms to liberalise the economy. That is actually rather fast – it can take much longer for economic reforms to feed through into economic growth. One recent study[18] indicates that economic recovery in a post-conflict situation typically begins about five years into the post-conflict peri-od, takes around a decade to reach the point where it appreciably reduces the risk of a return to conflict, but can take as much as two decades to return the country concerned to its pre-war GDP level. So it is very important to start economic reforms as early as possible. If the programme of reforms we instituted in 2002 had been put into practice in year one in Bosnia, rather than year seven, the country would be far further advanced today than it is.

It is important, however, to realise the pain and social instability which accelerated economic reform can bring. In the early stages, privatisation and economic liberalisation will almost always raise the level of unemployment and depress wages. We in Britain should not forget the pain of the Thatcher years of economic reform. Ironically, as a politician I campaigned against many of her reforms, arguing that they would lead to lost jobs and the selling-off of the national wealth; only to find myself instituting very similar reforms in Bosnia and facing the same arguments and opposition. What makes matters worse in most post-conflict countries is that they are poor, not rich – so the pain can be far greater. There is not much the interveners can do about this, except understand it and recognise that by insisting on accelerated economic reform we are often asking local politicians to take responsibility for a level of social disruption which our own politicians at home would reject without a second thought.

Sometimes difficult judgements have to be made which involve tempering the desire for economic reform with an understanding of the social consequences this can bring. There is real danger in dest-roying the old industries upon which a society depended for employ-ment too early, before the new economy of the country has started to grow. There are many who take the view that one of the early mistakes in Iraq, which proved almost as damaging in the end as abolishing the Iraqi Army, was Paul Bremer's decision in mid 2003 peremptorily to shut down all loss-making state-run industries, causing one US administrator to complain, *'Through aggressive de-Ba'athification, the demobilisation of the army and the closing of factories, the coalition has left tens of thousands of individuals outside the economic and political life of the country.'* The administrator went on to say that what his province, Anbar, needed was 'more Maslow[19] and less Friedman'.[20, 21]

Three other issues deserve special mention in any post-conflict programme of economic reform – currency stabilisation, privatisation and cleaning up the public utilities.

Currency Stabilisation

Inflation, like crime, is almost always a close travelling companion of conflict. All other economic reforms will be likely to have little effect until it is brought under control and the currency stabilised. This can often involve creating a whole new currency, or adopting some well accepted foreign one (such as the dollar or the Euro). International management of this process is best left to the IMF, with local management in the hands of a strong central bank, out of the reach of domestic political influence. The early adoption of the Konvertabilna Marka (KM), based on the Deutschmark, and the creation of a central bank and a currency board was one of the most notable early successes in Bosnia, leading to the formation of a vibrant banking sector and laying the foundation on which we were able subsequently to build our whole economic programme.

Privatisation

Privatisation can be a minefield for the implementers and a playground for criminals in all post-command economy societies. Conflict only makes this worse. The first programme for privatising the state's assets in Bosnia, mirroring that in previous post-conflict reconstruction projects, was based on a voucher scheme that gave each employee a share in the public companies for which they worked. It was a disaster. The old state companies, whose asset values were vastly over-inflated under Tito, were now largely defunct and desperately in need of new capital and effective management. The voucher system gave them neither. Their asset values plummeted and this was soon reflected in knock-down prices for the vouchers which poured on to the market place and were quickly snapped up by powerful political and business interests. These elites then either forced the government to invest taxpayers' money into companies they now owned, or alternatively stripped the assets (especially land), leaving behind abandoned wastelands. No new jobs were created and very few of the old ones were recaptured. The political parties painted privatisation as theft by foreigners – though often the truth was that the real theft was being managed either by them or their supporters. In 2001, USAID, World Bank and the EC jointly invested in a scheme to help restart privatisation. But as a consequence of the early failure there remains a huge backlog of public suspicion to overcome.

In Haiti the privatisation process resulted in similar opportunities for the ruling elite to engage in corruption. This, combined with resistance from 'workers' who were still 'employed' by largely defunct state firms halted the entire privatisation process, which has never been restarted.

Public Utilities

In most post-command economies, the state-owned public utilities offer another perfect vehicle for stealing from the public. Since they are owned by the state, they will often have been turned into milch cows for political parties and the powerful. In Bosnia the electricity generating companies (Elektroprivredas) and the state-controlled forestry industry, among other public utilities, were completely controlled by corrupt political forces and used for just this purpose. Cleaning them up prior to privatisation was an early economic reform task, in which our most powerful weapon proved to be auditors. If good, fearless auditors are not available locally, then they need to be trained up as quickly as possible and international auditors used to fill the gap. If I were asked to name one new organisation that might be able to help with post-conflict stabilisation in a troubled world, I would have no hesitation in choosing, as my nomination, 'auditors sans frontières'.

Incidentally, though these economic reforms should start very early, inputs of economic aid to stimulate growth may be best left to rather later. One recent study[22] concludes that the best time to provide aid to stimulate a post-conflict economy is not in the first year, but somewhere around the middle of the first decade, when the economic institutions are established, the utilities industries cleaned up and the economy is capable of absorbing this kind of assistance more efficiently than it can in the early days.

Security Sector Reform

Reform of the security sector and especially reductions in the size of the armed forces is also an important early task in the stabilisation phase. High post-conflict military spending has been shown to be a major factor in increasing the risk of relapse back to war.[23] Downsizing the military, however, can be fraught with danger as unemployed disgruntled soldiers can have a destabilising effect in the post-conflict environment. It is therefore important to downsize with care and to have a plan for either re-employing or providing an effective redundancy package for soldiers who are no longer required. The wholesale disbandment of the army in Iraq, without any such provisions in place, greatly increased the country's instability, with many disbanded soldiers joining the militias and adding to the strength of the insurgency. In Kosovo, by contrast, the Kosovo Protection Corps (KPC) was formed specifically to ease the transition of the disbandment of the Kosovo Liberation Army (KLA). In Bosnia, a programme run by the World Bank provided financial incentives to private sector companies to train and hire demobilised soldiers, while the IMF and OSCE had a joint scheme which provided an economic resettlement package for each disbanded soldier (but did not incorporate them into the local economy). This did not, however, prevent many disbanded soldiers joining 'private security companies' which had strong political and criminal affiliations, adding to the law and order problems we had to deal with.

Education

Although strictly speaking education is more a state-building agenda item, starting education reform early, so that the minds of the young do not get captured by the hates generated from the war, will be important in ensuring that the reforms of the reconstruction period are sustained and not reversed. Education is, however, often a much more difficult area to tackle than most interveners realise, for it touches centrally on core nationalist sensitivities, especially where a civil struggle has involved ethnic, religious or cultural divisions. Integrated education is a keystone to creating a sense of national unity and a strong civil society – but this is likely, as in Northern Ireland, Bosnia, Iraq and Afghanistan, to be strenuously resisted by the wartime generations for whom the preservation of ethnic religious and cultural identities were key war aims. I count our failure to make all but minimal progress towards a genuinely integrated education system, in the face of implacable local opposition, especially from the Croats, as one of the biggest failures of my mandate in that country.

Education is also an important part of the battle for hearts and minds – something which is all too often overlooked by the interveners and their political masters. The United States spends almost six billion dollars a year buttressing the armed forces of Pakistan in the global fight against terror (and probably a similar amount on intelligence support), but less than a billion dollars on education, aid and economic development in a country whose Islamic madrassas have become the world's foremost training ground for the radicalisation of Muslim youth.[24]

Elections

The sharp-eyed reader may well have noticed by now that among the things to be done in these early days, which I could have mentioned but haven't, are elections. This is quite deliberate. Because elections should not be held as early as possible, but as late as the interveners can get away with.

Perhaps because our decent liberal consciences make us feel embarrassed about occupying other people's countries, or, more likely, because we want our troops home early, the international community often makes the mistake of believing that what should come first is not the rule of law but elections. In Bosnia, holding elections was the international community's first priority and there were lots of them – six elections in seven years, in all. This was a mistake. The Bosnians got very tired of constant elections, belief in democracy suffered and, because elections were held before the rule of law was established, the result was that those who ran the war, and profited from it politically or criminally, reinforced their positions by becoming elected to government. Very frequently early elections prove not to be a short route to Western-style democracy, but rather a quick road to the criminally captured state.[25] Nor do elections, it appears, reduce the risk of conflict recurrence in the long term. A recent study[26] has shown that although the risk of a return to conflict goes down in the year of the election, it tends to rise again afterwards.

It is worth noting that in Germany after the Second World War, the first federal elections were not held until 1949, a full four years after the war ended.[27] By then the administration of Germany under the Allied Commissions had settled down, the economy was beginning to recover, the systems of the state were largely built and the rule of law had begun to be properly established.

We have a habit of confusing elections with democracy. In fact, democracy consists of much more than voting. To work properly, democracy needs the rule of law, an independent civil service, institutions of government in which there are built-in checks and balances to prevent the abuse of power, a free and vibrant press and an active civil society capable of holding the executive to account. It is better, if circumstances allow, to put as many of these other elements of democracy in place as possible, before launching into the business of voting. However, elections cannot be delayed indefinitely as, in the end, they are the only means by which the interveners can address the question of legitimacy. Without elections, how do the interveners have partners who genuinely represent the people? How can they justify occupying a country that has not yet had a chance to express its democratic views?

There are some temporary ways to overcome this legitimacy shortfall. Careful choice on the part of the interveners as to who to work with is one. Drawing legitimacy from the peace treaty which ended the war and which will in most cases have been endorsed by all parties (eg the Dayton Peace Agreement in Bosnia), is another. Regular opinion polling which is published (even if selectively so) can be a third. Getting buy-in for a programme of reform from the existing political parties is a fourth. And there is even the possibility of using plebiscites (for example on the published 'end state' or on a specific programme of reforms). All these can be means to delay the holding of elections in the short term. But sooner or later, the question of legitimacy must be addressed and elections are the only definitive way to do this, even if that means holding them earlier than is comfortable. This is what has had to happen in Iraq, where comparatively early elections were a necessity because the inter-veners were engaged in a battle for legitimacy with the insurgents.

The almost mystical belief of foreign interveners in the magical powers of elections can have other unintended consequences – one of them is cost. There is a tendency for interveners to institute a frequency of elections which may be bearable for rich countries such as ours, but can cripple the economies of those struggling to break out of destitution after war. In Afghanistan the initial round of elections cost $145.4 million. This represents more than half of the estimated total national income of the country ($260 million, or $11 per capita per annum). These first elections were largely paid for by the interveners. But subsequent ones will increasingly have to be paid for by the government – and the new Afghan constitution, assembled under the patronage of the interveners, requires that there shall be no fewer than eight to ten of these nationwide elections every decade, creating a completely unsustainable financial burden for the emerging Afghan state.[28]

Elections of course mean political parties. In a post-conflict situ-ation, especially where a civil war, nationalist struggle or inter-ethnic conflict has been fought, political parties will almost always be indistinguishable from the nationalist movements which fought the war. These are actually not political parties at all, but merely the political expression of the coalitions which came together for the conflict. In time, they will either convert into real political parties based around a programme of policies, or disaggregate into their conventional component political groupings. This is what happened with, for instance, Solidarność in Poland and the ANC in South Africa. In Croatia, Tudjman's hardline nationalist HDZ trans-formed itself into a conventional centre-right European party – and the same may be happening to at least some of the nationalist parties in Bosnia. It needs time for this process to occur – so interveners should not despair if the nationalist parties which fought the war continue to hold a powerful sway in post-war politics for a sub-stantial period after the conflict. Creating a modern democracy is a process, not an event.

There is a second phenomenon that frequently occurs in the post-conflict period. The emergence of 'boutique' parties based not around a set of political ideas, but on a single charismatic figure for whom the party becomes merely a vehicle for personal vanity. Bosnia has been plagued by this feature as have other post-conflict countries, like Haiti, where a large number of poorly funded 'ego' parties severely complicated the electoral and political process.

Factors Which Can Make Stabilisation Difficult

What the interveners can do, and in what order after the end of the conflict phase, will be strongly determined by the way the conflict ends. Some factors will make some actions easier and more of a priority; others will make them less so. For instance in Bosnia after four years of war, 90 per cent of the buildings were damaged and half the population became internally displaced refugees. Humanitarian relief, housing repossession and reconstruction had to be priorities. In Iraq there was much less physical damage and personal dislocation, but thirty years of Ba'athist rule and Saddam's tyranny had destroyed the country's governance systems and decapitated its liberal and democratic human capital.

A number of other factors can influence the process of post-conflict stabilisation and the sequencing of the tasks in this phase. Apart from the questions of human capacity and the state of the infrastructure given in the two examples above, these include: ethnic, tribal and religious divisions; the size and demography of the country; the existence or otherwise of democratic and free market based economic structures before the conflict; the attitude of the neighbours; the presence or otherwise of natural resources which can contribute to economic revival (such as oil); the presence or otherwise of militias etc.[29] One post-conflict factor, however, especially influences the early days of the post-conflict reconstruction phase: has there been a clear-cut victory for one side or not? The figures show that the split is about 50/50, with half of all civil wars ending in a clear outcome and half in stalemate.[30] If the conflict ended in a clear victory/defeat (as for example in Germany, Kosovo, Afghanistan and Iraq) then it is possible to impose a more protectorate-like structure for the stabilisation phase. If, however, the conflict phase ended in a stalemate (as in Bosnia) then an intervention package based more on shared sovereignty between the domestic forces and the interveners is more likely to be suitable.[*]

Stalemates also lead in almost every case to both sides in the conflict continuing to pursue their war objectives through the peace. This is what happened in Bosnia. In the early days (and still today to some extent), all three of Bosnia's warring ethnicities used the Dayton Peace Accords not to build peace, but to continue the pursuit of their war aims. The international community wasted two precious years of stalemate and obstruction to their reconstruction efforts before tackling this. It was not until December 1997 that the PIC finally decided to authorise the use of the so-called 'Bonn powers' which gave the High Representative the ability to break deadlocks by imposing legislation and sacking obstructionist officials and politicians. There is a message here, too. If it is necessary for the interveners be tough, be tough at the beginning and relax later, not the other way round.

Tough Love

Being tough also applies to the distribution of aid. Leaving humanitarian aid to one side – since this should be given according to need and nothing else – all other aid given to a country to help in the reconstruction phase should be firmly conditional. I had many heated discussions with my Bosnian counterparts when I explained to them that the aid Europe and the West gave to Bosnia came with strings attached – it was conditional on them making the necessary reforms. They used to accuse me of blackmail. I replied by pointing out that this aid was paid for by taxpayers in donor countries and, as the head of the international mission, I had to ensure that their money was spent on making things better, not keeping them the same. Tough conditionality became a key instrument enabling us to drive forward the reform process in Bosnia. In Croatia, the World Bank and the IMF both tied their lending to the fulfilment of the Basic Agreement on Eastern Slavonia and this became an important ingredient in the success of the UN mission there. In Kosovo, by contrast, the failure to make aid sufficiently conditional has been

---

[*] See p. 174 for a further discussion of 'shared sovereignty'.

criticised as one of the reasons for diminishing the leverage of the interveners.[31]

The United States is, frankly, far better at this kind of 'tough love' than Europe. It is of course up to a state and its people whether they want to reform themselves or not – and they are absolutely free not to. But it is also up to the aid-giving nations to decide what they want to give their money for, and to decide not to give it if that money is being used not to improve the country – but rather by corrupt politicians to keep things as they are.

The World Bank (WB) is pioneering a different approach which perhaps points the best way forward in this area. WB studies have found that conditionality works best if there is domestic government buy-in. They are increasingly shifting to giving the developing country governments responsibility for identifying and applying the conditionality under which the WB will disburse bank funding. Domestic politicians usually know best what their political and admin constraints are on this. More important, the domestic authorities then become fully accountable if they fail and can't blame the international community for 'imposing' unrealistic conditions. Obviously this requires rather hard-headed judgements when it comes to accepting the conditions set by the domestic government, so that the bar is not set too low (what the US call 'giving themselves self-licking lollipops'). But this approach to conditionality offers real advantages and is now being considered by the EU and championed by the British government development minister, Hilary Benn.

'De-Nazification'

There is one other key question that will need to be addressed by the interveners in the early stages of the stabilisation phase of post-conflict reconstruction. Whether to 'de-Nazify' as in Germany after the Second World War, or not. And if so, to what extent? One of the most common criticisms of the international community after Dayton was that it missed the opportunity to 'de-Nazify' Bosnia. According to this argument, the international community could have cleaned out all those who ran the war by refusing to allow them to continue in office or hold any official position. If this had happened, the argument goes, Bosnia would have made much more progress, much more quickly. What this argument ignores, however, is the fact that the only way to achieve peace at Dayton was to have those in power in the war sign up to the peace treaty. They would never have done so if the consequence had been that they would immediately be put out of office. Turkeys do not vote for Christmas. 'De-Nazification' may be possible in the case of a clearcut victory such as Iraq or Germany and Japan in the Second World War. But it is not possible in the case of a stalemate-based ceasefire, in which those in power have to sign up to the peace deal. But even if complete 'de-Nazification' is *possible*, as in the case of Iraq, it may not be wise.

Though de-Nazification was much talked about in Germany, it didn't actually happen, except at the very highest levels. The Allied powers occupying Germany after the Second World War declared that de-Nazification would be one of their principal early objectives. But they soon found that this was impractical, firstly because they did not have the manpower or resources to do it and secondly because it would have made it impossible to administer the state. Although a number of high-ranking officials were removed, the Allies' de-Nazification policy hardly affected lower levels. Of the 3,623,112 people considered to be chargeable under the de-Nazification laws in Germany, only 887,252 (considerably less than a third) were actually charged and of these only 117,523 were convicted – around 3 per cent of the original total.[32] Indeed Germany's third post-war President, Kurt Keisinger, had himself been a Nazi during the war.[33] One of General MacArthur's declared early aims in occupying Japan was similarly to purge the country of those responsible for the war. But he too soon discovered that this was impractical and the resulting clean-out of the wartime elements was even lighter than in Germany. The Emperor himself, the prime symbol of Japan at war, had in the end to be rehabilitated.

Iraq, on the other hand, provides a particularly graphic example of the danger of de-Nazification if taken too far. Ambassador Paul Bremer, who took over as head of the US's administration (ORHA) in Iraq in May 2003, little more than a month after the war ended, immediately launched a process of de-Nazification in the country, by removing very large numbers of senoir Ba'thist officials. This was resisted by some of the US generals in Iraq at the time, most notably the Commander of the 101st Airborne Division, Major General

David Petraeus,[*] who considered Bremer's policy to be dangerously out of touch with the realities on the ground. Petraeus allowed local officials wide discretion to keep on Ba'athist officials and set up employment programmes for those removed. Elsewhere, however, Bremer's policy of deep de-Ba'athification prevailed with the effect that the US administration soon found themselves with a vacuum where the government should have been. ORHA was too small to govern Iraq as MacArthur had governed Japan, and the state officials through whom they could have governed had either been sacked or gone home. The result was a state of administrative chaos in the early days from which subsequent governments in Iraq have not yet, three years later, recovered.

De-Nazification makes sense if it is confined to decapitating the political structures at the top of the state. But, as the Allies found out in Germany, there is a distinct limit as to how far down it should be taken. In the end the interveners are going to need a structure and officials through which to govern the state and it will almost always be the case that the best structure to use, at least in the early days, is the structure they inherited when the conflict ended. This will no doubt need to be amended, reformed and cleaned up later – but that is best done in the next phase – the phase of state-building.

Summary

The early hours after the conflict are the crucial hours. The interveners are now for all practical purposes the government. Their first task is to respond to the human needs of the population and here Maslow and his *Hierarchy of Human Needs* is likely to prove a better guide to their first actions than the prejudices or plans of the interveners. The first thing the population will want after war is security, and if the interveners won't or can't provide it they will look to someone else who can. So, it is essential to dominate the security space and introduce the rule of law from day one, moment one – even if, at the start, soldiers have to do it through martial law. The police, too, need to be operational as early as possible. But establishing the rule of law means more than improving the police.

---

[*] Petraeus is now Chief of Staff of the US Army and thus charged with oversight of the whole US operation in Iraq.

It means reforming the whole range of legal structures, from judges through to the penal services. This holistic approach is crucial elsewhere, too. Rebuilding states can't be done in a linear fashion by just concentrating on some sectors and ignoring others. But sequencing the challenges is also important. Economic reform should be an early priority, especially currency stabilisation, liberalisation, privatisation and cleaning up the public utilities. Security sector and education reform should also come early. But elections should be left as late as decently possible. Apart from humanitarian aid, all other aid should be conditional. Think twice before going too deep in de-Nazification, it nearly always rebounds.

5
State-building

Indeed the town changed rapidly in appearance, for the newcomers cut down trees, planted new ones in other places,
repaired the streets, cut new ones, dug drainage canals, built
public buildings. In the first few years they pulled down in the
market place, those old and dilapidated shops which were out
of line and which, to tell the truth, had up till then inconve-
nienced no one. In place of those old fashioned shops with their
wooden drop counters, new ones were built, well sited with
tiled roofs and metal rollers on the doors . . . The market place
was levelled and widened. A new *konak** was erected, a great
building intended to house the law courts and the local administration. The army too was working on its own account, even
more rapidly and inconsiderately than the civil authorities.
They put up barracks, cleared waste land, planted and chopped
and changed the appearance of whole hills.

The older inhabitants could not understand, and wondered;
just when they thought that all this incomprehensible energy
had come to an end, the newcomers started some fresh and
even more incomprehensible task. The townsmen stopped and
looked at this work, but not like children who love to watch the
work of adults, but as adults who stop for a moment to watch
children's games. This continual need of the newcomers to
build and re-build, to dig and to put back again, to put up and
modify, this eternal desire of theirs to foresee the action of
natural forces and to surmount them, no one either understood
or appreciated. On the other hand, all the townspeople, especially the older men, saw all this unhealthy activity as a bad
omen. Had it been left to them, the town would have gone on

---

* Municipal administration building.

looking as any other little oriental town. What burst would be patched up, what leant would be shored up, but beyond that no one would needlessly create work or make plans or interfere in the foundations of buildings or change the aspect which God had given the town.

IVO ANDRIC, On the coming of the Austrians to Višegrad.
Bridge on the Drina

At a ceremony in Petersberg on 22 November 1949 the Western Allies, who had administered West Germany since the Second World War, signed an agreement to hand over most of their powers to the newly elected government of the Federal Republic of Germany. During the four years of the Allied administration, the entire West German state machinery had been reconstructed, elections held, a constitution written and an economic system created which would in the years ahead produce what everyone acknowledged was 'the German miracle', making the country the most powerful economic force in Europe. Forty years later, in 1989, with the fall of Communism, West Germany was strong enough to re-absorb its broken and bankrupt East German brother and Germany was unified again, becoming a key member of the G8 group and of the Quint, the Euro-American grouping of the most powerful nations on earth.

Japan and the Japanese economic miracle followed the same trajectory, with the end of the Allied occupation under General MacArthur, in April 1952. Shortly afterwards, Austria followed, becoming fully independent in 1955. The albeit largely nominal supreme authority of the 'Allied Kommandatura' in Berlin, however, lasted for forty years after the war and only ended with German reunification in 1989, when the city was free to return to its old glory as the capital of a united Germany. The institutions created in the post-war reconstruction of all these three states have endured without major amendment and formed the basis in all cases of stable states that have become highly respected members of the international community of nations.

In Afghanistan the war against the Soviets ended with a complete Soviet withdrawal on 2 February 1989, after nine years of conflict. The world turned away. Afghanistan had always been a zone of chaos. Why should it not remain so? This was just another episode in the Nineteenth-Century Great Game, in which the Russians had lost again. The world had other priorities to deal with. What was there to worry about? The answer came on 11 September 2001, on the streets of New York. The United States discovered that even being the world's most powerful nation did not confer invulnerability to the consequence of lawlessness and ungovernability in some remote country on the other side of the globe. And the world discovered that ending the conflict is not ending the story. The job is not done until a durable system of government is rebuilt under the rule of law, capable of serving its citizens and of taking its place amongst the international community of nations.

*   *   *

In this chapter I shall outline the last phase of post-conflict reconstruction – that of state-building, leading to complete hand-over to the domestic institutions and the final exit of the interveners. For the purposes of making the argument, I have treated this as a separate phase. But there is in reality likely to be a lot of merging between the state-building and the stabilisation phases. Nevertheless the two phases are different in nature and approach, even if there is chronological overlap between them. In the stabilisation phase the emphasis is likely to be on security and law and order and creating the institutions that will deliver them. In the state-building phase the issues are those of governance and the institutions which will deliver it. There is, incidentally, a general lesson which applies to both of these phases – a kind of modern illustration of the old biblical proverb about putting new wine in old bottles. It is better, if you can, to reform the institution before you start reforming the people – for example it is better to create a modern police structure before trying to create modern policemen; better to reform judicial systems, before reforming the judges; better to reform political systems than to hope for the emergence of reformed politicians. Doing it the other way around risks having the good people who have been trained to new standards being quickly corrupted by the old practices of the as yet unreformed institutions in which they have to work. An example of this can be seen in Bosnia where the international community spent ten years training new policemen and asked them to operate in an old unreformed and corrupted structure, with predictable consequences.

Beware Creating Flawed Structures

In general, when it comes to creating the governance institutions of the state, such as its constitution and its political, economic and welfare structures, it is often best to wait, if you can, until the country is fully stabilised, or at least until stabilisation is well established. And there is a good reason for this. Institutions created before the conflict has been fully stabilised will reflect the character of the conflict, not what the country needs for a stable and enduring peace. Too early a shift into the state-building phase can easily lead to the creation of flawed structures. But timing is not always in the control of the intervener. Exogenous factors, such as crises else-where in the world, instabilities in the region, may end up driving the process.

In Iraq, the Coalition were forced by the insurgency to write the Iraq constitution in the middle of the stabilisation phase – not at the end of it. They had no other choice – but this has greatly increased both the difficulty of the task and the necessity to make short-term compromises based more on what was needed to resolve the conflict than on what the country needs in the longer term. We may be making the same mistake of trying to write the constitution too early in Kosovo, too. There will be a price to pay for this. The Iraqi constitution is unlikely to prove as enduring a document as that of Germany.

In identifying the differences between stabilisation and state-building, Bosnia makes, once again, an instructive case to look at. The Dayton Agreement had only one purpose – to end a war. Almost no attention was paid to creating a functioning state. This is not to criticise Dayton – with a single exception (that of language),[*] I believe that every one of the compromises made with functionality

[*] Dayton enshrined 'Bosnian', 'Croat' and 'Serb' as the three languages of Bosnia and Herzegovina, so encouraging a process of 'linguistic nationalism', which had begun during the war. The three are in effect no more than variations of what used to be known at Serbo Croat. This has added both to internal divisions within the country and to the cost of administration since all documents have to be available in all three 'languages'.

was necessary to secure peace – and I am sure that the vast majority of Bosnia's citizens and every responsible outside observer would rather have had an untidy peace than a continuing war. What is more, Dayton has proved a highly effective framework within which to conduct the stabilisation phase. It prevented the country from going back to war for ten years, against the early day expectations and predictions of many. That has been Dayton's greatest achievement.

For the first seven years of the international intervention in Bosnia, the emphasis was firmly on stabilisation and it was very successful. Nearly 90 per cent of dispossessed property was returned to its pre-wartime owners. A million refugees, half of those who had been driven out by the war, returned to their homes. Peaceful elections (albeit too many of them) were held, culminating in those of 2002 which were conducted entirely by the Bosnians to the highest international standards. Complete freedom of movement was established across the country and instances of ethnic violence dropped to almost nil. This was a very significant achievement, given the bitterness of the war in the early 1990s. During this period, some institutions were built, but they were in almost all cases the institutions of Dayton, not those which went beyond Dayton to create a functional state. Everyone knew that in due course this would have to be done – but it was not the priority at the time – the priority was to stabilise the peace, not to build a sustainable state in the future.

At the beginning of my mandate in mid 2002 it was clear that, whether it was convenient or not, we had to shift without delay to the state-building agenda because we had no option. A lot of opportunities had been lost through early mistakes in Bosnia – and now time was running out. We were very aware that we needed the full power of international leverage to push forward the state-building process – and we especially needed the ultimate guarantee of sufficient troops to hold the ring if things got tough. It was clear to us that with the other crises in the world we could count on these assets for only a short period of time. So we had no alternative but to embark on this phase immediately and push the process forward rather more brusquely than was comfortable, creating in a little over three years the outline structures of a modern, light-level state, governing a highly decentralised country.

In this reconstruction phase, Dayton proved (and is still proving) not so much a help as an impediment. For Dayton created a structure for a country of only 3.5 million, in which there are thirteen prime ministers, twelve of whom head up their own mini-sub-state governments with their own taxation systems, police forces, health, education and welfare structures. The result is that in some parts of this grindingly poor country, up to 70 per cent of the citizen's taxes are spent just on government and only 30 per cent on services for the citizens.

Furthermore, because the stabilisation phase had not been fully completed and the country's leaders were still locked into the psychology of the conflict, the old habits of seeking to pursue the aims of the war through the processes of the peace had not died. In consequence, it proved extremely tough to insist that these structures be created to a functionality consistent with European standards and not contaminated by the old enmities of the war and the dysfunctional structures of the Dayton Peace. In the struggles which ensued during my mandate with the wartime power structures still running the country, we had constantly to remind ourselves that we would have only one chance to build the long-term structures of the Bosnian state. It was better, we believed, to hold out for something which would work for the long term, rather than give in to short-term compromises which would leave the state burdened with the dysfunctions of Dayton.

It is important, however, to realise that while the stabilisation phase is temporary, the structures that are built in the state-building phase are permanent and must endure, if a return to disorder, dysfunctionality and, ultimately, possible conflict is to be avoided.

But Beware of Gold Plating, Too

The second mistake often made in this state-building phase is the opposite of the first. It comes not from compromising when you shouldn't, but from 'gold plating' – or insisting on standards which are relevant to the home countries of the interveners, but not appropriate to the country subject to the intervention. In Bosnia I had constantly to resist those who wished to create Whitehall, Washington, Paris or Berlin in the middle of the Balkans and were determined to stay until they had done so. It is not the interveners' job to replicate our own capitals in a foreign country. The task is, rather, to create the basic structures which can deliver justice and good governance and then leave and let the domestic powers do the rest. It is impossible to achieve in just a few years what it has taken our countries centuries to develop – and we shouldn't try. Once the right foundations have been laid to the right standards, it is up to them, not us, to build the structures of the state they want, not the one we would like them to have.

So, the task for the international community in this phase is to resist the twin temptations of accepting less than is necessary in order to get out earlier, and of building more than is required in order to stay longer. In my experience, it is capitals who will want out early and the interveners on the ground will want to stay longer.

The Itchy Palm

As the state-building phase progresses, the interveners will need to hand over individual institutions which they have been running to the domestic authorities. Exactly when this happens is often a difficult judgement to make. The moment when institutions are ready to be handed over in this manner is sometimes referred to as the 'tipping point'[1] and can occur quite early for some institutions. In Germany, the domestic authorities took over full responsibility for the delivery of local services in the US zone in 1948, just two and a half years after the end of the war. In Bosnia, the tipping point when the international community handed over all responsibility for refugee and property return to the Bosnian authorities was 1 January 2004, nearly nine years after Dayton was signed. The tipping point once passed, however, should be regarded as a watershed requiring a complete change of mindset on the part of both the interveners and the domestic authorities.

The people who will often have most difficulty with this are the interveners. Having run the country – more or less – for a number of years during the stabilisation phase, the interveners will have intervention in their bloodstream. They will probably have interfered in everything where they think they see error and will find it very difficult to stand back and *not* intervene when they think they see mistakes being made. But this is what they have to do. The job of the intervener in this phase is to oversee the creation of institutions, but not to interfere in what the institutions (parliaments, governments and courts) they have helped to create then do. You cannot give people freedom, without giving them the freedom to make mistakes – how else can a country develop?

In using the Bonn powers in Bosnia, I always took the view that it was more legitimate for me to intervene to help build an institution and less (much less) legitimate to interfere in what that institution then did. But I cannot pretend that my palm did not itch severely from time to time; or that I always managed to resist the temptation to scratch it. It is only human to find it difficult to watch something you have helped to create being – as you see it – damaged by someone else. It is even more difficult, when faced with this situation, to have the power to interfere but to resist using it. In my first year in Bosnia I used the Bonn powers to impose legislation some seventy times (about half left over from my predecessor); in my second year some thirty times; in my third year three times and in my last year once. My successor has continued to sharply reduce the use of the Bonn powers – and, in this phase, this is the right thing to do as Bosnia moves further from stabilisation and deeper into state-building and the heavyweight, intrusive era of Dayton and a High Representative gives way to the era of Brussels and a European Union special representative. When the international community arrived in Bosnia at the start of its reconstruction mission, what it found was a mortally wounded patient, close to death. The only option was to put it on the Dayton life support machine. As the patient progressed, it became possible to turn off the machine and get by with a pair of crutches. Bosnia can now complete its journey to full statehood and membership of the European Union on its own, with a helping hand from its international friends.

A similar gradual withdrawal took place in East Timor, where a series of successor UN observer missions have stayed in place in the capital Dili in order to provide support and monitoring for the new East Timorese government which formally took over government of the country in May 2002.

In Eastern Slavonia, however, the end of the intervention was decisive and swift. Although the UN mission was originally planned to last only a year it was subsequently extended by a further twelve months and then ended completely on 15 January 1998, the exact second anniversary of the start of the intervention. In Namibia and

El Salvador the end of the intervention ended in a similarly decisive fashion.

But whether this state-building phase ends gradually as in Bosnia and East Timor, or decisively with the departure of the interveners, as in Eastern Slavonia, it will almost always be followed by a setback in the country's progress. This is normal and to be expected. Running a country through democratic processes is more messy than running it through enlightened fiat. The difficult judgement for the interveners to make is not to do this too late, but not to do it too early either. If progress is set back a little, that is acceptable. But if the country reverses back to ungovernability and conflict, that is not.

The Dangers of Leaving Too Early

And here the most common mistake is to scale down the operation, or even leave, too early. In the Congo, Cambodia, Somalia, Haiti and in many other instances, leaving before the job was really finished, or scaling down too early, has resulted in failure. And in some cases (the Congo is a current example) it can mean having to return again to finish the job. Depressingly, this now appears even to be the case in what was until recently regarded as one of intervention's most notable successes – East Timor. It was always going to be a difficult task to bring that tiny, completely new country to full, peaceful and sustainable statehood. But it now appears that, when the UN decided it could scale down its mission there four years ago, it underestimated the catastrophic failure of leadership which would occur in East Timor's government and especially among those in it who had returned from exile. And so Australian troops once again had to deploy on the streets of Dili to keep the peace. Most believe that East Timor will still make it to sustainable statehood – but it remains a worrying example of the dangers of over-optimism in judging the right time to withdraw or scale down.

Peacemaking and state-building are measured in decades, not years. The price for not understanding that is to return to have to do the job again – and, as we have discovered in Afghanistan, the horn of Africa and the Congo, that can often prove much more expensive than the cost of doing it right the first time. I suspect that, in Afghanistan, building a fully functioning state capable of taking its place in the world is now a thirty-year project. I wonder how many of the leaders who turned their back on Afghanistan after the Soviets left ever thought that this would be the outcome?

Intervening where you have to is expensive in time, effort, political will and money. The only thing that is more expensive is not intervening when you should have done, or pulling out before it is finished and paying the costs and consequences of this afterwards. One of the reasons why it is easy to misjudge the exit point of the interveners is because a state consists of more than just the tangible – it also has intangible elements that cannot easily be measured. Of these intangibles, three deserve special mention here: identity, reconciliation and the existence or otherwise of a civil society.

Identity

A state with which its citizens do not identify, and therefore for which they feel no loyalty, will always be vulnerable. In most states split by a civil war, there will be at least a one-sided crisis of identity. In Bosnia the crisis was three-sided, with the Croats and the Serbs having fought a war to prevent the existence of the state in which they subsequently found themselves living. As a consequence most Serbs and Croats had little sense of identity with, or loyalty to, the Bosnian state.

But questions of loyalty to the state are not just difficult issues for post-conflict societies; they are vexing questions for all modern multi-ethnic and multicultural societies. In Britain recently there have been vigorous debates on just this, with Conservative politician Lord Norman Tebbit formulating the famous 'Tebbit cricket test' which claimed that an English person of West Indian origin could not be considered to be truly English unless they supported England when they played the West Indies at cricket. What Norman Tebbit overlooked is that in our modern world the idea that you can have only one identity is not simply out of date, it is dangerous. The mono identity belonged to the days of the monolithic nation state and they are either over or on their way out.

Let me put it personally. If, forty years ago, when I was a British soldier, you had asked me who I was I would have said that I was British and that would have been enough. Today, if you ask me that question, I would have to give a more complex answer. I am Irish by blood and proud of it; but the West Country of England is my chosen home and the place I represented in the British Parliament – so I am a West Countryman, too. And I am British and proud of that as well. And I am a European. And unless you allow me to call myself all these things, I cannot describe who I am, or the space in which I want to live and in which I want my children and grandchildren to live as well.

So having a multiple identity is not only all right – it is for many people the only way to live and, for some, the only way to have peace. If you say to a Catholic in Northern Ireland that he or she cannot be Irish as well as being British, or tell a Serb that he cannot proudly be a Serb as well as being a Bosnian, or a Tajik in Afghanistan that they have to choose between being a Tajiki and an Afghanistani, then you will probably end up with blood on your streets. Our nations are diverse and becoming more so. The only way to accommodate that fact is to accept it and be proud of it – to celebrate it. And very frequently symbols and flags and national anthems are the enemy of this. In Bosnia, as in most states after a civil war, these were the cause of more trouble than almost anything else. There are a few occasions when badges and flags have to be taken seriously – as for instance when those the state depends on for its security, such as soldiers or police, reject the symbols of the state they are supposed to serve. But as far as possible and whenever possible the best thing to do with these symbols in a post-conflict state is to ignore them if you can and try to get others to do so too. The British government simply failed to react when the city council of Derry flew the Irish tricolour above the city hall, rather than the British union jack; and I always tried to be resolutely blind to the Croatian flags or the Serbian double eagles which constantly flew throughout the Croat and Serb areas of Bosnia.

Loyalty to a state cannot be legislated for, cannot be imposed by outsiders and does not come from standing up for the national anthem or saluting the flag. Creating identity with the state and loyalty to it is not an event – it is a process. It comes from intangible things – like winning an international football match or having a citizen do something which the whole state can feel proud of. In my four years in Bosnia there were at least three events which created more sense of pride in and attachment to Bosnia than anything I, or any of my predecessors, or any international, had ever done in the ten years of the international community's involvement there. The first was when Bosnian citizen and renowned film maker Danis Tanović won an Oscar for the best foreign film;[2] the second was when the Bosnian football team beat Denmark in the European Championship qualifiers in 2004 and the third was when the triumphal re-opening of the Mostar bridge was shown live on the TV sets of the world.

The second way to build a citizen's loyalty to the state is for the state to provide the citizen with what they want: good health services, decent education for their children, the rule of law, the prospect of a job, decent welfare services and the hope of a good pension. These are the product of a well functioning state. Citizens' identity and loyalty are therefore the product of good state-building, not a pre-existing condition for it.

Truth and Reconciliation

One of the ways that citizens identify with their state is to have a united view about its history. In a country which has experienced a civil war, this cannot be arrived at easily and is unlikely to be arrived at quickly. But the process of arriving at it begins with the process of dissolving the enmities of war. There is no substitute here for time, which is the great dissolver.

But time can sometimes be assisted through a process of truth and reconciliation. The best example of this is, of course, South Africa. But the South African model has proved very difficult to replicate in other post-conflict countries. The reasons are simple to identify. First of all, few civil wars or struggles end in such a comprehensive and bloodless victory as that of the ANC in South Africa. Once they had swept to power, the apartheid losers had no option but to accommodate to the new force in their country. That was the realpolitik necessary for their survival. Secondly almost no countries after that kind of struggle are fortunate enough to have people with the extraordinary qualities of leadership and moral vision of Nelson Mandela and his generation of ANC leaders. All of them had suffered too – in most cases more than their people. If they were to be satisfied with the acknowledgement of evil, rather than its punishment, how could others not be? These two conditions – and especially the latter – are unlikely to be replicated in many other countries after conflict. I know that I could have found neither the words nor the means to persuade a mother from Srebrenica that she should accept that recognition for his crime was all that was needed from the Serb policeman who she saw every week in neighbouring Zvornik and who she believed had murdered her son.

For her, only justice would suffice – and I am sure that for me in her position, it would be the same. So neither truth nor reconciliation is likely to be possible in most countries after conflict until at least the primary tasks of justice have been carried out. There must of course come a time when the pursuit of every last perpetrator can give way to the process of truth and reconciliation – but not early and not until the principal perpetrators of the horrors have faced justice. Herein lies the importance of the ad hoc tribunals established in post-conflict situations around the world, such as the Hague and Rwanda tribunals. In all there have been five of these since the Second World War.[3]

So justice first – and after justice, in most cases the next step will be truth, the simple act of recording what happened where and when through a Truth Commission.[4] One way to do this is through an 'open system' which does no more than note down everyone's story, as they would wish to tell it – without any attempt to establish truth or to pursue any other outcome. In this way a body of knowledge, or claimed knowledge, can be established. And then, after the truth has been exposed, the next and last step can be reconciliation, if the conditions can support this.

Finally, probably many years later, the nation will be able to arrive at a common view of its history. It is said to have taken four or more generations after the English Civil War before a united view of what had happened could be arrived at. The old tensions and even the animosities of the American Civil War still remain just below the surface in the United States, nearly 150 years after its ending. In Japan, more than half a century after the ending of the last war, a visit by the prime minister to the Yakusuni shrine celebrating Japanese war heroes can be a contentious event, both domestically and internationally.

The Civil Service

One of the hallmarks of a modern sustainable democratic state is the existence of a merit-based civil service, free from political interference. Creating such a civil service is one of the key tasks for the interveners in the state-building phase.

Before I started in Bosnia I asked a wise old friend[5] who had been a young man in the days when the post-Second World War Allied Control Commissions ran Germany what he thought should be my priorities. He replied without hesitation that I should follow the example of the British in Germany and concentrate on the creation of a modern, state-wide independent civil service. This was indeed one of my priorities when I started. I hoped to be able to set up a single college which would train the servants of the state from each of the ethnicities, in a single location. I fear I failed. Try as I did I never managed to get the individual international community players, who were involved in penny-packet programmes aimed at tackling some element of civil service reform, to combine together into a single nationwide programme. And I knew that, if I could not persuade my international colleagues, I would never be able to persuade the competing local ethnic vested interests to agree to submit to a single nationwide structure.

The creation of such a modern civil service is not an easy task. In most post-conflict countries the notion that the civil service is an exclusive playground for the patronage of those who govern will be very deeply ingrained – especially if the country has previously been subject to imperial rule and/or dictatorship. The existence of democratic elections will not, by itself, change this. Those who win the election will simply assume that appointing their own civil servants (and police chiefs and often generals, too) is a natural part of the spoils of victory. And the civil servants appointed will continue to view their jobs as sinecures which open the way to wealth through bribery, or taking a share in their political masters' take from the profits of government. Reforming a civil service is, once again, a process, not an event. And like all processes it is most difficult at the start. When the new standards requiring that civil servants should be appointed on merit and not through political connections come in, they will almost always initially apply to the old civil service, appointed on the old system of patronage. This will be difficult to explain to an incoming government which has just won an election. The last government appointed their civil service – so why shouldn't we appoint ours? Why should we have to work with a civil service appointed by the people we just beat in the elections? Etc etc.

These difficulties will be magnified in places like Bosnia, Iraq, Northern Ireland and Afghanistan, where one of the destabilising factors is a volatile ethnic or religious mix. In these countries the formation of governments will very frequently be constitutionally prescribed so as to represent the ethnic mix of the country and prevent the dominance of any single ethnicity. The same, of course, has to apply to the civil service. This means that there will be two factors to be considered when appointing civil servants: merit and ethnic or religious origin. The effect of this complication will frequently be to increase the scope for 'hidden patronage' and for the creation of 'parallel structures' which can undermine the unitary operation of the state.

These issues caused us many headaches in Bosnia and have plagued post-conflict state-building in most other recent interventions. A recent evaluation of the current operations in Afghanistan[6] identified the failure to create a merit-based civil service as a major deficiency and attributed this to the fact that there had been insufficient priority given to this area by the international community. Moreover, where the international community was involved, they had focused on fulfilling the minimum requirements in key ministries (finance, army and police) by establishing parallel systems of internationally paid and funded project staff. This had resulted, the report concluded, in buying in outside capacity rather than building it locally within the civil service. The problems this caused had been sharply exacerbated by the fact that bought-in staff were paid by the international community far more than their permanent civil service counterparts.

This highlights another very common problem in the state-building phase – the unwitting tendency for the interveners to create an 'internal brain drain' in the country they are trying to rebuild.

When I took up my mandate in Bosnia I was shocked to discover that nearly all the key posts in the Office of the High Representative were filled by foreigners, while excellently qualified and able Bosnians held only lower positions in the organisation. I started a policy to open all positions to Bosnians and in the process put together one of the most talented teams I have ever had the privilege of working with. As is often the case, however, there was an unintended consequence to this policy. I unwittingly accelerated the internal brain brain caused by the fact that the international community pays its staff far more than the local going rate. My driver earned more than the prime minister of Bosnia.* Inevitably this resulted in the best and brightest – just those who should have been running the state – working instead for the international community. As we closed our organisations, we tried to migrate these talented people across to the institutions of the Bosnian state. But we were hamstrung by the fact that, having worked for the foreigners and enjoyed 'foreign salaries', they were regarded with extreme suspicion in the Bosnian government and civil service. Some international organisations have excellent programmes for helping disbanded soldiers with transition payments – but I could never persuade any of my international colleagues to fund a transition support scheme for talented local people who have been working for the international community, to enable them to move across to the state, where their skills were desperately needed.

The Civil Society

Lastly, paralleling the need for an independent merit-based civil service, a sustainable modern democracy also requires a strong and vibrant civil society – I mean the term in its broadest sense, encompassing the professional, cultural and business world and incorporating an understanding of the importance of human rights, gender equality and other issues.

A sustainable, well-functioning state is made up of two elements: efficient democratic institutions which make it work, and a civil society strong enough to protect these from the abuse of power and from the actions of an over-mighty executive. Without a civil society performing this function, even the most perfect of institutions bequeathed by the wisest foreign intervener will become corrupt over time. So creating or reconstructing a strong civil society after conflict is important. And here we have a paradox. Although a strong civil society is one of the conditions which will make the exit of the interveners more secure, the interveners themselves cannot create that civil society – the only people who can do that

---

* According to the Oxford Research Group paper 'What would Military Security look like through a human security lens?', a similar problem has occurred in Kosovo, where the president earned some 800 Euros a month, while a junior official from NATO or the EU earned some ten times that amount.

are members of the society itself. That point is so obvious that it ought to be – well – obvious. But it isn't.

There is a cosy and very common assumption among interveners that, since they have strong civil societies at home, they can re-create them abroad. They can't and when they try they almost always fail. Huge amounts of money were wasted in Bosnia importing well-meaning *Guardian* readers from Hampstead Garden Suburb to set up NGOs and civil society organisations. They made precisely no impact apart from creating handy employment projects for the middle classes. Indeed there was a time in Bosnia when this was one of the country's only real employment growth industries. And not just for the Bosnian citizens but also for NGO 'experts' from developed countries who were given significant sums of money in the belief that they could export their know-how. In this, Bosnia is no exception. In Iraq, human rights and women's rights were one of the early priorities, even in some cases taking precedence over the establishment of the rule of law, ignoring the fact that such issues, while vital, are the products of a stable society based on the rule of law, and not the means of establishing one.[7] Despite the expenditure of considerable sums of money and effort, I know of no single case in any intervention where the interveners have been successful in 'creating' the civil society where it did not already exist. Many have tried, but all have failed in the same way.

There is an obvious reason for this. While the foreigners are there controlling the abuses of power, why should anyone trouble themselves to set up an organisation to do the same thing? When I used to berate my Bosnian friends for not preventing their government's excesses, they replied, very reasonably, 'Why should we Paddy, when you are doing it for us, with all your powers?'

When it comes to the creation of a civil society strong enough to protect what they have created, the best that interveners can do is to help with technical assistance in setting up laws for NGOs, encourage the establishment of media regulatory bodies, provide enabling training for individuals[8] and then hope that a true civil society will emerge after they have gone.

Summary

State-building has different characteristics to stabilisation. But the two phases will usually run together. The twin dangers in building institutions are making compromises for the short term, which damage the long-term sustainability of the institutions, and gold plating institutions when you do not have to. As institutions are handed over, the interveners have to learn to stand back, even when mistakes are committed. The most common error in this phase, however, is to pull out too early, before the job is done. This most often leads to them having to return later, often at greater cost, to finish the job. Creating a merit-based civil service is a crucial and difficult task in this phase. The interveners may be able to do a lot when it comes to building state institutions, but they can do far less when it comes to creating the intangibles of statehood – the way people think. Loyalty to and identity with the state cannot be manufactured by foreigners, it has to grow naturally. So does truth and reconciliation – and so does the civil society. Creating these things is a process not an event.

Part III

How can we do it better?

6

Right analysis – wrong solution

Gentlemen, when you do a good thing, you may do it in so bad
a way that you may entirely spoil the beneficial effect.
GLADSTONE, 'On the Domestic and Foreign Affairs of
England', 27 November 1879 – Midlothian Campaign

In recent times the Western interveners (chiefly led by the US) have
pursued an approach to peacemaking and peacekeeping which bears
a striking resemblance to British 'gun boat diplomacy' of the nineteenth century. Although the problems these interventions are
intended to resolve are chiefly diplomatic and political, the arm
chosen to solve them has been primarily military and the policies
pursued have been based on the assumption that the countries in
which we are intervening want nothing more than to have the
benefit of our systems, our organisation and our values. The attitude
of the military has tended to be 'in – out; sort them out; and let the
diplomats pick up the pieces later.' In pursuit of this policy whole
armed forces have been re-shaped into expeditionary armies (see the
British Defence Review of 1998 for a classic example of this), in
which the centrepiece has been the projection of power to win
wars, rather than the projection of influence to prevent them and of
resources and good governance to win the battle for reconstruction
afterwards.[1] This policy has initiated a revolution of thinking and
posture in military circles, but almost none in the circles of
diplomacy and politics.

This expeditionary approach is not working. Where it has been
followed in its starkest form it has sometimes led to painful failure
(Somalia), often led to greater difficulties (Iraq) and mostly fallen
short of success in the way originally hoped for.

If we are to be serious about peacemaking and peacekeeping and want to do better in the future, we will need to think much more radically than military expeditions with a few diplomatic 'add-ons'. And we will have to accompany this with a revolution of policy, posture and integration across governments domestically and between them internationally.

The good news is that the recent experience of burnt fingers seems at last to have produced a glimmering realisation that we need to do things differently, even if the result still falls far short of the deep changes which are necessary to be more successful. There is now a growing acceptance that prevention, intervention and post-conflict reconstruction are no longer to be considered as unusual events which from time to time take us by surprise, but as part of the regular heartbeat of international military and political affairs in an increasingly interdependent world.

In November 2005, the US Department of Defense issued Directive 3000.05, defining stability operations as a *'core US military mission'* that *'shall be given priority comparable to combat operations'*. In July the previous year the US State Department created a new unit, the Office of the Coordinator for Reconstruction and Stabilization (S/CRS) and tasked it to plan for and carry out post-conflict reconstruction.[2] The British government recently established a similar organisation, the Post-Conflict Reconstruction Unit (PCRU) and two Global Conflict Prevention Pools (GCPP) – of which more later. Meanwhile, the Canadian government has followed suit with its Stabilisation and Reconstruction Team (START).

A number of reforms have also been undertaken in the international community. The UN, on the advice of the High-Level Panel on Threats,[3] has established a new Peace-Building Commission (PBC) to advise and propose integrated strategies for post-conflict recovery. The UN's Department of Peace Keeping Operations (DPKO) has also beefed up its planning, exercise and deployment capabilities, establishing for the first time its own strategic planning cell. The strengthening of UNIFIL in the Lebanon, both numerically and in terms of a more muscular mandate, seems to indicate a willingness among the international community to see the UN moving back to peacekeeping in non-permissive environments, which were abandoned after the Congo in 1960. The EU, for its part, aims to raise its level of readiness so that it would, by 2008, have

adequate resources to act as a global player in civilian crisis management. To this end it has stood up several Battle Groups, which
can act as the military backbone of future operations. There is now a
Civil-Military Cell in the EU Council Secretariat and the arrangements for cooperation between the EU Council and the EU Commission have gradually improved. Meanwhile, on 17 September
2004 the then EU Presidency announced that several of its member
states had agreed to establish a multinational European Gendarmerie Force (EGF). NATO, still the most capable and experienced
military alliance in the world, has also developed its Rapid Reaction
Force, which, although still hamstrung by inter-alliance disagree-
ment in its development of civilian capabilities, has, through its
Kosovo and Afghan missions, now arguably accumulated more
civilian stabilisation experience than the EU. Finally the African
Union is in the (slow) process of building its skills, with the establishment of a new Committee on Post-Conflict Reconstruction and a
ten-year programme of help from the UN is now in the process of
being formulated.

These initiatives should be welcomed as evidence that this issue is
at last being taken seriously and that thinking is shifting in governments and international organisations. Unfortunately, however,
the setting up of new institutions has not in the main been followed
by the adoption of the radical new thinking which is required to
enable them to work effectively.

In the following chapters I will outline what that radical new
thinking might entail.

7

The seamless garment

Any administration must bring to the task . . . singular integrity and diligence, combined with a just comprehension of the competing claims of different classes of the population. It must also command the confidence of the people so as to secure the co-operation of public opinion, without which so complex a tangle could not be unravelled.

GERTRUDE BELL, Baghdad 1918, writing on the setting up of the post-First World War British administration in Iraq[1]

MONDAY 16 JUNE 2003 – **Washington**
(two months after Saddam Hussein's statue fell in Baghdad)

Off in the car to the Pentagon. We were whisked upstairs and into Rumsfeld's meeting room, where we all sat around and chatted with his key advisers.

There was much nervousness about the Iraq situation. They are losing about one American a day now and there is real concern that they are also losing control of the situation and that, sooner or later, American casualties will become the issue, probably in the context of the Presidential election campaign that starts in the autumn.

While we were chatting, Paul Wolfowitz came in. He said he was sorry not to meet me in Sarajevo, and we chatted about the recent operation Balkan Vice.[2] He asked me if there was anything they could learn for Iraq, from us in Bosnia? I said that there might be some general things – but Iraq and Bosnia were different and anyway, it was probably a bit late now since presumably they had already launched their plans?

Before Wolfowitz could reply, Rumsfeld burst in, a bundle of energy and gimlet-eyed as ever. It is extraordinary how good he

*looks for seventy-two. He was wearing a pair of pin-stripe trousers
and a polo fleece. He sat down opposite me and cracked off at his
usual pace. As always, he challenged me in almost the first thing I
said, which was about the economy, claiming that usually judgements made about the economy overlooked the grey economy. I told
him that we hadn't and gave him the figures.*

*The conversation on Bosnia was perfunctory, before turning to
the subject he clearly wanted to discuss – Iraq. He had heard I was
making a speech on peacemaking and state-building – could I send
him a copy? He continued along the lines Wolfowitz had started,
saying that he believed that, in Iraq, they could learn from what we
had done in Bosnia. They had just decided to put a team together
to come and see us in Sarajevo with the aim of doing a paper on
'lessons learned from Bosnia for Iraq' – would we help them? Would
I be prepared to fly out to Iraq to see Bremer (the new American
'High Representative' there) to give him my views? I replied that,
since it was two months since the war had ended, wasn't it a bit late?
But of course I would be happy to help if they felt I could if they
could make the arrangements. He agreed to fix it and the meeting
ended.*

The US State Department began their preparation for the post-
conflict phase in Iraq in April 2002, assembling some seventeen
working groups made up of experts from a wide number of dis-
ciplines. Among other conclusions this group reached, one was that
there would be an insurgency and that the wholesale disbandment of
the Iraqi Army would be disaster. Nor was forward thinking about
the situation the US would find itself in after the end of the conflict
in Iraq confined to the State Department. The Pentagon's own
thinkers had been considering this, too, and in a prescient minute
of early 2003, concluded that:

*Rebuilding Iraq will require a considerable commitment of Amer-
ican resources, but the longer US presence is maintained, the more
likely violent resistance will develop . . . An exit strategy will
require the establishment of political stability, which will be difficult
to achieve given Iraq's fragmented population, weak political
institutions, and propensity for rule by violence . . . To tear apart
the [Iraqi] Army in the war's aftermath could lead to the destruction*

of one of the only forces for unity within the society. Breaking up large elements of the army also raises the possibility that demobilised soldiers could affiliate with ethnic or tribal militias . . . The possibility of the United States winning the war and losing the peace in Iraq is real and serious. Rehabilitating Iraq will consequently be an important challenge that threatens to consume huge amounts of resources without guaranteed results.[3]

In late January 2003, however, just two months before the start of the Iraq war, President Bush issued Presidential Directive NSPD 24, making the Department of Defense, under Secretary Donald Rumsfeld, responsible for the entire post-war reconstruction effort in Iraq and establishing the Office of Reconstruction and Humanitarian Assistance (ORHA) as the organisation charged with this task.[4] The thinking appears to have been that the need for clear command was paramount and, since the military were the best planners and the only people who would have the post-war structures on the ground to make things happen, they, and not the State Department, should lead the process.[5]

Retired US general Jay Garner was chosen by Secretary Rumsfeld to head up ORHA and instructed to ignore all previous State Department preparatory work, which was unceremoniously dumped and replaced with new and hastily drawn up plans based on assumptions laid down by Rumsfeld and the Department of Defense. These assumptions were as follows: first that there would be a humanitarian disaster, including a massive refugee crisis and substantial environmental damage from the igniting of Iraq's oil fields, including possible contamination from the use of weapons of mass destruction; second, that the US and Coalition soldiers would be welcomed into Iraq as liberators and that the Iraqi police and security forces would maintain law and order; third, that basic services, such as electricity and water, could be assured in a short period of time; and finally that an interim Iraqi administration could be inaugurated within weeks of the end of combat which would swiftly lead to a brief transitional period, before a full state apparatus was up and running and the US could withdraw . . . And finally, that the Iraqi Ministries, including the police, would remain intact throughout this period. As the *Los Angeles Times* put it, officials at the Pentagon assumed that the invaders would '*inherit a fully functioning modern state, with government ministries, police forces and public utilities in working order – it would be a "plug and play" occupation, [because] the resistance would end quickly.'*[6/7]

During the seven weeks Garner had to write a plan ('that's what it takes to get a computer connection at the Pentagon' commented a Defense Department Official)[8] he had at best only minimal communications with the Office of Special Plans who were actually planning the war. He quickly set up a governance team to manage the transition process across Iraq. At the time the war started it consisted of fewer than two dozen people, the core of whom were, like Garner, retired service officers[*] and had inadequate communications, only a few Arabic speakers, almost no computers with internet access and neither desks nor stationery.

Garner's original plan was to take the ORHA into Iraq right behind the frontline troops, so that they could set up the administration as soon as the fighting stopped. But he was prevented from doing this by the Pentagon, who told him that the military plan did not foresee ORHA in Baghdad until 120 days after major combat operations were over. In the event, and after much high-level lobbying, Garner and his ORHA team were finally allowed into Iraq on 21 April, nearly two weeks after Baghdad fell. What they found when they got there is described in one US report as follows:

With the Coalition victory, Iraq's national government disintegrated. Only in the Kurdish northeast, where two Kurdish political parties reached a peaceful modus vivendi in the early 1990s, was there anything resembling legitimate civil authority, although it was supported by party-based militias (peshmerga). In the southern, Shi'a-dominated areas, Iraqi religious authorities held sway; while in the Sunni-dominated west, scattered remnants of the old regime persisted. Baghdad, Iraq's proud though shabby capital, had no army, no police, no courts, no city government, no Parliament and

---

[*] They were known in the Pentagon as the 'Space Cowboys' after the Clint Eastwood film in which ageing astronauts set off into space for one last mission. According to Thomas E. Ricks in *Fiasco: The American Military Adventure in Iraq*, Garner wanted to include staff who had been involved in the State Department's planning project in ORHA, but these had been refused by Cheney (pp. 81 and 102–3) because they were regarded as 'not people who stood up for the party line' (i.e. they were regarded as State Department, rather than Department of Defense people).

virtually no ministries. Iraq's borders were unguarded, its customs posts unmanned, and its army defeated . . . All . . . assumptions the Department of Defense had made about post-conflict Iraq were wrong. No humanitarian or environmental crisis emerged. After a decade of sanctions and misappropriation of oil-for-food money, nearly all basic services in Iraq were on the verge of collapse. Hospitals and schools were in shambles. Sewage flowed through the streets and directly into the Tigris River. The provision of electricity was erratic. Iraq also lacked even the most basic building blocks of democratic governance. Political opponents to Saddam and non-governmental organisations had been driven into exile. Civil society had been silenced and replaced with an entrenched culture of corruption and fear. Finally, police, military and intelligence assets mostly evaporated during the invasion and those that remained had little experience with the rule of law – they had all answered to Saddam Hussein. Given these unexpected realities, the plans ORHA had developed immediately proved inadequate.

Moreover, as Baghdad fell, widespread lawlessness swept across the country. Rampant looting and criminality took hold, resulting in the gutting of government ministries, museums, schools, hospitals, and power plants. Seventeen of the twenty-three ministries were completely destroyed. Lacking the force structure and orders to impose martial law, Coalition forces stood by and merely watched the rampage. Washington-based officials dismissed it as minor and understandable in a new state of freedom. Secretary of Defense Rumsfeld, in response to the looting, merely claimed, 'Stuff happens.'

The impact of the looting and lawlessness was devastating. It compounded the already dilapidated state of Iraq's infrastructure, making it far more difficult to provide basic services such as water and electricity. The destruction of the ministries made it impossible to operate according to the 'decapitation' plan ORHA had devised, and the looting and lawlessness undermined ORHA's standing in the eyes of the Iraqis. Even Iraqis who had greeted the Americans as liberators disapproved of their failure to uphold law and order. Impunity rather than accountability seemed to be the first product of liberation. While many in Baghdad and southern Iraq had hated Saddam Hussein, the goodwill that the Coalition forces had earned for defeating the Hussein regime quickly dissipated when the victors failed to deliver law and order, basic services, or even a clear plan for the future.[9]

In one sense, this situation might be regarded as scarcely surprising – since the United States did not really have anything worthy of description as a 'plan' for the post-war situation in Iraq. COBRA II, the classified US war plan, did not even include in its overall aim the establishment of a viable administration in Iraq, but declared instead that *'the end state for this operation is regime change'*.[10] The very carefully assembled and fully rehearsed plan for the war was entirely separate from and largely unconnected to the hastily thrown together, under-resourced and unrehearsed plan for what followed. Commenting on this afterwards one US Air Force general said, *'Once they made the decision, that there would be a separate plan for the postwar, that was the mistake.'*[11]

*   *   *

What makes this story so depressing is that, when it comes to failures of planning for the post-conflict phase, Iraq is not the exception, it is merely a rather dramatic example of the rule. There were no plans for what would happen after NATO occupied Bosnia either, beyond sending the first High Representative in Bosnia, Carl Bildt, into Sarajevo with a suitcase full of money and instructions to get on with it. Here is how the international community's first High Representative described his first days in Sarajevo on 21 December 1995, four weeks after the Dayton Peace Agreement was initialled:

> *I had to ask the Swedish Ambassador, Erik Pierre, to borrow his Land Rover in order to get around, and the members of my team had to go on similar national begging raids to prevent us from being stranded at the airport. Moreover, since NATO had occupied the few hotels, we had to sleep on the sofas and floors of the ambassador's tiny apartment . . . We shivered in Sarajevo during those first few weeks of January. It was impossible to work in the office without an overcoat and gloves – but even that was not enough to keep the cold at bay for more than a couple for hours. There were traces of bullet holes in my desk, and no sign of life whatsoever from the old telephone. As darkness fell, we had to work with candles and torches, with pens and paper, and with whatever we could borrow*

or bring in. There was never enough time to cope with the combination of looming political crisis and all the practical things that needed to be done to set up.[12]

The late and usually unprepared arrival of the reconstruction mission following the conflict has been an almost standard feature of all recent interventions. In Kosovo, despite the fact that NATO began to plan for its deployment several months in advance, the UN was given only a few days' notice of its role and was therefore very slow to deploy its civil administrators, leaving a governance gap of several months, which was quickly filled by the Albanian and Serb extremists. The UN civil police (CIVPOL) were even slower and did not reach their full deployment strength until well over a year after the end of the fighting, again creating a gap in the establishment of the rule of law in Kosovo which NATO's soldiers could not fill, but which the criminal elements could, and did. Late deployment of civilian administrators and police, together with the variable quality of those deployed, was also a feature of the immediate post-conflict period in East Timor, where the UN found itself woefully under-resourced in the early days to cope with a situation where all 8,000 Indonesian civil administrators had left and 70 per cent of the public administration infrastructure and housing had been destroyed. By contrast, detailed planning for the civilian occupation of Germany in 1945 started in 1943 and the civil administrators who implemented it went in just behind the frontline troops, with 'town majors' frequently taking over the local administration within hours of the frontline troops moving out.

The truth is that nowadays, while we are very good at military planning for war and lavish huge resources on getting it right, we spend neither time, nor resources, nor energy on the civilian planning for what will happen the moment after the war ends. Time is of the essence here. I well recall being welcomed by the Catholics on the streets of Belfast with cups of tea and sandwiches, when British troops first arrived to protect them from the Protestants. Less than a year later we were seen by most Catholics not as saviours but as hated occupiers. Exactly the same happened, only even quicker and more dramatically, to US troops in Iraq. Armies of liberation have a distinct and usually rather short half-life before they start being seen as armies of occupation. Making best use of the 'golden hours' after the war ends can make a huge difference to the chances of success in the long struggle to reconstruct a conflict-ravaged country.

In this chapter I will lay out how we could approach the planning for the post-conflict reconstruction phase more rationally in order to give a greater chance of success. I shall do this by looking first at the nature of the battle that has to be fought to reconstruct a nation, secondly at how this ties in with the prevention and the war phases that preceded it and thirdly at what a good plan might look like. However, as in the rest of life, post-conflict reconstruction involves compromises between what it is best and what it is possible to do. What is outlined here is a recommendation of perfection which will more often than not have to be amended because of prevailing realities.

Public Opinion

In his seminal book *The Utility of Force*, General Sir Rupert Smith argues that, since all modern wars are fought among the people, the crucial battlefield to win on is that of public opinion and that, therefore, *'we fight in every living room in the world as well as on the streets and fields of a conflict zone.'*[13] It is self-evident that, even more than wars, post-conflict reconstruction is also carried out 'among the people'. So to say that you cannot rebuild a state by force of arms, you can do it only by consent of the people, ought to be no more than stating the obvious. Yet from the way we behave in too many interventions it is clear that this fact appears not to be obvious to some. In fact, soldiers, though absolutely necessary, are the least *useful* people to have around when you are attempting to rebuild a state after conflict. Their job is limited to creating and maintaining security; to holding the ring while a political solution is found. In reality, when it comes to the period after the conflict, providing security has been established, a dozen water engineers are probably more useful than ten times that number of soldiers – unless of course the soldiers are willing to turn their hand to reconnecting water supplies, which few of them are.

The reason for this is simple. After security has been established, it is the establishment of the rule of law, the connection of basic services and the setting up of effective administration which enables you to win the battle for hearts and minds at this stage. Even more than fighting the war which preceded it, the struggle to reconstruct a state and society cannot be won without first gaining the support of the local population. This central fact has to shape all that you do and all that you plan to do.

Our enemies understand this very well. For them the battlefield of public opinion is the crucial battleground – the only one that matters. When they blow up an American Humvee in Iraq, their most important aim is not killing the enemy, but gaining a media spectacular which will be available on the internet in a matter of minutes. And this crucial battlefield is growing exponentially in size, scope, geographical reach and influence. One US expert has calculated that, whereas at the time of the Vietnam conflict, the average citizen had access to only ten media outlets, of which almost half were under government control, the average citizen today has access to some twenty five sources of news and information (counting the internet as only one) of which very few are under official control.[14] This is the crucial battlefield which we have to dominate and win on, quite as much as on the terrain of the country concerned. And in Iraq at least, it is here that the Coalition is losing and our enemies are winning.

Giving full recognition to the importance of this battle for hearts and minds means understanding something else which is fundamental and very important: that the interveners are, even if only informally, *accountable* to the people of the country in which they are intervening and their actions must, therefore, be as transparent to them as possible. This fact is one which is almost completely ignored in most interventions – not just in Iraq. In Kosovo, the UN has little or no sense of accountability to local people and very little sense of the need for transparency either. Despite repeated requests from the government in Afghanistan, the UN agencies and the NGOs operating there have refused to make their accounts and audit reports available to the public.[15] I like to think that we tried to understand the importance of local accountability in Bosnia, by making the audited accounts of the OHR publicly available, accepting that where I used the 'Bonn powers' to impose legislation this should be open to challenge before the Bosnian Constitutional Court, by being regularly available for questioning before Bosnia's parliaments and by trying to be as open as possible with its press. But there was no formal structure which required this and I fear we fell short of what was really necessary.

There are in effect two public opinion battlegrounds to consider – the international one and the domestic one in the state that is the subject of international intervention. The international battleground is the less important of the two. It is possible, especially for the powerful, to intervene successfully without having world opinion on your side – though it is much easier if it is. But democracies cannot succeed in these exercises if their own domestic opinion is opposed. Ho Chi Minh understood, even if the US did not, that the battle to get the Americans out of Vietnam was won on the streets of America, not in the jungles of Vietnam – perhaps modern history's most powerful example of the basic truth that the crucial battleground in these exercises is that of public opinion.

There is a theory of modern conflict which divides war into three theatres: the advanced battlefield (which is the enemy's rear area or homeland); the close battlefield, which is where the troops are; and the rear battlefield, which is your own rear area or homeland. In order to win on the close battlefield it is first necessary to win on the advanced battlefield – the enemy's territory – and prevent him from winning on his advanced battlefield – your home territory. Whoever wins that battle then wins on the battlefield where the troops are – the close battlefield.

It is possible to look at the battle for public opinion in post-conflict reconstruction in the same way. It is helpful to have world opinion on your side. But, in a democracy (though even totalitarian states are not immune from this – think Russia in Afghanistan) it is essential to have the support of your own domestic opinion. It is even more essential, however, to have opinion in the state in which the intervention is taking place, if not actively with you, then at least believing that what you are doing is in their interests. This means that the messages that are sent as to why the intervention is taking place are vital. And so is the means of getting those messages across. I shall discuss later the role of the press in these operations. For the moment, it is the message not the means that is important. Why is the international community intervening and what is it trying to achieve? If that message cannot be communicated in terms that elicit the support of the audience in the country in which the intervention is taking place, then the battle for reconstruction cannot be won, it is as straightforward as that.

In reality, however, this battle begins long before a single international soldier or peacemaker puts a single foot on the territory of the country concerned. It begins way back in the prevention phase, for this is the time when the messages start to be formulated.

The Seamless Garment

And this is the second crucial message of this chapter. If we are to succeed, we have to stop viewing post-conflict reconstruction as a stand-alone event that somehow takes us by surprise when the fighting has stopped. We should view it instead as only the last phase in a process which began with the attempt to prevent a state failing, or to change its actions which threaten the wider peace. We need to start looking at these three phases – prevention, war fighting and post-conflict reconstruction – as a single seamless garment, where each piece pre-shapes and flows into the next and where, throughout all three phases, the overall aims remain unchanged. As a recent high-level US conference looking into why the US continues to make the same mistakes over and over again in its intervention efforts puts it, there is *'a more or less seamless web of relationships and activities . . . that extends from the beginning of a crisis to its final resolution, a process that may take years or even decades.'*[16]

Clausewitz once said that war was an extension of politics by other means. But the opposite is also true. That the aims of the politics of prevention and reconstruction are the same as those of the war pursued by other, non kinetic, means. Or, to put it another way, there is no defined 'beginning' or 'end' to this kind of 'conflict'; it simply transforms itself over the process, creating new structures, actors, means and dynamics, according to the phase in progress.

In this way the prevention phase and the messages sent during it transition into the messages for the war-fighting phase, if there has to be one. And then the messages of the war phase similarly transition into the messages necessary for the post-conflict reconstruction phase which follows. Indeed, the way each phase is conducted influences the phase that follows – most notably the way the war is fought will critically determine the reconstruction phase, especially in the early days. It follows therefore that the way the international community intends to go about the reconstruction task should influence the way it plans to fight the war which precedes it. After all, international involvement is not finished when the war is over – it is finished only when the reconstruction phase has been successfully completed – and that may still be many years and many millions of dollars or Euros later.

Our biggest mistake in past interventions has lain in our failure to adopt this 'seamless garment' approach and most particularly to think and plan *through* the war phase to what follows *after* the end of the fighting, so losing the opportunities of the 'golden hour' through the late arrival of the civil administrations and the civil police structures which can begin early to establish the rule of law.

The Case

Central to the 'seamless garment' approach are the messages which the international community sends throughout each of these phases. The important thing here is that the core message has to be the same throughout, even if the details vary according to the phase. What is needed here is a public narrative, or 'case' which defines in clear terms capable of winning public support why the international community must act, what its intentions are and what it is trying to achieve. The very broad outlines of a case could be sketched out in a UN Security Council Resolution. But it is important to remember that the 'case' itself is a *political*, not a legal document – its purpose is to convey messages, not legal arguments. A 'case' might thus cover the following points:

Because of its internal acts of repression state X is in breach of international human rights law, threatening a humanitarian catastrophe and causing floods of refugees which place in jeopardy the peace of the region. The international community, having tried all other means to persuade state X to change its actions in order to conform with international law, has concluded, through a resolution of the Security Council, that it cannot stand idly by and has therefore resolved to act, with a view, initially, to persuading state X to alter its policies in order to conform with international law, end the repression of its people and cease undermining the peace of the region – if it fails to do so, then the international community reserves the right, if necessary, to act.

The 'case' thus needs to be constructed in language which can gather the widest public support, domestically and internationally. It should have particular regard to the voices in the country which is the subject of the intervention and be framed in a way which appeals to them. This will often not be easy to do, since the international community will frequently find itself in head to head conflict with the regime of the country concerned. That regime is likely to have control of the media outlets and be able to whip up nationalistic fervour about foreign invaders. But, however difficult this battle is, it has got to be won. If it can be won in the prevention phase, then there will be a greater chance of that phase being successful. If it is not won in the prevention phase, it will have to be won in the post-conflict reconstruction phase, because unless public support in the country is secured for the reconstruction phase, it cannot succeed. This 'case' applies in, and is relevant to, all phases from prevention through to state-building.

The 'Intervention End State'

A central part of the public 'case' put forward by the international community for its intervention should be a clear definition of what is to be achieved by the action – i.e. the 'intervention end state' which describes the international community's desired final outcome. Each of the three phases – prevention, conflict and stabilisation – should be seen as a single integrated process leading to this declared 'intervention end state' or destination, which is known and understood by all the players. While the utility of the 'intervention end state' depends on it being a public document, there can and sometimes must be elements of it which are kept from publication until the appropriate time – that is until after the post-conflict reconstruction phase has actually begun.

In seeking to modulate both the 'case' and the 'intervention end state' so that they have maximum appeal among ordinary people in the country concerned, it will often be tempting to listen to the voices of exiles. This can be very dangerous. Exiles almost always have an axe to grind, or old scores to settle, having in many cases fled for very personal reasons. More importantly they are often regarded with suspicion, even hostility, by the people who stayed behind. One of Bosnia's most grievous losses during the 1992–5 war was the exodus of its middle class, the majority of whom fled abroad. They were, in many cases, the country's most able and gifted. Bosnia needed them after the war and some returned to help rebuild their homeland – only to find that they were met, not with gratitude, but with hostility, because they had fled when the war came and had not suffered like those who stayed behind. In Iraq, the United States' failures of planning and anticipation were in part the result of listening too much to the voices of the exiles – and the US's attempts to establish early administrations were severely hampered by local hostility to the exiles whom the US put in positions of power.

Deciding on the 'end state' which is the core of the case for intervention, is a vital exercise. In the prevention phase the 'end state' provides a point of leverage and a clear marker which the state concerned has to achieve in order to avoid intervention; in the conflict phase it provides a crucial part of the justification for action; in the stabilisation phase, it provides the purpose of the mission. And in the final state-building phase it provides the exit strategy.

Both the 'case' and the 'intervention end state' can change through the process – the 'end state' required of a recalcitrant nation in order to prevent intervention will be less intrusive and radical than the 'end state' which is the aim of an intervention that follows a conflict. But these should be different iterations of the same general theme; they cannot be contradictory. You cannot argue one case for the prevention phase, a completely different case for the conflict phase and a different case again for the stabilisation phase without losing effect on the ground, international understanding and popular support in the country in which the intervention is taking place.

There is a piece of semantics which is important here. Too frequently interveners speak of 'nation-building' when what they mean is state-building. The difference between the two can be crucial. As Francis Fukuyama puts it: *'Nation building in the sense of the creation of a community bound together by shared history and culture is well beyond the ability of any outside power to achieve . . . only states can be deliberately constructed. If a nation arises from this, it is more a matter of luck than design.'*[17] Interveners may, if they are very lucky, be able to rebuild a state. But very few, if any, can build a nation. Only the people of the country can do that.

To be successful an 'intervention end state' must (a) be achievable, (b) be acceptable to the IC and (c) have broad popular acceptance in the country concerned. Some of the definition of the 'intervention end state' can be framed in general terms – what *kind* of country is envisaged. But an 'intervention end state' ought to be much more than just a wish list made up of motherhood and apple pie. The more specific and detailed it is, the more useful it will be – but only up to a point. It is important to keep ambitions modest and achievable. In far too many cases, foreign interveners have set themselves targets which are unachievable, chiefly by adopting unofficial 'intervention end states' which replicate (or even sometimes exceed) the best standards of their own Western governments.

Within these broad limits, a publicly declared 'intervention end state' can define what *kind* of country the international community, in partnership with the local people, is aiming to reconstruct during the post-conflict phase – for example, one that is sustainable, subject to the rule of law and free from tyranny, whose currency is controlled by a central bank, whose economic system is based on broadly free market principles and which will be capable of joining the relevant regional groupings if there are any, and becoming a member of international organisations such as the World Trade Organisation, the United Nations etc . . . In the case of an ethnically mixed population such as Bosnia, Iraq or Afghanistan the 'intervention end state' might also, for instance, commit the international community to a constitution, founded on checks and balances which do not permit any one ethnic group to dominate.

I have severe doubts about including democracy in this list of 'end state' desirables, as I am not at all sure that it is legitimate to intervene for the purposes of imposing your preferred form of government on someone else. It is up to the people of a country to decide the form of government they want, not the international community. As General John Abizaid, the Commander of US Central Command in Iraq, has frequently said, '*The mission of Coalition forces . . . is to enable the indigenous political process to go forward to establish a state of consent, not to dictate its politics.*'[18]

I heard it said recently that '*democracy is our [the West's] big idea*'. I do not think this is correct – we in the West are not even particularly good at democracy ourselves. Good governance is our big idea; the rule of law is our big idea; a free market-based economy is our big idea. I am very confident that if people have these things they will almost certainly choose democracy as their system of government – because that is the best way to protect these assets. But this is the secondary outcome of the intervention, not its primary purpose.

There has been a tendency recently to use interventions as an excuse to export our ideologies to countries in which they are wholly inappropriate. As we are painfully discovering in Iraq, the ideologies of America's Midwest are not necessarily suited to the culture and traditions of the Middle East. And there are often good reasons for this. For instance, when we seek to bring our democratic structures to an Islamic country, we all too often ignore the democracy which already exists in the Muslim world, either because of ignorance or because it does not conform to our ideas of the importance of secular democracy. Islam is the world's most democratic religion. There is no Pope; no Archbishop of Canterbury. Every Imam is, in theory at least, elected. What this means is that there is a form of religious democracy already in place that will run in parallel with the formal democratic structures of the state, and this has to be taken account of. In Bosnia, if I wanted to get an accurate view of opinion amongst the Muslim majority, it was necessary to listen not only to what was said by their elected representatives in parliament but also to what was said by the Imams at Friday prayers. To get an accurate judgement of what is happening in Iran today it is necessary to listen not just to President Ahemdinijad, but also to the voice of the Mullahs – and they are not always the same. When creating secular democratic structures for an Islamic state, it is foolish simply to import Western models which do not take account of the religious democratic structures alongside which these will have to work.

This habit of the interveners not to take account of local traditions and cultures does not just apply to the Middle East. When I arrived in Bosnia I found a young group of committed, hard working and highly talented international lawyers writing the new criminal codes for the country based on English common law. Their product would have made any Washington or London law school proud. But it had no connection whatsoever with the established traditions of Balkan and ex-Yugoslav law, or with the European legal system into which the country's judicial structures were going to have to fit. It is not the interveners' job to replicate their own countries in faraway places. It is their job to give the people of the country concerned the chance to choose their own ultimate form of government – even if the result is one which makes us feel uncomfortable. For instance, though there is a Western principle that governments and systems of law should be secular, in some Islamic countries theocracies and theocratic laws are the norm. We may not like that – but that is for the people of the state to choose, not us.

There is a very important point here which once again highlights the necessity, in constructing the 'intervention end state', of listening to the genuine voices of the country concerned. Being aware of and sensitive to local traditions and cultures is pivotal to getting public acceptance for the 'intervention end state' and the plan which springs from it. If the interveners are to have any legitimacy and any chance of success they have to be prepared to listen to the voices of those who genuinely represent the opinions of the people and have an influence on them – whether they like them or not. It is possible (though not often wise) to conclude that it is inappropriate to have contact with the elected representatives of a foreign country or entity – as, for instance, many Western countries have decided in the case of Hamas in Palestine. But this is a luxury which, in the main, interveners cannot afford in a country in which they are engaged. When, how and in what form these 'uncomfortable' voices will be brought in will be a matter of judgement which depends on the circumstances, the level of their support, the extent of domestic hostility to their inclusion and their strategic importance. But as Britain discovered with Sinn Fein in Northern Ireland and the Coalition are rediscovering in Iraq, if a group is supported by a substantial swathe of public opinion, particularly if they have been elected, then in the end they must be heard and, if possible, incorporated into the solution, if they are not to become an even more intractable part of the problem.

Interveners will be wise, however, to recognise that, in a post-conflict situation, moderate opinion is likely to be marginalised and they may have to consider how to give expression, or at least extra weight, to these voices. This can lead to one of the most difficult decisions of all for interveners. When do they interfere with freedom of expression? The answer is not often, but not never either.

Freedom of expression, including the freedom to criticise the international community, is a core democratic principle which should be preserved wherever possible, except where this freedom is being abused to promote a return to conflict. In the early days (1997) in Bosnia, the full might of NATO's forces had to be employed to close down the 'Udrigovo towers' transmitter which was putting out a constant stream of ethnic hate and anti-Dayton propaganda. The then High Representative, Carlos Westendorp, understanding the need to get balanced messages across to the population, established a local independent TV station to provide a more balanced view.

In the battle for public opinion it will be very helpful, if possible, to get some form of public endorsement for the agreed-on 'intervention end state' shortly after the post-conflict reconstruction phase has started, for it is at this time that the question of the interveners' legitimacy has to be faced. I shall discuss this and the role of elections in more detail later, but one of the conclusions from peacekeeping operations so far is that elections too early in the process can be a mistake. It may therefore not be possible to obtain public endorsement through a formal plebiscite process. In which case, opinion polling to gauge public reaction to the 'intervention end state' will be useful. We conducted regular opinion polling in Bosnia to keep in close touch with shifts of public opinion and to ensure that what we did had overall public support, especially at the most difficult times. It may also be possible to secure the formal endorsement of the political parties involved. In Bosnia we drew up, with the government, a document called 'Justice and Jobs' at the start of my mandate. This was essentially the declared 'intervention end state' which we undertook to achieve with our domestic partners, before the end of my time. Every political party in the country signed up to this and that gave us both legitimacy and leverage in pursuing the reforms outlined in it. The importance of getting the 'intervention end state' right cannot be over-estimated. For it has five very important functions to play.

Firstly, it is the 'intervention end state' which should frame the UNSC mandate given to the interveners. It is important here that the mandate is as clear, specific and tough as possible, in order to give the interveners the leverage necessary to do their job. Diplomats love ambiguity for it gives them room to manoeuvre. But in this instance ambiguity is fatal; clarity is what is required. Secondly, it is around the 'intervention end state' that the interveners will seek to build public support in the post-conflict reconstruction phase, so creating the common gathering point around which the international community and the constructive forces in the country can assemble, to enable the reconstruction to succeed. Nothing helped me more in Bosnia than the fact that everyone across all political parties and ethnicities agreed the 'intervention end state' – membership of the EU and NATO – and were prepared to make sacrifices to achieve it. A clear, understood and agreed 'intervention end state' was also a key ingredient in the successful interventions in El Salvador, Namibia, East Timor and Eastern Slavonia.

By contrast, nothing has undermined the success of the stabilisation phase in Kosovo more than the fact that no one in the international community was prepared to articulate the 'end state' they sought for the country they were intervening in. Worse, by not even being prepared to say at the end of the war what everyone knew to be the truth, that Kosovo could never again be governed by Belgrade, the international community left a vacuum to be filled, not by the constructive forces in Kosovo, but by the destructive ones. The fact was, and everyone knew it, that the Serbs, by their actions prior to and during the Kosovo war, had forfeited the moral and practical right to govern a province in which they were only, at most, 10 per cent of the population. The international community's failure to say this after the war meant that they could never answer the 'intervention end state' question, which was the only one which every Kosovar was interested in. This had the unsurprising result that the forces of violence in Kosovo sought to fill that vacuum with answers of their own. And so the gathering point around which the constructive forces could have assembled with the international community became, instead, a gathering point for the destructive forces seeking to frustrate the work of the international community. This is not just the wisdom of hindsight. Together with Senator Joe Biden of the US, I wrote a paper which was sent to both our governments just after the Kosovo war ended in June 1999, proposing that the international community should immediately declare that Kosovo could not again be governed by Belgrade. We should then adopt a policy which accepted that Kosovo could make a claim for full statehood, but only when it had fulfilled the attributes of a state – that is, universal human rights within the state, protection of minorities (the Serbs), free and fair elections and good relations with its neighbours. This policy later became known as 'standards before status' and was eventually adopted, but not until April 2002. By then the opportunity had been lost, the golden hour had long passed and the destructive forces in Kosovo already had the upper hand.

The most sophisticated form of 'intervention end state' driven policy is, of course, that pursued by the European Union through its Stabilisation and Association (SAA) process. This defines in minute detail the precise conditions which have to be achieved by would-be member states of the EU before they can join. This policy has been credited with being the driving force behind the transition of nearly all the ex-Communist Eastern European countries to full democracy, market-based economies and membership of the Union, making the EU the world's most successful state-builder, albeit in a context which did not include rebuilding after conflict.

Finding an 'intervention end state' is easier in some cases than others – Iraq and Afghanistan obviously have neither prospect nor probably wish to join the EU and NATO. But even in these cases it is not impossible to do. In January 2006, the United Nations, the international community and the Afghan government drew up the 'Afghanistan Compact', laying out a five-year framework for co-operation between them in order to achieve a specific 'intervention end state'.

Throughout 1989, the year before Iraq invaded Kuwait, James Baker, the US Secretary of State, travelled extensively in the Middle East in an attempt to get Iraq's neighbours to buy in to a plan to resolve the Palestine problem. The five-point 'Baker Plan' of September 1989, while very far from being an 'intervention end state' within the meaning envisaged in this chapter, was nevertheless an attempt to articulate the overall aim of US policy in the Middle East and thus assisted in the creation of a coalition, when the war came, which included local Arab participants.

Which leads to the second invaluable contribution a declared 'intervention end state' can make to successful peacekeeping – a contribution which George Bush senior understood and his son, it appears, does not.

There are not many really golden rules in peacemaking and post-conflict reconstruction. But one is that these operations have a much greater chance of success if the neighbouring countries constructively participate in the process. We began to succeed in Bosnia, only after Zagreb and later Belgrade shifted from wreckers to helpers in the process. The help of the so called 'four friends'* – was crucial to reconstruction in El Salvador, as was the constructive engagement of Japan, China and Australia in Cambodia and the assistance of neighbouring states in Mozambique. The British government, similarly, began to create opportunities for peace in Northern Ireland only when it recognised that Dublin had a legitimate role in the process. The need for buy-in from the neighbours is also the reason why the Baker Plan of 1989 was so important to the first Gulf War – it provided a vision of the future 'intervention end state' for the Middle East to which the neighbours could subscribe. It is also why it is so catastrophic to US ambitions in Iraq that, except for a brief period to make Tony Blair feel better, there was no US understanding that a sustained attempt to solve the Palestine problem was a crucial step towards solving the Iraq one. In Iraq we seem, by contrast, to have gone out of our way to make enemies of the neighbours. Even the rhetoric we have used seems designed to make this worse. One of the US's stated aims in the Iraq invasion was to bring democracy to the region. I happen to agree with that and continue to hope for it. But Iraq's neighbours – from Saudi Arabia in the south through to Syria in the north and Iran to the east – do not. Whether we like it or not, with the exception of democratic Turkey to the north, Iraq is surrounded by regimes for which democracy, in the way Washington means it, is something for which they have, at the very least, an extreme lack of enthusiasm. Of course we in the West would like to see democracies in this area, but I am not at all sure it was wise in the context of Iraq to elevate this into one of the primary purposes of the war. I do not think that the problem of Iraq can be now solved purely within Iraq. In the end there will have to be a regional solution, which the neighbours can buy into. That means bringing the neighbours in, not shutting them out. It will also mean doing business with some pretty unsavoury players – but no more unsavoury than Milošević and Tudjman, and we had to deal with them.

As it happens there has existed for some time a ready-made grouping which could be used to get Iraq's neighbours to buy into the process of creating stability in the country. In January 2003 Turkey launched

---

* Spain, Colombia, Mexico and Venezuela.

the Neighbours' Forum, made up of the foreign ministers of countries that have borders with Iraq, plus Egypt.[19] This grouping was originally envisaged as a coalition whose aim was to prevent the war in Iraq. But, largely due to the fact that a number of its members did not want to be seen to be openly opposed to the United States, it has become instead a forum for discussion of issues such as border security and terrorism (for which purpose the group also now meets at interior minister level). At the time of writing, the Forum has held some nine formal and two informal meetings, which are also attended by an observer from the UN. The Iraqi foreign minister joined the Forum at its meeting in Kuwait in February 2004, and at a later meeting in Istanbul in April 2005 the EU was invited to join as was the Organisation of the Islamic Conference.[20] The Neighbours' Forum thus offers a ready-made framework through which the positive engagement of Iraq's neighbours might, with the assistance of the UN and EU, be brought into play to help stabilise Iraq.

The third function of the 'intervention end state' lies in providing a mechanism to hold the international interveners to account for what they do. The 'intervention end state' becomes, in effect, the publicly avowed aim of the post-conflict reconstruction phase – and thus the heart of a Mission Implementation Plan for the interveners, which serves to prevent mission creep and provide a means of accountability for the work of the mission, both to the international community and to the people of the country concerned. This, preferably endorsed by the international community at UN Security Council level, then becomes, in effect, the work programme for the international community as a whole and provides the international mission leader with the authority to co-ordinate the various international and non-governmental players to ensure they are working to the same plan and speaking with the same voice. And finally, the 'intervention end state' provides the last way marker which defines the moment when the mission is over and the international community should go home.

It is the 'case' and the 'intervention end state' which constitute the framework around which the seamless garment of the three phases of prevention, war-fighting and post-conflict reconstruction should be woven. This is what gives coherence of action between the phases, each flowing naturally into the other. The use of force should be seen as part of and subservient to this process and not separated from it. This is especially true for the prevention phase where the credible threat of the use of force will, in many cases, be the sanction at the end of the diplomatic effort if that effort fails. The threat of the use of force becomes itself, therefore, part of the diplomatic effort, not separated from it. It was our failure to understand the importance of this synergy which fatally hobbled David Owen and Cy Vance's attempts to find a diplomatic solution to the Bosnia war in the mid 1990s. There was a total disconnect between what the two negotiators were trying to do in Geneva and what our forces were doing on the ground (observing conflict, not stopping it), and this was exacerbated by the acknowledged unwillingness of the international community to have them do anything else. Crucially, the United States, which many believed actively undermined European diplomacy in ex-Yugoslavia prior to 1995, declined to back the Vance/Owen Plan. Because of this, the Bosnian participants at Geneva (especially the Serbs) knew that there was no cost to them of filibustering at the negotiating table, while their armies continued to gain on the battlefield.

We are facing the same issues currently when it comes to the cases of Iran and North Korea. We will stand a better chance of succeeding in persuading these two countries not to continue with the development of their nuclear programmes if there is a credible and understood sanction in place at the end of the diplomatic phase, if that should fail. If no such sanction is possible (i.e. the sanction of force is not available and economic sanctions are either impractical or ineffective) then this must temper the actions we can take in the prevention phase – such as doing whatever is necessary to get Russia and China on board for the diplomatic effort (which raises the effect of the sanction of isolation, if they do not acquiesce).

The Plan

It follows that it is the 'case', and especially the declared 'intervention end state' that is central to it, which should drive the formulation of the plan in each of the phases. The plan, including in the war phase, serves the 'intervention end state' not the other way round. The military may be the best planners, but they are the worst people to lead this planning process. For this is essentially a political process, not a military one. Clemenceau once famously said that war was too important to be left to the generals – and the same is true of intervention. To make a good plan, it is first necessary to make some accurate judgements about the nature of the country you are intervening in and correct assumptions about the situation you are going to find when you get there. This requires an ability to think *beyond* the end of the conflict phase and accurately assess what will happen afterwards. In general, ministries of foreign affairs (MFAs) or ministries of development are better equipped to make these judgements than ministries of defence. But, since the essence of successful implementation (which I shall expand on in a later chapter) is a cross-disciplinary approach, the essence of a good planning team is to be cross-disciplinary in nature. So ideally a planning team should be foreign affairs or development-led, but contain experts, including, crucially, military experts, from all the fields required.

It is not my purpose here to go into the details of a good plan – largely because these will differ widely according to the specific nature of the country concerned and the situation after the conflict is over. But some general points are worth emphasising. Firstly, the plan for post-conflict reconstruction should start from the very moment after the midnight hour when the war ends. This is the 'golden hour' and what is done at this time will have real and long lasting effect well into the reconstruction phase. Most essential of all is the immediate establishment of the rule of law. It will also be necessary to set up the civil administration with immediate effect. What this means is that the civilian administration teams should go in, as they did in Germany after the Second World War, immediately behind the frontline troops and take over as the leaders of the operation as soon as the fighting is over. Generals have to realise that, although they are in charge in the fighting phase, as soon as the fighting is over, they are acting, as we used to put it in Britain's post-colonial internal security operations, 'in aid of the civil power' and that means in support of the civilian administrators, not in charge of them. This obviously becomes more difficult if, as in the case of Iraq, the intervention is dealing not with post-conflict reconstruction, but with in-conflict reconstruction. But the principle has to remain the same – after you have taken over the country, the prime drivers must be political, not military.

Secondly, a good plan should be based on the worst case scenarios, not the best case. Here the US and the UN seem to have reversed roles. In most of its interventions the UN has underestimated the difficulties it will face on the ground and the amount of resources, especially troops, it will require; while US-led interventions, typified by the Powell doctrine of overwhelming force, always planned to the worst case and deployed maximum resources and especially troops in the early stages. But in Iraq, the US plans seem to have been based not on reality, but on little more than hope, with consequences outlined at the beginning of this chapter. The hard truth is that more troops may be needed to secure the peace in the early days than were needed to win the war which preceded it.

The military have a saying; *the first casualty of war is the plan.* The same is true for post-conflict reconstruction. For here the law of unintended consequences reigns supreme. However good the appreciation and however solid the assumptions, Murphy's Law always applies: things never turn out quite as they were expected to – and sometimes they turn out precisely the opposite of what was expected. Having fought a war in Kosovo to get the Albanian Kosovars home, no one imagined that the most difficult problem they would have to deal with, once they succeeded, was to protect the Serbs in their homes (though to be fair, this should have been fairly easy to predict). No one ever thought that the Bosnian Serbs, who started off hating Dayton, would end up hanging on to it like grim death – or that the Bosniak Muslims would start seeing Dayton as their saviour, and end up seeing it as their enemy. No one predicted that, while General Mohamed Aideed and the warlords remained in charge in Somalia, they would take most of the international aid pouring into the country and distribute it first to their own supporters, so further strengthening their position in the country at the international community's expense.* As Donald Rumsfeld famously said, 'stuff happens', and although the stuff he

---

* In the Scottish distilling industry, the whisky which is lost through evaporation during the maturing period in barrels is known as 'the angel's share'. Aid which passes through or near military forces during or shortly after conflict, is also subject to loss, sometimes referred to as 'taking the soldier's share'. I remember complaining bitterly to the UNHCR's Larry Hollingworth, who was in charge of feeding the city of Sarajevo during the siege, that the opposing armies were getting more of the aid than the civilians it was intended for. He shrugged his shoulders and explained it was always like this. The army was the dominant power and they would take their share first – only after they had been satisfied would the aid get through to the people – that was what happened in a war zone and aid agencies had to plan for it.

was referring to should have been perfectly predictable, much that occurs after the war is over is not. So plans should allow a lot of latitude for local decision-making on the ground, should be 'living strategies' capable of iteration quickly and should be subject to regular audits and, especially, reality checks from those at the front end. In Iraq and in Afghanistan there was plenty of early evidence from those at the sharp end that the plans were not working – but this information was largely ignored as inconvenient by those setting the policy at the centre.

Next it is important that everyone realises that planning is for the long term, not the short. It may be possible to win our sharp little modern digital wars in a few days or weeks. But building the peace which follows is measured in decades. The average counter-insurgency in the twentieth century has lasted nine years. We British have been trying to bring peace to Northern Ireland for thirty-five years, and we are still not there yet. The international community has been peacemaking for more than thirty years in Cyprus, but it is still a divided island. So it is not helpful to say, as we did initially in Bosnia, that the troops would be out in a year. Indeed it is unhelpful ever to give timelines for withdrawal – all that happens is that those who would wish to wreck the rebuilding will sit you out. Exit dates should be driven by milestones of achievement, not arbitrary dates picked off a calendar. And even these can be dangerous at times. It is relatively easy – and relatively quick – to create the hardware of a state, its governmental, judicial and economic institutions. But it is much more difficult to change the software of a state – what is in people's minds; that is, the extent to which they still feel enmity for their neighbours; their feelings of insecurity; their sense (or lack of it) of identification and loyalty to a state. With luck and good judgement, building a state's institutions can be done in perhaps ten years – but building a sense of statehood in people's minds takes much, much longer and usually is not finally achieved until the wartime generation have died, or at least are no longer in power. It is important to realise that state-building is a process, not an event – so the plan has to be a long-term one which gives sufficient time for the processes to play out to a successful conclusion.

As we discovered in Chapter 4, plans also have to be multi-disciplinary and holistic. They have to cover the whole range of peacebuilding and not just a few sectors. Having a plan for the army is fine. But one is also needed for reconnecting the water supplies, rebuilding the civil service, re-creating a judicial system, reconstructing the prisons and creating an efficient modern market-based economic system – along with much else.

Next, a plan is useless without the resources to implement it and the key resource is money. The planning and the estimation of the resources to enable it must go hand in hand. Indeed there is even a case for assessing the resources likely to be available before beginning to draw up a plan. There is no point in producing the ideal plan and then finding there is insufficient money available to make it a reality. When resources fall short, begging for more to achieve ambitious objectives will often prove less practical than scaling back objectives to meet available resources.

The international community has in the past been expert at adopting grandiose ambitions for its missions and then refusing to provide the funds to make these a reality. Peacemaking – and especially post-conflict reconstruction – is very expensive. It has been calculated by the World Bank that, whereas the maximum a 'normal' developing country can usefully absorb in aid is around 20 per cent of its GDP, for countries emerging from conflict this limit doubles and can even reach as much as 70 per cent in the first year after the conflict ends. Zalmay Khalilzad, former US ambassador to Afghanistan and now in Iraq, estimates that in the case of Afghanistan, *'It will take annual assistance of more than $4.5 billion or higher for five to seven years to achieve our goals.'*[21] Meanwhile the operation in Haiti is said to have cost more than $2 billion, while those in Somalia and Bosnia have so far cost $2.2 billion and $23 billion respectively.[22]

Typically funding for a mission is easy in the early days when the crisis is on the front pages of the world's newspapers. But donors soon lose interest. It is important, if possible, to plan funding on a 'through life' basis, so that there are adequate funds available for the mid and end terms of the reconstruction phase. But this can prove very difficult to do with national exchequers budgeting on annual cycles and politicians who think in electoral ones. Recently the international community has taken to setting up trust funds for each intervention, usually administered by the World Bank or the United Nations Development Programme (UNDP). This approach facilitates borrowing against future donations, so helping with 'through life' funding, while making it easier to audit donations, reassure donors about their proper use and provide for greater transparency.

Having assembled a plan for the post-conflict reconstruction phase it is important, if possible, to test it before initiating it on the ground. The military use a technique which they call 'sand table modelling' their plans, to ensure that they work. This consists of working through their plans in sequential order and testing them against various scenarios. Following the 'seamless garment' approach, it goes without saying that the civilian administrators who will follow the military should be part of this 'sand table' process and have a say in the way the war is fought, because they are going to have to deal with its aftermath. But there is also a case, if time and circumstances permit, to sand table model at least the first phase of the post-conflict reconstruction plan too, bringing in all the stakeholders involved.

The Press Operation

Finally, since the crucial battleground is the battleground of public opinion, a special place should be reserved in the plan for media and public information campaigns. For these are just as important in successful interventions as are armies and civil administrators. The US effort in Iraq was severely hampered by the fact that the Coalition Provisional Authority (CPA) press operation was isolated, inadequate and incompetent.[23] What is important here, however, is not just the resources dedicated to press matters and the competence of the people doing the job. The press operation personnel cannot fulfil their full purpose if they are treated simply as 'add-ons' who are brought in and told the message once it has been arrived at – to do their job properly, they need to be embedded, right at the start and at the highest level, in the decision-making process.

The interveners' press and public information operations need to be structured to enable four functions. The first is the 'offensive' operation of selling the interveners' core messages to the media. The second is 'defensive' press operations, aimed at countering as quickly as possible inaccurate information that is damaging to the interveners' cause, both in the international and the domestic arena.

Mark Twain is supposed to have said that the lie 'is a swift little thing. It is half way round the world before the truth has got its boots on.' This is especially true in post-conflict situations, where lies are very easy to spread among populations still traumatised by war and correcting inaccurate stories quickly can be crucial to winning the battle for public opinion. The third task of the press and public information operation is to run public information campaigns on key messages through posters and the media. And the fourth is to oversee a regular process of measuring public sentiment through opinion polls so that the interveners are kept constantly in touch with the state of public opinion.

Summary

The crucial mistake made and remade in interventions has been the failure to 'think through' the conflict phase and plan for the post-conflict phase which follows. Here the key battle which must be won is the battle for public opinion – especially in the country where the intervention is taking place. To win this, the international community needs to be clear about its reasons for acting – this is the public 'case' – and what it wants to achieve – the 'intervention end state'. Both must be constructed with a view to winning the battle for public opinion. The 'intervention end state' also provides the publicly stated tasks for the intervention mission and therefore forms the core of the mission implementation plan which governs and directs the actions of the interveners. To maximise the chances for success it is necessary to view all three phases – prevention, conflict and post-conflict reconstruction – as a single 'seamless garment' with each phase interlocking with the next. The plan for the intervention can then be constructed. It should be properly funded, based on the worst case, not the best, founded on an accurate assessment of the conditions in the country concerned, sensitive to changes on the ground, capable of iteration, leave maximum room for local decision-making, have an important place for press and public information and, if possible, be 'sand table' tested before the operation begins.

8

Who's in charge?

I don't care who's in charge, Sir. Just so long as somebody is.
THE ROYAL MARINES SERGEANT WHO TRAINED ME

In August 1995, following the massacre at Srebrenica and the mortaring of a Sarajevo market place killing sixty-eight, the international community, in the shape of NATO, finally decided it had to intervene in Bosnia. The white-painted vehicles of the UN Protection Force (UNPROFOR) were repainted military khaki. UNPROFOR's soldiers from NATO member countries exchanged their UN blue berets for regimental ones and, in co-ordination with NATO air strikes and sweeping advances by the Croatian and Bosnian Muslim forces, marched into Bosnia to end the humiliation of UNPROFOR and stop the war.[1] What is notable here is that the troops did not change and the flag under which they operated remained that of the UN. But now, for the first time, the UN in Bosnia was backed by a robust mandate, the political will to enforce it and the overwhelming power of NATO just over the horizon. A few weeks later, the three-and-a-half-year blood letting was over and in December the US contingent of NATO's 60,000 occupying force crossed the Sava river in the snow to take up their duties in the international community's peace implementation force in Bosnia and Herzegovina. In the ten years since, not a single one of those soldiers nor any one of the civilian peacemakers who followed them has been killed by hostile action in Bosnia.

In East Timor, in February 2000, the initial fighting force of troops led by Australia, having taken only a little over four months to establish a secure peace and effective order in the country by force of arms, handed over the task of maintaining that peace to the

United Nations Mission in East Timor (UNTAET), of which they
then became a part.

In these two stories lies all you need to know about both the
utility and deficiencies of the UN as a leader of international interventions in non-permissive environments. The UN is necessary as a
prime mover in performing many tasks in our increasingly interdependent world. But it is not good at managing conflict in difficult
circumstances.

*   *   *

For the purposes of this book I have divided the process of
peacemaking and reconstruction into three basic phases: the prevention phase, the war-fighting phase and the post-conflict reconstruction phase (sometimes referred to in US circles as 'Phase IV')
operations, which, in Chapters 4 and 5 has been further subdivided
into stabilisation and state-building.

The Prevention Phase

The prevention phase could be defined as the period in which a
nation or nations, acting alone or in concert, uses non-military
means, either to intervene to prevent a state from failing (usually
through the outbreak of civil war), or to persuade a rogue state to
change its ways, which are judged to threaten the wider peace.
Given that the chief instrument here is persuasion, backed either by
sanction or by reward, the UN usually has a large role to play in this
phase. It is through the UN's organs, most notably the Security
Council, that world opinion can be expressed and actions (such as
sanctions) can be legitimised. There is also a rule of thumb about
international actions which confers a special utility on the UN in
this phase. That is that the broader the multilateral coalition, the
greater the chance of success. This is not a perfect equation. It is
nearly always the case that it is easiest to build the widest coalition
around the weakest action. So there is a trade-off to be made
between a broad coalition on the one hand and sufficiently strong
and cohesive action to cope with the problem on the other. It will
most often be in and through the UN that that this trade-off takes
place.

But in the end successful prevention, especially in the harder cases, is likely to depend on more than persuasion, whether gentle or otherwise. Diplomacy succeeds better – and indeed in some cases, such as that of Milošević and arguably Iran today – can only succeed at all if there is a credible sanction at the end if it fails. And here the UN has far less leverage than many states, especially the most powerful ones.

Sanctions are the only real UN sanction – and there are always doubts about their utility. That is not to say that there is no role for sanctions – just that we should not overstate their effect. Sanctions can be a powerful way of expressing the world's opprobrium and for that reason alone they can be useful. But I can think of only very few cases where the effects of economic sanctions by themselves have caused a state to alter its actions in the way that was hoped for when they were applied[2] – and many cases, as in Milošević's Serbia and probably in Saddam Hussein's Iraq, where they actually strengthened the regime internally, and weakened the moral case of the international community amongst the population of the state concerned.

There is a way, however, to improve the effect of sanctions by targeting them more precisely. Almost all authoritarian regimes depend for their existence not on the support of their people but on that of a relatively small number of what the Communists used to call the 'nomenklatura'. These include the generals and the intelligence chiefs and the political hierarchy and, crucially, the corrupt businessmen who benefit from the regime. They also include their families. Targeted sanctions, hitting at these people and their dependants by instituting visa bans and freezing foreign bank accounts usually require more technical work and detailed political application. But they can often have much more effect than blanket sanctions, whose effects too often make the already difficult lives of ordinary people more difficult and can strengthen the control of the regime against whom they are intended.

Balkan watchers have been fascinated by the reasons behind Milošević's sudden and largely unexplained capitulation at the end of the Kosovo war, just when, by common estimate, he was winning. He had, after all, resisted UN sanctions and NATO's bombing had only strengthened his grip on Serbia. Meanwhile, his forces were practically untouched and well-prepared for NATO's impending attack on Kosovo. NATO, on the other hand, was facing horrendous choices as to how to attack. The main crossing from Kumanovo into Kosovo was a nightmare of easily defendable high ridges, easily demolished road tunnels and very difficult logistics. There was another way through the Preševo valley to the east – but this was much longer, still difficult enough and would have meant invading Serbia proper. There was a third crossing through the high mountain passes of Albania, but it would have been excruciatingly difficult to provide logistic support for this route. Meanwhile, NATO's internal cohesion was weakening by the day. Many predicted that NATO could not hold together for more than a few weeks.

And then – suddenly – on 13 June 1999, Milošević threw in the towel. There are, of course, well-known reasons which account in part for why Milošević did so. He was finally convinced that, despite many unwise statements to the contrary from Western politicians at the start of the war, NATO and especially the US had now taken the decision in principle to invade Kosovo with ground forces in overwhelming numbers, if necessary. The Russians had also told him that, in these circumstances, he was on his own and should expect no help from them. There were even rumours of a mild heart attack. But none of these seemed to provide a sufficient reason for this extraordinary example of snatching defeat from the jaws of victory.

It has more recently come to light, however, that there was one final act of pressure which we did not know about at the time. Among his chief business supporters was the head of the Serbian Post and Telecommunications (PTT) monopoly, Milorad Jakšic. In the few days prior to Milošević's sudden capitulation, Jakšic had gone on a business trip and had been refused entry into Cyprus, a favourite haunt for corrupt Serb businessmen. He had flown on to London and was shocked to be refused entry there, too. It is said that he returned to Belgrade, demanded an immediate interview with Milošević and told him that a war which affected young men's lives was one thing, but one which affected business was something entirely different. It should stop immediately.

In Bosnia we used personally targeted sanctions extensively against those who assisted the network protecting Karadžić, Mladić and the other war criminals – freezing bank accounts and placing individuals on the US and EU visa ban list. This was one of the key factors in finally breaking the nine-year dam of Serb obstructionism in capturing war criminals, as a result of which eleven of the fifteen major International Criminal Tribunal for the former Yugoslavia (ICTY) indictees were transferred to the Hague by the Serb authorities within a year or so.

Though broader economic sanctions may be a useful way to show international disapproval of a state, more extensive and imaginative use of 'smart' sanctions targeted at the individuals of a regime and its supporters may be a better way of changing minds – especially if applied early enough.[*]

There are places where the UN can play a marked role in preventing conflict, as the successful UN prevention exercises in Haiti, the Congo in 2005 and the Bakasi peninsula show. In many areas, however, beyond sanctions and international condemnation the UN has less real leverage on the actions of rogue states or on the internal forces which threaten their failure than many of its individual member states. While there are UN Security Council resolutions aplenty on Israel, the influence which acts as the most powerful restraint on the Israelis does not lie in the UN building New York; it lies in the White House in Washington. In seeking to restrain Iran from further development of its nuclear technology, the most powerful force is not the UN, but that of the nations of the G8 (especially Russia) and China.

In a recent case, the British ambassador to a central American state in which Britain has considerable influence identified that the state's institutions were at threat from capture by organised crime structures related to the drug trade. At the invitation of the state concerned, Britain took a series of actions ranging from strengthening the domestic rule of law institutions, to the use of UK special forces in order to overcome the threat and prevent the imminent failure of the institutions of the state. These are all examples where individual relations between states can often prove more effective *in* the prevention phase than action by the UN. As a general rule, in

---

[*] The UN Convention on Corruption, which came into effect on 14 December 2005, has a whole chapter devoted to preventive measures, which focuses on both public and private sector measures and targeted sanctions as well as asset seizure etc. Recent UN-imposed sanctions on North Korea have specifically targeted luxury goods as a means of putting pressure on the country's elites without making the very difficult lives of ordinary North Koreans even more difficult.

order to have influence on a nation, you have to have influence *in* a nation – and only other nations have that. Before the Iraq war, the UK Foreign Office (FCO) looked in detail at what actually sustained the regime of Saddam Hussein and concluded that the key to his survival was the illegal sale of oil to Jordan and Syria, which Saddam relied on to pay his army and security services. The FCO spent a good deal of time devising ways to tackle this complex problem and came up with proposals to engage Iraq's neighbours in an anti smuggling programme, with appropriate financial and other inducements attached. However these measures were either ignored or overridden or lost in the headlong rush to war.[3]

Macedonia

The best example of a successful prevention is that of Macedonia – and here it was the EU, assisted by NATO and the US, which played the key role, with the UN retrospectively legitimising the outcome in a UN Security Council presidential statement.

To be honest, I didn't think it could be done. In March 2001 I happened to be visiting Kosovo when the flag of rebellion was raised by the country's Macedonian Albanian minority in the hills above the cities of Tetovo and Gostivar, adjacent to both the Albanian and Kosovo borders. This had always been a hotspot for trouble. The Kosovo Liberation Army (KLA) had been launched in these cities. In the third week of March, shots were fired, people were killed on both sides and tensions heightened towards what most people believed was an inevitable civil war and the fifth act of the Balkan tragedy which followed the death of Yugoslavia.[*] The danger of Macedonia lay in the fact that, whereas the previous Balkan wars had been confined within the borders of ex-Yugoslavia, a civil war in Macedonia would be likely to spread beyond them, potentially drawing in Albania, the Macedonians' Slav brothers from Bulgaria and possibly even, pessimists said, NATO members Greece and Turkey on opposing sides. Macedonia was the bomb in the Balkans, experts believed, and all the other Balkan wars merely the fuses leading to it. The stakes were very high.

[*] After the wars in Croatia, Bosnia and Kosovo.

The Macedonian president, Boris Trajkovski, had been asked to meet European leaders gathered for a summit in Stockholm on 23–24 March. While he was there, a nervous ceasefire was called resulting in a stand-off between the Macedonian army and the Albanian rebels, led by Ali Ahmeti in the hills above Tetovo. On 21 March, at Downing Street's request, I was asked to visit the rebels and to try to calm Macedonian nerves in the hope of preventing an assault by the Macedonian army on the rebels' positions, believed to be planned for dawn the following morning. My first stop that day was with the Macedonian foreign minister. My diary records the day as follows:

21 MARCH 2001

Off with the British Ambassador to see the Macedonian Foreign Minister, Srjan Kerim. I found him urbane, intelligent and very moderate. I urged him not to unleash the Macedonian army until we saw what the rebels' demands were in detail. We might be able to pull back from the brink, but it would require only a single provocation from the rebels, or one stupid act on behalf of the Macedonian army and all would be lost. He agreed but indicated that he thought it would probably be difficult to persuade the hot heads in the Government to turn round now, since they have really got the bit between their teeth and the Macedonian army was determined to unleash a military offensive.

I checked with London (John Sawers in Blair's office) that they were intending to use tonight's meeting in Stockholm to put pressure on Trajkovski to be restrained.

Then into the car and down to Tetovo. We went in to see Menduh Thaqi and Arben Xhaferi. We sat talking for an hour in their smoke-filled office. Contrary to what the SIS had said to me in Skopje, Xhaferi, it turns out, is prepared to negotiate on behalf of Ahmeti and the rebels if the negotiations are serious. As we talked I could hear sporadic shooting up in the hills and around the town, but concluded this was just the Albanians letting off their guns to cheer themselves up, as usual.*

I dashed back to Skopje leaving behind a deserted and frightened Tetovo and passing Macedonian army units on the move in the

---

* The political leaders of the Macedonian Albanians.

opposite direction on the road. On arrival, I contacted Sawers, who was now in Stockholm with Blair. I related what Xhaferi had said and went through the rebels' demands, all of which, it seemed to me, were easy for the Macedonian Government to accept – indeed many of them had already been carried out by the Macedonian Government. This should not be difficult to sort out if only we can get people starting to talk. But time was precious. The Macedonian army were already positioning themselves for an all-out but almost certainly doomed assault which would plunge us back into war.

I then spoke to Rupert Smith* and asked him whether or not he could use all his influence on the Macedonian army for moderation. He told me there was a British army training team actually in Macedonia at the moment. They might be able to do it. But when I contacted their Brigadier,† it became apparent that, following the appointment of a new hardline head of the Macedonian army, all contact between the British military team and the Macedonians had been broken off. I advised the Brigadier to ring Rupert to get him to ring the Prime Minister's office (Sawers again) and get Blair to lean on Trajkovski when he sees him tomorrow to reopen communication with the British army . . .

The next task was to get confirmation that Ahmeti had accepted that Xhaferi should negotiate for him. I contacted Andrew Lloyd, the head of the British team in Kosovo who had told me earlier that he had contact with Ahmeti in the hills. He promised to do what he could to find out from our sources amongst the rebels whether they would accept Xhaferi as their negotiator. He also said that the Troika‡ had been in Kosovo that day and had extracted from one of the Kosovo Albanian leaders§ a very tough statement calling the Albanians in the Macedonian hills 'extremists' and calling for restraint. I asked Lloyd to fax this through so that I could show it to the Macedonians – it might just do the trick. When I received it I faxed it through to Kerim, the foreign minister, who immediately contacted me on the phone and agreed that this could change things.

---

* General Sir Rupert Smith, who was at the time the Deputy Supreme Allied Commander Europe at Mons in Belgium.
† Brigadier James Short.
‡ A European high level group consisting of Javier Solana and Chris Patten, accompanied by the then EU Presidency foreign minister, the late Anna Lindh and the next Presidency foreign minister, Louis Michel.
§ Ramush Haridanaj.

He would now try to persuade the Government that they should hold back so as to give time for the Albanians to react, provided I would myself go down to the Government buildings to try to persuade the hardliners who were driving the case for immediate military action, especially the Speaker, Stojan Andov. I had known Andov as one of the Macedonian 'liberals' who I had helped at the time that Macedonia was breaking away from Yugoslavia. So, accompanied by the British Ambassador[*] we paid a late night visit to Andov. The meeting lasted beyond midnight and much was drunk. But Andov was immovable. The only time he seemed at all unnerved was when, in a fit of passionate pleading, the British Ambassador, a very decent man who loved Macedonia, burst into tears! Threats he had seen before, but this was something he had not experienced and it made him stop. But only for a moment. He insisted that the Macedonian people wanted rid of this Albanian scum and that military force was the only answer. The opposition was already calling them cowards etc. I said that it was important to do the right thing, even if it was not necessarily the popular thing. If he wanted to kill his people in tens of thousands then more war was the best way to do it. The assault could not succeed now; it was bound to fail. Of course they had a right to control their borders but they ought to use the time to prepare a proper military action and in the meantime see if they could test whether the Albanians are serious.

We might have done it, but I doubt it.

The Macedonian army did indeed launch a dawn assault the following morning and it was, as predicted, a military failure. They couldn't dislodge the rebels. Indeed, in a sense, we were saved by the Macedonian army's incompetence as a further stalemate soon ensued and Solana was able to return and broker a deal. He was greatly assisted in this by his EU colleague, Commissioner Chris Patten, who was able to offer powerful inducements in the form of European Commission money for infrastructural projects, the US, who used their muscle to help broker the final Ohrid peace settlement, and by Lord George Robertson, NATO's secretary general, who threw the Atlantic Alliance's weight behind the process,

[*] Mark Dickinson.

offering to take on the security aspects of the deal, such as overseeing the ceasefire and disarming the Ahmeti rebels. Indeed, George
Robertson's personal engagement became known as the 'Bowmore
process', after the seventeen-year-old Scottish single malt Islay
whisky which lubricated negotiations far into the night over five
weeks of intensive talks. Finally, on 13 August the Ohrid Agreement
was signed. It included a plan to develop decentralised government,
new laws and principles on non-discrimination, equitable representation for the Albanians and the appointment of an EU special
representative, François Leotard, reporting directly to Solana, with
responsibility to oversee the deal. What started as a peace which
many believed was too fragile to last, has, over time, become a
secure and relatively stable process that is leading Macedonia on
the path to Europe.

This successful act of prevention probably saved tens of thousands of lives and avoided a war of incalculable consequences.
Although there had been a preventative UN mission in Macedonia
for some time before the crisis broke, only the European Union had
the leverage that mattered at the crucial moment when war seemed
inevitable in Macedonia.

One aspect which is especially prone to being overlooked in this
prevention phase is the part that can be played by the provision of
development aid. There is a very close correlation between state
failure and poverty and inequality[4] which is far too little understood
by intervening states. It frequently costs far less to inject substantial
sums of development aid into a country in order to avoid a war,
than to pay for its military occupation afterwards. And yet we spend
far more on our ability to fight wars than we do on development
assistance to avoid the conflict in the first place or on rebuilding
after the fighting is over. The cost of keeping a single US Division
in the field in Iraq is $1.25 billion per month, which is about the
same as the entire annual budget for the American government
development agency, USAID, in the country ($1.3 billion).

The Chinese have a saying that it is better to sweat over the peace
than to bleed in the war. We all too frequently put less emphasis on the
prevention phase than we should, given the dividends that are attached
to success. A war prevented is not just tens of thousands of lives saved,
it also means that the whole panoply of heavyweight intervention and
the extremely costly and usually very long term accompaniment of

post-conflict reconstruction, can be avoided. Failing and rogue states are not difficult to spot ahead of time. I shall discuss in later chapters how we could approach the task of prevention in a more structured and efficient way. For the moment, however, it is sufficient to note that, in this crucial phase, there is a distinct, if often limited, role for the UN. But the best chance of success is likely to come from those nations who have the greatest influence in the state or states concerned, working in combination with multilateral organisations, including especially the UN, where appropriate.

The Conflict Phase

In the war-fighting phase the position is much clearer. Wars are best fought by organisations designed to fight wars – and the UN isn't one of them. Bosnia and East Timor proved that.

This is not the UN's fault. Originally the UN's role in peacemaking was conceived as one which included a war-fighting capacity and it was equipped with the means to do this in its first intervention in the Congo. But since then, the UN members, and especially the Permanent Five, have declined to give New York the things a war-fighting organisation needs. The UN has no fixed military command structure: no standing general staff, no standing army, no intelligence, no logistics, no battlefield communications, quite often no soldiers of the right quality and almost always no clear-cut rules of engagement that make sense on the battlefield – in short nothing that is required to successfully prosecute a military action in which live bullets are likely to be used and young men and women run the risk of being killed. To reinforce the point, since the Congo, the UN's member states have never so far allowed the UN to carry out a Chapter VII (humanitarian) intervention (which tend to be opposed) and only ever allowed them to carry out Chapter VI (peacekeeping) tasks, which tend to be 'permissive'.*

---

* There have been instances where UN forces, operating under a Chapter VI mandate, have started off with fairly strict and 'traditional' peacekeeping mandates and then, through subsequent UNSCR resolutions, have gained in muscularity because the situation has demanded it (e.g. UNPROFOR in Bosnia). The UN resolutions for the recently deployed UNIFIL force in the Lebanon seem to have taken a further step in this direction with an initial mandate which goes more towards a Chapter VII mandate than previous UN missions. For this reason UNIFIL's mandate has been referred to as a 'Chapter VI.5' mandate.

The UN's incapacities as a war-fighting organisation were cruelly illuminated in Bosnia, where soldiers were put in the position of impotently watching slaughter, but being unable to intervene, and its darkest hour, Srebrenica, was a product. But the horror stories which can arise when the UN tries to run a war are by no means confined to Bosnia. In the early days in Sierra Leone, fatal confusion over the rules of engagement set by the UN Security Council, and misunderstandings between the UN Secretariat and the troop-contributing nations, were among the major reasons why the operation so nearly failed and the rebels so nearly won, before the British forces arrived and took over. When it comes to a non-permissive environment where kinetic (military) force may be required, it is better to place leadership of the war phase in the hands of a military alliance, such as NATO, or of a coalition of the willing, under the professional leadership of a single nation's armed forces, such as the Australians in East Timor.

On the other hand, in more permissive circumstances, the UN can bring real advantages to the table. For a start, its troops, most of which come from developing countries, are cheaper – much cheaper. The cost of putting a single US or NATO soldier on the ground is estimated at $200,000 per year. The equivalent cost for a UN soldier is around $45,000.[5] This cost is multiplied by the fact that, in non-permissive environments (which NATO would be more likely to take on), some five to ten times more soldiers may be required than in permissive environments, making US or NATO interventions as much as twenty to forty times more expensive than the equivalent UN peace mission in a similar size of country. The United States currently spends about $4.5 billion per month to support its military operations in Iraq, which is more than the UN will spend to run all seventeen of its current peacekeeping missions in a year. Put another way, the cost of one year of US peacekeeping in Iraq is approximately the same as that for all UN peacekeeping operations from 1945 to the present day.

Secondly, the UN can mobilise a wider coalition of support than a regional alliance or coalition for the willing – and this can be important when it comes to winning the battle for public support, both international and domestic. Next, the UN provides the most effective structure for burden sharing. The US and EU pay 50 per cent of all UN operational costs. But they pay 100 per cent of NATO's much more expensive operations, and, by agreement, nearly 100 per cent of the cost of recent African Union operations. And lastly the UN can reach parts of the world which no one else can reach – that is, parts of the world (such as Africa) where no strong, professional regional military alliance exists which can do better. Or places where individual nations are reluctant to get involved nationally and an intervention under UN cover is the only acceptable context for action. In fact the UN currently has some 90,000 soldiers and police[*] deployed worldwide, making it the second largest expeditionary power in the world after the United States.

Two points, however, apply to this kind of operation, whoever leads it. Firstly, this kind of soldiering is the most difficult of all. It requires good discipline, excellent training, strong leadership qualities down to the lowest levels and a high sense of political awareness. Using troops of inferior quality, whether these come wearing the UN's blue beret or not, can considerably increase the chances of failure – often through destroying the moral credibility of the whole intervention operation. This rule can apply as much to troops from the world's most powerful nations as it does to the world's weakest ones – as the recent scandals of Abu Ghraib and Haditha in Iraq show.

Meanwhile, the world's most powerful nations on the Security Council have become rather good at declaring interventions in faraway places to which they are happy to send other people's troops, but would not dream of committing their own. And some of the world's developing nations, especially in Africa and Asia,[†] have become equally good at seeing interventions as excellent opportunities to earn foreign currency from UN payments for themselves and their soldiers. Higher salaries, accompanied by opportunities to engage in local corruption, were among the chief reasons why it was never difficult to find Russian and Ukrainian[‡] battalions to serve

[*] Of these, 58,000 are soldiers and the remainder police and ancillary personnel.
[†] India, Pakistan and Bangladesh are particular offenders in this area.
[‡] I remember watching Ukrainian troops in besieged Sarajevo in 1993, trading black market cigarettes behind the UN headquarters building in the city. They were widely believed also to be running the trafficked women network and some of the brothels in Sarajevo. One UN official told me he was powerless to stop this, and believed that when they left the battalion took away with them more than a million Deutschmarks of profit from black market trading in this starving city, which they had come to protect.

in UNPROFOR and afterwards NATO's Stablisation Force (SFOR) in Bosnia – and the same dynamics are still much in evidence among other interventions today. If the international community wishes to go on intervening at the current rate, it should take urgent steps to raise the quality of the troops from some contributing nations. I shall discuss later in this chapter how this might be done.

There is a second problem affecting both UN forces and those of the most proficient regional military alliances (such as NATO) that is worth a special mention here – the problem of national caveats. Contributing nations' forces often come with specific instructions from their capitals (many set by their parliaments) as to what they can and cannot do – and always more of the latter than the former. In 2003, I was with the general in charge of NATO forces in Bosnia when he was doing a search of a small town where the indicted war criminal Radovan Karadžić was believed to be hiding. The cordon included roadblocks on all the exit roads and went in before dawn, when the search operation began. Suddenly we heard over the radio that two of the key roads which should have been blocked were open. The German contingent, which was supposed to be there, wasn't. The general got in touch with the commander of the German forces and asked where his troops were. 'In their barracks,' came the reply. 'Why?' asked the general (in rather stronger terms than that monosyllable would indicate). 'Because the German parliament says that German troops don't do roadblocks,' was the response.

Likewise, in Kosovo the UN was often impeded from getting its job done by troops citing national caveats as a reason for not carrying out certain instructions. One example, again involving German forces, occurred when the UN sought to support the decision of the locally elected municipal assembly in Prizren to remove contentious statues in the town centre. The German military contingent based there refused, citing national caveats. The UN mission was unable to bring any pressure to bear on the Germans, and it had no other means of following through on its promise. The statues remained in place, discrediting both the UN and the democratic structures they were trying to foster. German and Greek troops were also prevented by their national caveats from even leaving their barracks during the troubles in Kosovo in March 2004, while churches and non-Albanian areas were being demolished by rioting mobs all around them. In a similar way national caveats among African troops proved a particular problem in the early days of the intervention in Sierra Leone. In Iraq Japanese troops don't do patrols, aren't allowed to come to the aid of others under attack and have to rely on Dutch troops to protect their bases; the Italians do only vehicle patrols and the Thai battalions' rules prevent them from leaving their bases at all.[6] In Afghanistan there are a total of seventy-two different national caveats distributed between the thirty-two nations contributing to the NATO force there. One of these, it appears, is that German troops don't do patrols either.[7] The number of nations who come without national caveats attached is a minority and the exercise of these (known by commanders of multinational forces as 'pulling the red card') has frequently bedevilled efficient multinational operations under both NATO and the UN.

So there is work to be done to improve the performance of troops in the war-fighting phase and afterwards, whether this is led by the UN or not. As to who should lead in this conflict phase, the rule might be: where context is permissive, the UN is possible; where it is not permissive, a militarily proficient coalition of the willing such as NATO is preferable.

The Post-Conflict Reconstruction Phase

The necessity for military proficiency extends into the post-conflict reconstruction phase, too – especially in the early days when there is a paramount need to gain and maintain control of the security space and enforce the rule of law even if only in a rudimentary way, until a police force takes over. This is even more necessary when, as in Iraq and Afghanistan, the task is not post-conflict reconstruction, but in-conflict reconstruction against a powerful insurgent challenge. These, too, are issues we shall touch on in a later chapter.

At this point the question to answer is who should lead in the post-conflict reconstruction phase? The short answer is that someone should. Far too frequently, no one does. International co-ordination is one of the most golden of the golden rules – and we are not very good at it.

The key unity here is that which exists between those responsible for the military and the civilian aspects of reconstruction. Tensions and disagreements between the military and civil arms, both in

Washington and on the ground, have also been a feature of the US operation in Iraq. By far the best solution is to have a single unified command structure, preferably under civilian command. In Bosnia, the Dayton Peace Agreement created a double-headed monster with a NATO general responsible for the implementation of the military aspects, and the High Representative responsible for the civilian aspects of the Agreement. This caused considerable problems from the earliest days of the international intervention in that country. Before I arrived in Bosnia there was barely disguised hostility between NATO and the Office of the High Representative. During my mandate in Bosnia, my NATO colleague and I made it our business to have the closest possible contact – what the Americans call 'handcon' (hand-to-hand contact) – because we understood that indivisible unity between us was the fundamental pillar on which the success of both our missions depended. This ought, however, to be a structural issue, not one dependent on personalities. The principle of unity of command under civilian control, or at least supremacy, is followed in most UN operations.

But the question of who commands in the reconstruction phase has been fought over between the US government's military and civilian departments, right from the days when the US first established a 'Bureau of Insular Affairs' in 1899 to oversee their occupation and reconstruction efforts in the Philippines, Cuba and Costa Rica. In 1939, the Department of Defense finally lost the battle to the US Interior Department. But modern US practice again separates and insulates the military chain of command from the civilian one, a practice which has led to dangerous muddle and damaging consequences to the overall US effort both in Somalia and, more recently, in Iraq.[8] Instead of unity of command, the US now stresses *unity of effort* (i.e. coordination). But this has merely had the effect of muddling the issue without resolving it. As a recent US paper put it: '*Unity of effort ultimately fails to ascribe the same level of importance to the political and military parts of any intervention plan. While military forces operate under a well-established chain of command that includes accountability, links to resources and clear operational guidance, "non-military" actors generally do not. Moreover, explicitly delinking key activities like the rebuilding of infrastructure and the reconstruction of government services from military activities on the ground further separates the political*

objective of war from the very military operations supposedly con-
ducted in support of such objectives . . . Furthermore, there simply
are no civilian government agencies that even remotely duplicate the
serious strategic planning culture that exists in the US military.
Absent a single integrated planning organization designed to address
both military and political requirements in any intervention, unity of
effort risks merely endorsing the current ad hoc disconnected ap-
proaches that almost invariably tilt toward military modalities to
solve essentially political problems . . . Unity of effort embodies a
classic government response – meetings and more meetings – to an
operational problem . . . Everyone owns part of the problem, but
no one has the authority, responsibility or resources to actually get a
job done.'[9]

NATO, regrettably, follows US practice on this question. It would be far better to follow instead the UN practice of unified command under a civilian lead, but realistically speaking I doubt that they ever will. In which case, care should be taken to provide institutional mechanisms to ensure unity of voice and action between the military and civilian pillars in any post-conflict reconstruction mission.

Interestingly one such mechanism emerged (after much pain) during the Vietnam conflict, when in 1967 the CORDS organisation was established, creating a hybrid civil-military structure in which soldiers and civilians drawn from all service arms and all US civilian departments (including the White House) were brought together in a single integrated structure in which the military served under civilians and vice versa, at all levels. The US, however, seems to have forgotten this Vietnam lesson and has never replicated it since, though the need for it, not least in Iraq and Afghanistan, remains just as great, and the damage done by not having it just as painful.

But the importance of unity is not confined to that between the military and civilian pillars – it extends across the whole international community effort. Squabbling among the international community has been a very common and damaging feature in intervention missions, from the Congo right through to Sierra Leone[10] and Kosovo[11] and beyond. To overcome this the Brahimi Report recommends the establishment of an Integrated Mission Task Force for future operations.[12]

When I visited Bosnia just before the start of my mandate I found that members of the international community there spent more time criticising each other, often in public, than they did working together. It was as if they had concluded that the best way to deal with the Balkans was to start off by Balkanising themselves. Although technically the Dayton Agreement gave the High Representative the formal task of coordinating the international community effort, this provision was more honoured in the breach than in the observance. Each international organisation worked separately, reported separately to their parent headquarters and had separate mandates and aims. And all resented any attempt to achieve a more coordinated approach.

The recent Iraq Study Group identified the same problem in Iraq in the following words: '*A lack of coordination by senior management in Washington still hampers US contributions to Iraq's reconstruction. Focus, priority setting, and skilful implementation are in short supply. No single official is assigned responsibility or held accountable for the overall reconstruction effort. Representatives of key foreign partners involved in reconstruction have also spoken to us directly and specifically about the need for a point of contact that can coordinate their efforts with the US government. A failure to improve coordination will result in agencies continuing to follow conflicting strategies, wasting taxpayer dollars on duplicative and uncoordinated efforts. This waste will further undermine public confidence in US policy in Iraq. RECOMMENDATION 67: The President should create a Senior Advisor for Economic Reconstruction in Iraq.*'[13]

Exactly the same problem has bedevilled the current operations in Afghanistan. There are no fewer than twenty-four national and multilateral organisations providing aid and assistance in the international intervention in Afghanistan, which began in October 2001. But it was not until five years later, in mid 2006, that anyone thought to appoint a co-ordinator for all this effort. So massive amounts of money and far too many precious opportunities have been lost. One example of this is the opium poppy eradication programme, which is one of the international community's key priorities. According to a recent report[14] there are in all some fifteen international and local agencies working on poppy eradication, but almost no coordination between them, despite the fact that harmonisation of this effort was a task which Britain agreed to take on. The consequence has been that, despite an expenditure of some $400 million on poppy eradication, the Afghan poppy harvest in 2006 hit a new record of 6,100 tons, up 49 per cent from the previous all-time record in 2005,[15], while the area devoted to growing the opium poppy has risen from 7,606 hectares under the Taliban to 165,000 hectares today – the highest level ever in Afghan history.[16] And incidentally this failure to control poppy cultivation has not just had an effect on the illegal trade of global narcotics. It has also had a direct and damaging effect in the battle for control of Afghanistan. Part of the Taliban strategy for wresting control of territory from NATO has been to use threats and intimidation (particularly at night) to persuade farmers in Helmand Uruzgan and Kandahar to convert to poppy growing because this draws them into illegal activity and makes them easier to control.

Bosnia and Afghanistan are, of course, very different. But they have two things in common. They are both mountainous areas where tectonic plates of religion and ethnicities collide. And both have been a playground for invaders for a thousand years and more. Their inhabitants have become very practised at knowing how to cope with occupiers by driving wedges – it is just foolish of us to make it easier by dividing ourselves. To overcome this problem in Bosnia, we established a 'cabinet' structure which we called the Board of Principals.[17] This consisted of the heads of each of the main international organisations and took its decisions on a collective basis. The unity of voice and action that this achieved became one of our most powerful instruments for getting things done in all of our respective missions in Bosnia. Elsewhere, however, division and lack of coordination among the international community remains the rule and unity the exception.

The situation can be even worse when it comes to individual nations' bilateral aid. With some noble exceptions (in Bosnia these included USAID, the UK's DfID and the Swedish and Norwegian aid organisations) most bilateral aid is just that – completely bilateral with neither coordination nor consultation with the main international effort. Huge amounts of money were wasted in this way in Bosnia and sometimes real damage was done. On one occasion we found two national bilateral aid projects building two schools either side of an inter-entity border line within two kilometres of each other, thus encouraging ethnically based education, while the rest of the international community was trying to encourage integrated education.

In many cases the transaction costs of aid delivered through bilateral and NGO donors can be outrageously high. In Afghanistan the United States offered to provide money for a road to be built, but insisted on using US contractors (while unemployed Afghans stood by and watched). After the cost of flying out the personnel and equipment to do the job had been paid for, there was insufficient money left to finish the project. Hardly any work was completed before they all flew home again. Elsewhere, out of a $59.6 million Afghan health aid package delivered by the World Bank, only around 1 per cent, some $0.5 million, had to be deducted for delivery costs. But, in a similar $60 million USAID health aid package, no less than $23 million, more than 30 per cent of the total, was consumed in delivery costs.

But if the situation with bilateral national aid can be bad, the situation with respect to NGOs is usually much worse. Some NGOs, usually the bigger and better known ones, are well run, responsible and take care to keep themselves properly briefed on the priorities of the international community. But many are not and do not. They flock into a country brimming with good intentions and crowded with well-meaning people. But they often soak up huge amounts of national aid (being supported by home governments) which they spend in wholly uncoordinated and often deeply damaging ways. They usually come in droves when the country is high profile in the news but melt away when the cameras go. I have often entertained the uncharitable thought that some at least find that having a presence on a high profile foreign field does no harm to fundraising at home. They can also spend unsupportable sums on their own administration and return scandalously low amounts to the country they are in. In Afghanistan (as in Kosovo and elsewhere) this practice of taking more money out of the country in salaries than they put into it in aid is causing real resentment, with President Karzai complaining that far too much of the money NGOs received was spent '*on high salaries, on overhead charges, on luxury vehicles, on luxury houses and lots of other luxuries that Afghanistanis cannot afford*'.[18]

Reconstructing nations after conflict is difficult and expensive enough without wasting time, money and vital opportunities by failing to coordinate what we do. There is, therefore, a strong case for insisting that all international aid and reconstruction assistance, multilateral and bilateral, should be made subject to coordination by the person nominated to lead the international mission concerned. As for NGOs, they are real players on the field with an important role to perform, especially in the distribution of aid, where they can often ensure that aid goes to the most needy and not into the pockets of the most powerful. NGOs deserve to be taken seriously as key stakeholders in the process and should have a formal place at the table when plans, priorities and strategies are decided. But the deal should be that, in return, they too should work with, rather than against, the grain of the international community's efforts and contribute to the coordination process.

So who should manage the process of the reconstruction phase: the UN or a coalition of the willing? I have tried in this book not to let my prejudices show. But on this subject I fear I might.

I am not a great fan of the UN's 400-strong Department of Peace Keeping Operations (UNDPKO) in New York. One of the weaknesses of the international community in general when it comes to managing the processes of peacemaking is a tendency to be risk averse. But this deficiency is especially marked within UN structures and UNDPKO is by no means immune from this general trend. I appreciate that UNDPKO is itself locked within the intestines of the UN bureaucracy and has to clear its actions with many equally senior units within the UN structure, especially legal and political. Nevertheless, I have found them slow, bureaucratic and insensitive to the needs of their people on the ground – especially when it comes to realising that crises do not have a habit of neatly occurring during weekday working hours in New York. Not being a government themselves, they have only a vague notion of what it is like to construct a government and run what is, in effect, a shadow administration. They also do themselves no favours by failing to give the leaders of their missions on the ground sufficient room to use their own judgement. You cannot run a peacekeeping mission at the end of a 5,000-mile screwdriver operated from New York. UNDPKO's greatest success was in Eastern Slavonia and that was with a head of mission, Jacques Klein, who made an art form out of ignoring them.

In Kosovo, UNDPKO's interference in day-to-day matters has

often seriously hampered the smooth running of the operation on the ground. On one occasion, in 2002, the UN's head of mission, the Special Representative of the Secretary General (SRSG), ordered a quarter of his mission staff to move to the northern town of Mitrovica in order to give the Serbs a greater say in the operation. His orders were quietly countermanded by New York and were never applied. Meanwhile, New York's requirement to be kept constantly updated, sometimes by cabled reports every two hours, together with their tendency to second-guess their people on the ground, has on occasion significantly reduced the UN Kosovo mission's ability to deal with crises and press forward advantages at key moments. The administration of the mission is affected, too. The SRSG does not even have the authority to get rid of incompetent or insubordinate staff without permission from New York. Some aspects of UN bureaucracy are equally irksome for lower level UN staff. For instance, in the early days of the Kosovo mission, permission had to be obtained from UN headquarters in Pristina before a fax could be sent from its northern headquarters in Mitrovica. The only way to do this was to send a fax to Pristina, asking for permission to send a fax to Pristina!

So, although, in Bosnia, I had to spend a great deal of time managing the individual country representatives of a coalition of the willing (the Steering Board of the Dayton Peace Implementation Council – or PIC), it was worth the effort because I could call them up twenty-four hours a day every day and what they gave me was real time answers and real political support when I needed it and where I needed it. And being representatives of governments themselves, they had a better understanding of what politics and government is actually about.

My colleagues in charge of our sister Balkan reconstruction mission, the UNDPKO-run operation in Kosovo, envied my position in Bosnia, as it had developed under the PIC. And I did not envy theirs in Kosovo, under New York. Of course this is too sweeping a judgement. There are areas where the UN can add real value which multilateral coalitions of nation states cannot. The UN can usually gather wider coalitions of support and this can be important. They can have better access to the 'gene pool' of international experts in the field. And through them the powerful support of the UN Secretary General can be mobilised. But there, I fear, you have it.

I am a passionate believer in the UN. If we did not have a UN we would have to invent one. And, if the world is to be safer, its role in the future is going to have to grow, not diminish as some would like. In Chapter 9 I will discuss in greater detail how we could strengthen the UN's capacities in the peacemaking field. For the moment, however, leaving aside the UN specialist agencies such as UNHCR and UNDP etc, the main body of the UN is, I regret, not an organisation designed for executive action, whether in war or in reconstructing peace. Although this deficiency has not so far proved significantly debilitating when intervening in permissive environments, it does undermine the UN's ability to carry out the very serious business of warfare and post-conflict reconstruction in non-permissive circumstances.

There are those who argue that we should change this – that we should equip the UN with specially earmarked forces who can be called on to be placed under UN command in order to undertake action and with a standing capacity to command these forces in the field. Brian Urquhart, United Nations Under-Secretary-General for Special Political Affairs from 1974–86 has argued the case for a highly trained rapid reaction force, made up of voluntary contributions from member states to be placed at the disposal of the Security Council in order to give the international community the capacity to intervene quickly in situations of civil war or anarchy. In a perfect world, I would agree. But we do not live in a perfect world and I just can't see nations, in these days of military over-stretch, providing what is needed to make such a system effective.

So my preference remains that, wherever executive action is required in non-permissive environments, it will normally be better for the UN to subcontract the management of this, where possible, to coalitions of the willing under broad Security Council supervision. In Bosnia, the High Representative's direct line of responsibility is to the PIC, not the UN. But he is still required to report twice annually to the UN Security Council. And this is right because, even though the day-to-day management of the Bosnian operation is not a matter for the UN, its international legitimacy springs from a UN Security Council Resolution.

The Role of the UN

So what then should be the role of the UN in a world where carrying out successful interventions, from prevention right through to post-conflict reconstruction, is going to be more and more necessary and more and more part of the normal conduct of international affairs?

The answer is that the UN's first role should be to act as the repository, guardian and developer of international law and the legitimiser of international action. But when it comes to executive action it should not be the 'doer' of first resort – especially in 'non-permissive' circumstances – but, where possible, the subcontractor and overseer of international action taken in its name. This, incidentally, is precisely the role which the UN played recently in Afghanistan where, through UNSCR 1510, it legitimised NATO's expanded operation in that country. It needs to be recognised, however, that there will be some circumstances and some parts of the world (Africa for example) where the UN has to get involved in executive action because there is no one else to do it.

But here too, we should be thinking rather more for the long term, than the short. There could be a real role for the UN in creating capable 'subcontractors' in places where they do not already exist. Firstly, by enhancing the quality of troops available for action through a process of 'accreditation' of forces capable of being deployed under the blue beret. Given the desire of some third world countries to earn money through providing troops for UN operations, a system of accreditation could prove a strong incentive towards improving troop quality. And secondly the UN should actively promote and enable regional military alliances such as that of the African Union (whose 5,000 force currently in Darfur are rarely paid regularly and have been described in one report[19] as '[having] very poor cohesiveness, highly limited communications and intelligence-gathering ability and desperately inadequate transport capacity – [who] cannot possibly provide security for humanitarian personnel, operations or convoys') so that they can intervene successfully when and where necessary.[20] There are dangers which need to be recognised in this approach. Creating more militarily capable 'coalitions of the willing' risks encouraging the increase of third world armies when we should be decreasing them and not creating new instruments and opportunities for military adventurism and illegal interventions. So any such policy would have to be very carefully proscribed and firmly tied to legitimisation through UN structures.

Nevertheless in a world where 'over-stretch' is already a crucial issue limiting the engagements even of the strong, these are issues which have to be considered. There is, additionally, both a moral imperative and a practical advantage for the world's most powerful nations to assist in this process – given that it is their decisions on the Security Council which call for these interventions in which they rarely take part and, all too frequently, their troops who have to bail the UN out when things go wrong, as in Somalia and Sierra Leone.

All this, however, begs the key question of whether, post-Iraq and Afghanistan, the UNSC will be so willing to grant mandates to coalitions of the willing to do its work. The UNSC's reluctance over Darfur (although no doubt also influenced by China's activities in Khartoum) seems to indicate that the Security Council is becoming less 'biddable' and the 'good old days' when it could relied upon to legitimise operations in such places as Kosovo may be over. I suspect that this new reluctance on the part of the UNSC to license operations taken in its name is not going to change. The UNSC will require, at the very least, a greater say in future in the conduct of these operations and stronger lines of accountability for those who conduct them.

Trusteeship Council

One means of providing this would be to resuscitate an old idea – the concept of the UN Trustee Council. In recent years, the international community has been very coy about facing up to what it is doing in countries subject to international reconstruction after conflict. We seem prepared to go to any lengths in order to invent increasingly complex mechanisms to avoid the accusation of running protectorates. Yet that is what we are, in most cases, doing. How else would you describe international missions which in some cases: *'enforce local laws, exercise total fiscal management of a territory, appoint and remove public officials, create a central bank, establish and maintain customs services, regulate the local media, adjudicate rival property claims, run schools, regulate local businesses and reconstruct and operate all public utilities, among numerous other functions'?*[21] Far better to face this openly and set up proper mechanisms for providing UN oversight of the actions of individual nations or coalitions of the willing, subcontracted by the UN to help a state pass from the chaos of conflict to full membership of the international community of nations. The UN Trusteeship Council, which provided a means of doing just this, was, with that perfect sense of timing that often attends international affairs, retired from active service in November 1994, just as the pace of UN interventions was picking up after the cold war. It was then finally and formally effectively killed off a year or so ago in December 2005, when the UN Peace-Building Commission (PBC) was established, even though the PBC – a welcome development in its own right – was neither designed nor intended to perform the same function as the old Trusteeship Council.

The UN Trusteeship Council process was originally created as a successor to the League of Nations Mandate system. Through this process, the UN Security Council granted the administration of certain territories to individual member nations on the condition that they would take their charges through to full independence and membership of the UN, under the oversight of the Trusteeship Council. The last such territories were Palau, the Marshall Islands and Micronesia, whose interim administrations were conducted by the United States until they gained full UN membership in November 1994.

The trusteeship/protectorate concept is, however, limited in its application. Firstly, it envisages a rather intrusive style of intervention at a time when the whole thrust of new thinking in this area (led by Britain's DfID) is now moving towards more local ownership, with the international community acting as a safety net if things go wrong, rather than an agenda setter and temporary governor. Secondly, as with any other intervention, to succeed it requires local support or at least acquiescence and this may not always be forthcoming for what is overtly a protectorate structure. And thirdly, since establishing a trustee/protectorate-style administration involves the international community in taking on the full burden of government, it is likely to work better in small countries than in large ones (the UN considered the possibility of setting up a full protectorate-style government in Afghanistan, but rejected this option because of the size of the country.* The debate is still continuing when it comes to Gaza.

There is also a fourth, constitutional difficulty in reviving the Trusteeship Council. The UN Charter (Article 78) explicitly states that the provisions of the Trusteeship Council will not apply to UN member states[22] – so any attempt to subject existing UN member states to the activities of a revived Trusteeship Council would require a Charter amendment, which is not easy to obtain.

Some propose that one way of overcoming the 'size limitation' of the Trustee approach would be to revert to the old concept of shared sovereignty – similar to that established in Germany after the Second World War, where the international community takes on full responsibility for some but not all aspects of government.

But all these approaches – trusteeship, protectorate or shared sovereignty – entailing as they do, *'the temporary third party control of some or all of the principal governance functions of a state or territory'*,[23] raise serious issues of legitimacy.[24] In part these are mitigated by the temporary nature of the engagement. They would be further mitigated by the establishment of some formal modern equivalent of the UN Trusteeship Council, perhaps under the oversight of the UN's newly established Peace-Building Commission (PBC),[25] which would provide for greater legitimacy, greater oversight by the Security Council and a greater capacity to mobilise multilateral support for post-conflict reconstruction than exists in the present rash of freelance reconstruction exercises currently being carried out by individual nations, or coalitions of the willing.

As with so much else on the peacemaking agenda, there is not a 'one size fits all' solution to the question of who takes charge of the post-conflict phase. The key is to have the flexibility to match the model with the situation on the ground.

---

* Another factor was also UN reluctance, led by Lakhdar Brahimi, for the UN to have more than a 'light footprint' in the country.

Finding the Right Person

But leadership is not just an organisational question, it is also a deeply personal one. So, leaving aside the question of which organisation should be in charge, there is also the question of what *kind* of person should we be looking for when choosing the leadership of a civilian post-conflict reconstruction mission?

The answer that the international community almost always arrives at to this question is a diplomat. And it is the wrong answer. Running one of these missions is a quintessentially political operation, not a diplomatic one. It requires an ability to balance political forces and take political decisions, something which politicians spend all their lives doing, while diplomats are trained to be political observers, but not political actors. It requires a facility to move and manipulate public opinion through the press, which politicians revel in and diplomats are taught to avoid like the plague. It requires an ability to confront crises, which politicians often use to advance their agenda, and diplomats are taught to avoid. This not to say that no diplomat should ever lead one of these missions – some diplomats are more politicians than many politicians. Michel Steiner, who led the Kosovo operation, is one example. And some politicians are more ponderous and risk averse than any diplomat I have ever met. And some generals have the right qualities too (think of MacArthur in Japan, probably the most successful post-conflict reconstructor of all time – or, on a much smaller scale, General Jacques Klein in Eastern Slavonia.)

This is not about categories of people, but skill sets. Some diplomatic skills are required, to be sure. After all the leader of one of these missions will probably have to spend more time managing the international community than getting things done in the country under reconstruction. Some military knowledge would be helpful, too, given that the key partnership will be with the commander of the military forces who will secure the peace, without which there can be no success in rebuilding the country. But the greatest skills required for leadership of one of these missions – the skills that will be called on and tested every day, twenty times a day, will be those of political judgement, political manipulation and political manoeuvre.

Finally there is the question of how the international community chooses its leaders for these intervention missions. The current process of making these vital choices is almost completely haphazard and governed more by who knows whom in the UN (especially in the Secretary General's office) and by the principle of 'buggin's turn' – which major country's turn it is to have a senior post such as this. The procedures are, moreover, completely opaque, relying heavily on 'corridor conversations' beyond the sight of the wider world. The country which is subject to the intervention is never meaningfully consulted – and often never even informed before the matter is announced publicly. There is no interview process, little or no attempt to draw up a job description and no training or formal handover process for the fortunate (or unfortunate) person chosen. It is scarcely possible to imagine a more disorganised way of choosing someone for such an important position. In Chapter 9 I discuss what improvements could be made to improve and rationalise these appointment procedures.

Summary

So the answer to the question 'Who's in charge?' is that there isn't a simple answer. There is not a 'one size fits all' answer to the question of who should lead in a peacemaking and post-conflict reconstruction mission. In some cases the right answer will be the UN, in some a coalition of the willing will provide the best result and in some the best answer is a combination of the two, depending on the task in hand. In the prevention phase, the UN's role may be large, but the role of those nations with greatest influence over the country concerned will often be decisive. In the conflict phase a professional military coalition of the willing should lead where the strength of opposition makes this necessary, and the UN where the permissive nature of the operation makes it possible. In the reconstruction phase, the UN's constant role should be to legitimise and oversee – but a coalition of the willing and the engaged, if one can be found, may be better to do the work. The overarching rule, however, is to be flexible and to ensure that there is a range of options that can match the means to the conditions on the ground. When it comes to choosing the person to lead the mission, a wide range of skills will be required – but a high level of political skills will be more important than a high level of diplomatic ones. It is unlikely that the international community will do better than it has done to date in choosing the right people for these posts, if it continues to do this through a process that remains almost totally untransparent, unstructured, inappropriate and, to anyone outside the charmed circle of diplomacy, completely incomprehensible.

9

New structures – new thinking

> There is nothing more difficult to take in hand, more perilous to
> conduct, or more uncertain in its success, than to take the lead
> in the introduction of a new order of things. Because the
> innovator has for enemies all those who have done well under
> the old conditions, and lukewarm defenders in those who may
> do well under the new. MACHIAVELLI, *The Prince*, 1532

New ways of structuring our actions and thinking about prevention,
military intervention and post-conflict reconstruction will require
new structures and institutions in governments and international
bodies. This at least seems now to be commonly accepted by most of
the key players in this field, as the establishment of new bodies
dedicated to this task in the UN, EU, NATO and individual nations
listed in Chapter 6 show.

But so far most of these innovations have been confined to
'add-ons' to current structures, rather than the kind of substantial re-ordering of the way we do things which will be necessary
if we are to make more of a success of these activities in the
future.

The Post-Conflict Reconstruction Unit (PCRU), newly established by the British government, illustrates the point. The task of
the PCRU is defined in its mandate as follows:

To improve the UK's contribution to post-conflict stabilisation by:
— developing strategy for post-conflict stabilisation, including link-
ing military and civilian planning; working with wider international
community; and
— planning, implementing and managing the UK contribution to
post-conflict stabilisation, including practical civilian capabilities

needed to stabilise environment in immediate post-conflict situations.[1]

Note how the words 'post-conflict' appear no fewer than four times in the above short passage – but the word 'prevention' appears not once.

Speaking in the House of Commons on 16 September 2004, Hilary Benn the development minister underlined this aspect when he identified that the purpose of the PCRU was *'first, to develop government strategy for post-conflict stabilisation . . . and, secondly, to plan and direct activities designed to create stability in post-conflict environments in the period immediately following the cessation of hostilities.*[2] This statement illustrates the fact that we have not yet appreciated that success in creating *'stability in post-conflict environments'* does not begin, in Hilary Benn's words *'in the period immediately following the cessation of hostilities'*, but long before in the prevention and conflict phases which preceded it.

The original thinking behind the PCRU approach and that of its US cousin are broadly the same. Both were established after the interventions in Iraq and Afghanistan had highlighted the almost total lack of capacity in the two governments to conduct this kind of operation. They were originally conceived as national organisations, working under national flags, rather than plugging in with each other and with international bodies to enhance the effectiveness of multilateralism. Although the staff of PCRU and S/CRS are knowledgeable, deeply committed and genuine experts in the field, the political ethos behind their founding was a paternalistic one which presumes that the countries in which we intervene crave nothing more than the adoption of the full panoply of Western values and institutions. And they both initially worked on the principle that the best way to rebuild after conflict is, as it were, to stack up boxes of diplomats, development experts, water engineers, military strategists et al, ten to the box in some dusty Whitehall corridor waiting for the conflict to end, before unleashing them in flights on the unsuspecting country concerned.

This *prêt à porter* approach is not the best way to succeed in post-conflict reconstruction – first and fundamentally because it completely ignores the 'seamless garment' principle. It treats post-conflict as a stand-alone phase, rather than as part of the continuum which stretches from prevention, through involvement in the planning of the conflict, right down to the final exit of the interveners. But the reasons for failure of the PCRU approach to fulfil the mandate originally conceived for it are more than conceptual.

Firstly, the PCRU and its sister organisations in other countries were conceived as 'add-ons' for government, not as integral co-ordinating and directing parts of it. Creating little bureaucracies, each with a national flag on them, is the easy bit. The hard bit is to re-think our whole approach to this, re-shaping the inter-relationships of government, creating a national capability to match these and, perhaps most importantly, investing in an international structure to carry it out.

Secondly, the PCRU is an interdepartmental unit set up by the Foreign Office, DfID and the Ministry of Defence.[*] This means it has no single minister to whom it is solely responsible and who can be relied on to argue its case in Cabinet – and this is necessary when cross-departmental resources are required, for instance troops or extra development aid, or diplomatic pressure or extra financial resources at a key moment. Moreover, precisely because of its cross-departmental nature, the PCRU has suffered from the natural 'tissue rejection' process of large bureaucracies who find a newcomer, owned by none of them, in their midst. The Whitehall and Washington bureaucracies were never going to allow high-priced experts to sit around kicking their heels, waiting for a crisis to happen. So the PCRU's role has been reduced from an organisation whose primary purpose was strategy development and crisis planning, to one whose primary purpose is to be an occasional service provider facilitating those already engaged in the existing crises in Afghanistan, Iraq and elsewhere. In consequence both the US and British organisations have become under-funded, under-resourced, under-used and under-regarded.

Commenting on the S/CRS a recent US study says this: '[S/CRS] . . . has been consistently under funded, its work has remained limited, and it has had trouble getting consistent representation from other US agencies despite its mandate to be an interagency office. S/CRS only received seven million dollars in

---

[*] Although defined as an interdepartmental organisation, the PCRU is administratively housed and paid for by DfID, who regard themselves as its lead department.

funding during Fiscal Year 2005, despite a Presidential request for $17 million. As of this writing, it seems as though the President's request for $124 million for [Fiscal Year 2006] will only result in a fraction of that amount at best. Another promising development was the issuing of National Security Presidential Directive (NSPD) 44 in December 2005, which addresses the management of inter-agency efforts for reconstruction and stabilisation. It reaffirms the role of S/CRS as the focal point for such efforts, and it creates a Policy Coordination Committee to oversee these issues. Yet it remains to be seen whether its provisions will be implemented effectively or whether bureaucratic disagreements will continue to plague the coordination process.'[3]

The Bespoke Approach

Instead of the *prêt à porter* approach to peacemaking and reconstruction, what is needed is a bespoke approach, in which potentially failing or rogue states are identified early and teams of country experts – at first relatively small – are assembled to manage the prevention process. Since development is frequently a key means of prevention – especially in the case of failing states – these teams should include development experts at the earliest point. If it then becomes obvious that prevention will fail and conflict cannot be avoided, these 'bespoke' teams can be further augmented with military planners and those who will be involved in the post-conflict reconstruction phase. Their job will not be just to prepare for the conflict phase, but also to influence the military plans as they are constructed so as to ensure that they take account of the post-conflict reconstruction phase which follows. It is at this point that it will be helpful to bring in the aid agencies and the NGOs operating on the ground – for they will know local conditions, perhaps better than anyone. Those whose task will be to establish the rule of law will also need to be closely involved in this early planning and have the authority to begin to assemble, or at least earmark, the police and judicial resources they will need in those early hours after the conflict ends. These bespoke teams should then form the core of the post-conflict reconstruction mission who should go in to begin their work, just behind the frontline troops.

This bespoke approach depends, of course, on the early

identification of potential failing or rogue states. Spotting potential rogue states, such as Saddam Hussein's Iraq and today's North Korea, is an entirely subjective and political matter to be decided on by politicians. But when it comes to potentially failing states, more objective measures can be used. A lot of work has been done, notably by Oxford academics Collier and Hoeffler, on measures for identifying failing states and what steps can be taken to stop them failing. Ultimately, however, the application of the bespoke approach will depend on political leaders being prepared to take clear-cut policy decisions on which states are at risk of failing and what are the limits of policy in addressing these.

The germs of precisely such an approach already exist in the British government's Global Conflict Prevention Pool (GCPP) and African Conflict Prevention Pool, which oversee some fifteen or so development/prevention strategies, each covering a country or region. This brings together officials from the FCO, MoD and DfID to discuss country strategies from a prevention/development perspective and to spend money jointly on the basis of shared conflict risk assessments and strategic plans. The approach is excellent, but there are problems which make these Pools far less effective than they should be. Firstly they tend to be run by rather junior Whitehall desk officers and local staff in post and have neither the horsepower nor the attention from senior levels to make them a serious forum for real political and military planning, and programme spending. In consequence, the funds designated for use by these Pools are extremely limited compared to the task at hand. They have become, in short, too large to ignore, but too small to be taken seriously. Because of this the Pools are frequently raided for post-conflict operations, rather than being allowed to focus on conflict prevention. If these interdepartmental conflict prevention teams could be institutionalised, given more attention by senior levels, provided with more resources and underpinned with the political support to change policy, then they could become the nucleus of a new joined-up bespoke approach to this process.

Beyond the major developed nations, however, there will be few nations who will have the resources to assemble such teams in this kind of orderly and resource-intensive way. But since international coordination in all phases is central to success, there should be no reason why a group of like-minded nations who share the same policy analysis should not work together and assemble bespoke teams which are international in character – reflecting what will anyway be required in both the conflict and the post-conflict phases.

For European countries, the obvious framework within which to do this is the Council of the European Union and the Common Foreign and Security Policy structures. These could provide the EU with the instruments to apply the 'seamless garment' approach, with bespoke teams following individual countries deemed to be in danger of failing or becoming rogue states. The EU has certain key strengths in this area. It can act quickly and deploy significant leverage in support of prevention, as the Macedonia experience showed. It can in theory provide strong executive leadership under Dr Solana and his successors. It has a sizeable assistance budget to support prevention, crisis management, and post-conflict interventions. And it has staying power – at least in theory. The Commission and the Council would need to work more closely together to maximise the Union's political influence and back this with the resources necessary. The two still pursue separate agendas far too often. And the Council would need to re-think its staffing policies to allow for the hiring of practitioners with the right kind of experience on long-term contracts, with the aim of arriving at significant numbers of deployable 'civilian forces' who could rotate between the field, headquarters and their own national administrations, depending on need. The EU is still predominantly staffed by civil servants and diplomats in Brussels without operational field experience. Member states will no doubt wish to retain independent capabilities. But an EU complement could bring about a more joined-up approach to policy-making and the rapid deployments of state-building teams.[*]

There could also be a powerful role for the UN in such a global 'bespoke' approach, in identifying potential failing states, providing the primary forum for the conduct of the prevention phase, establishing an international database of experts for bespoke country teams and in ensuring that the expertise and country knowledge of

[*] The UK, during its Presidency of the EU in 2005, launched a process of reflection known as the 'Hampton Court' process, on how to improve the EU's operations. If this initiative is to come to anything it will require a major re-think about how the Union manages its human resources. Provided this happens, it could lead to a significant boost in the EU's operational capability.

its specialised agencies, such as UNDP and UNHCR, are fed into the process. There is even a theoretical case for conducting the whole bespoke approach through, say, a sub-committee of the UN Security Council – but I fear that this would be so inhibited by the UNSC veto process and so tied up with the internal politics of the Council that it would prove too sclerotic to be practical. Besides which, UN member states would no doubt object to their own organisation declaring them as potentially failing states. There should be no reason, however, why the Security Council should not mandate the Department of Political Affairs (DPA) by way of a general resolution to produce a list of potential conflict areas at regular intervals. The success of the bespoke approach will depend on executive action and, for reasons already discussed the UN, while good at enabling and facilitating, is less good at managing concrete action to get things done.

Joined-Up Government

Adopting the bespoke approach would, however, require a whole new way of joined-up thinking from within governments – to say nothing of a whole new way of structuring government itself. 'Joined-up thinking' has been one of the buzz words of the Blair government – and indeed has been attempted, in one form or another, by every British government back to Churchill, who first proposed 'overlords' to co-ordinate across government depart-ments.* But we are still not very good at this – especially when it

---

* In this experiment, individuals, largely drawn from the House of Lords, were appointed to oversee and coordinate across departments on thematic issues. In identifying the reasons for the ultimate failure of this approach, Harold Macmillan (then a cabinet minister) put his finger on the basic reason why all subsequent similar attempts at 'joined-up' government have also foundered when he said: '. . . *where there was no statutory basis, even of the slenderest kind, the new structure began to break down for two reasons: first, because the position of an overlord, armed with little but an office and a private secretary, soon becomes shadowy and indeterminate; secondly, because however loyal to their nominal chiefs, the subordinate Ministers begin to feel over-riding obligations to their separate departments. Moreover, since the Ministers were in the House of Commons, and the House was already jealous of a Cabinet in which the peers had so large a part, this contrivance, however valuable in principle, became unworkable in practice*'.

comes to thinking about prevention, armed intervention and post-conflict reconstruction.

It is not possible within the scope of this book to analyse the government structures of all the key nations involved in global peacemaking and peacekeeping. In what follows below I have therefore taken the present structures of the British government as an example, in order to illustrate the current practice, the nature of the challenge and what might be done to improve things.

In the British government coordination in this area begins and ends with the GCPPs and the PCRU. These organisations apart, there is no legislative framework to ensure coherence between departments; no mandate for the Cabinet Office to provide this coordination and leadership; no regular, joined-up oversight of overseas and domestic policies, except at the highest level i.e. the prime minister and cabinet; no joined-up, working-level staff structure to coordinate the full range of overseas commitments and ensure effective implementation of ministerial decisions; only limited cross-over between the diplomatic and home civil service and no cross-departmental coordination for related subjects like conflict, security policy and development. Departments are still focused primarily on their own policies, their own budgets, their own cultures, and their own minister's slot on BBC *Newsnight* or in the *Sun*. Furthermore, the way departments are structured and managed still militates against cooperation. The FCO's division of the world's nations in its departments bears no relation to the MoD's organisation, which, in turn, is different from the security agencies' approach. There is no overarching policy framework to guide departments working in the same field; the MoD prepares Defence Reviews and the FCO has Strategic Priorities, and DfID has a Conflict Policy. Furthermore, coordination is weak between those departments that focus on foreign issues (FCO, DfID, MoD) and those that are mandated to focus on the UK (e.g. the Home Office). There are no fewer than six Whitehall units that deal with conflict issues and many of these have overlapping mandates.* This position is exacerbated by practical problems such as the lack of a common

---

* CIG – Conflict Issues Group; SecPol – Security Policy Group; CHASE – Conflict and Humanitarian and Security Affairs Department; SSDAT – Security Sector and Defence Advisory Team; the PCRU; D Strat Plans – Defence Strategic Planning.

departmental language, an absence of inter-operable IT systems*
and the fact that there is no common approach to risk management.

There is also no recognised pan-government planning process led,
for example, by the Cabinet Office. In the military, once a political
decision is taken, the Chief of Defence issues a Planning Directive to
the Chief of Joint Operations. Then a Military Strategic Estimate is
written, which, once ministerial decisions are made, leads to a Chief
of the Defence Staff (CDS) Directive. This in turn leads to the Joint
Commander's Mission Directive and so on down the chain. No
other government department has an equivalent planning process
and the creation of interdepartmental plans, for example for post-
conflict missions, is at best unsystematic and ad hoc. In addition, the
personnel who operate the system – the civil servants – are not
incentivised to work for anything but departmental goals. Schooled
in large bureaucracies that promise promotion and a pension in
exchange for institutional loyalty, they quickly find that seeking
cross-postings into other departments or trying to promote interdepartmental cooperation can be debilitating to a career.

The few cases of successful cross-departmental cooperation have
required a calamity or the direct interest of either No. 10 or a
powerful Secretary of State. On a day-to-day basis, what should be
the centre for coordination – the Defence and Overseas Policy
Committee – has not been able to fulfil the function it was created
for. Critics argue that the Committee serves *'merely to rubber stamp
decisions previously made by the relevant official in the individual
departments, without any critique or input from others.'*4 'Policy
osmosis' between different missions, for example in Iraq and
Afghanistan, may occur at the highest levels of government,
but this hardly permeates at all to lower levels. The Cabinet
Office's Overseas and Defence Secretariat is understaffed and
overstretched.

As the Office of Public Services put it: *'Despite clear intentions to
the contrary and good examples of working together, the gulf between policy and delivery is considered by most to have widened.'*

---

* Whitehall uses at least five different computer/network systems and can therefore transfer documents and briefs between departments only with the greatest
difficulty. The exception to this is, perhaps, COBR (the Cabinet Office Briefing
Room) which, as a location, has quite good IT linking it to relevant government
departments.

This failure to make a reality of joined-up government on the peacemaking and peacekeeping agenda is not confined to Whitehall. The House of Commons' approach to scrutinising government is also exclusively departmentally based. As the Defence Select Committee wrote in 1998: *'Scrutiny of joined-up government will require a joined-up Parliament.'* Bruce George, the former Chair of the Defence Committee, has gone further. He told the House of Commons in October 2005: *'What has come out of the events of the past few years is that the Government's response needs to cut across all Departments, horizontally and vertically . . . Is our Select Committee system remotely fit to monitor that range of inter-departmentalism? No, it is not. We excel at stove-piping better than the most stove-piped industry or Government Department in the country.'* In short, the centrifugal incentives – compelling ministers and officials to work more closely together – are still too weak to alter the status quo, which in structure, culture and thinking continues to act as though it is living in the era of 'stove-piped' governments of a hundred years ago.*

If cohesion and a cross-disciplinary approach is one of the golden rules of conflict prevention and post-conflict reconstruction, then it is impossible to avoid the conclusion that we still have a long way to go to achieve it. There is a separate discussion to be had on whether the wider purposes of government would now be best served by abandoning the Haldane Committee's proposals of 1918, which, mirroring the vertical hierarchies of the industrial revolution, proposed that government should be structured on the division of labour principle into vertical functional departments organised according to service. Perhaps in its place we should now completely re-shape government so as to mirror modern economic structures which are horizontal, cross-cutting and organised according to clients' needs. But what is clear is that, when it comes to peacemaking and reconstruction, that is the approach that is needed.

However, the purpose of this book is to concentrate on improving things as they are and not spend too much time dreaming of things as they might be. So until such a revolution in government

---

* Many of the deficiencies outlined in the above paragraphs are acknowledged implicitly or explicitly as areas for improvement in a report prepared by the Prime Minister's Strategy Unit in 2005, but without, so far, very much follow-up in terms of action.

thinking occurs (and I suspect this is not about to happen quickly), how can we make best use of the architecture that we have?

A Stronger Centre

In the absence of a large-scale restructuring of government to improve its capacity for joined-up action, the only place from where cohesion and coordination across government can come is the centre. Perhaps the best way to do this would be to strengthen the prime minister's office in order to create a peacemaking and peacekeeping equivalent of the French SGAE (*Secrétariat Général des Affaires Européennes*) which works directly to the French prime minister to ensure cross-departmental coordination on all EU matters.

The alternative in the British system would be to locate this task in the Cabinet Office, increasing its resources and altering its structure so as to create a capacity to formulate generic policies, identify potential rogue or failing states, do the long-term planning and generate individual country-specific strategies. But this will require a change not just of structure and tasking but also of approach by the Cabinet Office, which would have to abandon its somewhat dreary ethos of always relying on the consensual approach to problem solving in favour of a more directive attitude which would enable the Cabinet Office itself to take decisions, once all the voices have been heard. It would also require the Cabinet Office greatly to improve its understanding of the importance of coordinating internationally and its capacity to dock with other involved states and international organisations. This would, in turn, require some internal re-organisation as to how the Cabinet Office goes about its business. Given the current lack of coordination between foreign and domestic policies in this field, there is a need for the Cabinet's Overseas Policy Committee to be, at the very least, working as closely as possible with the Cabinet's domestically focused committees meeting at COBR (the Cabinet Office Briefing Room), and maybe, even, a case for a merger between committees focusing on domestic and foreign matters. The UK has a successful mechanism – the Joint Intelligence Committee (JIC) and the JIC Intelligence Requirements system – to manage the collection of information on threats. Bodies like the Joint Terrorism Analysis Centre (JTAC) and

the Serious and Organised Crime Agency (SOCA) are now beginning to coordinate how we handle those threats domestically. But
there is no equivalent process or body for coordinating our national
activity to counter instability abroad, which, as we have recently
and painfully found, is so often the generator of threats at home.

We should consider the creation of a government-wide National
Engagement Strategy as a framework for this, which should be
debated and endorsed by parliament. But strengthening the centre,
though necessary, is not sufficient. There is now widespread recognition that avoiding conflict where we can and rebuilding after it
where we have to is one of the key governmental tasks of our age. It
follows therefore that there should be one 'big beast' in government
responsible for it. Someone who has the power to enforce coordination where it does not exist and argue for the right resources and
staying power where they are needed. What this, of course, means is
a cabinet minister. But which department represented at Cabinet
level should have oversight of the bespoke approach and the job of
ensuring that the 'seamless garment' principle is followed?

There is a clear negative answer to this question. It should *not* be
the Ministry of Defence. They may be the best at planning and at the
logistics required in the early stages of the stabilisation phase. But
their job is fighting wars, not preventing them or building the peace
which follows.

There remain two obvious candidates for this role; the first is the
Ministry of Foreign Affairs or MFA (FCO in British terms), for it is
here that the diplomatic skills required for the prevention phase and
much of the individual country expertise will lie. But development
also plays a large part in this enterprise – especially in the prevention
phase where it can often perform the crucial role in the avoidance of
state failure – as Hoeffler and Collier say in their study on civil war,
'*reducing the global incidence of conflict [points] to the importance
of economic development as critical to peace.*'⁵ This gives a special
role to Departments of Development. Britain's Department for
International Development (DfID) already has wide knowledge,
many experienced staff and a good track record in this area. But it
suffers from one debilitating drawback – its funding is legislatively
tied to long-term development and disbursed largely according to
criteria based on objective poverty levels which, specifically, are not
permitted to be influenced by issues of national interest. Rogue and

potentially failing states can very frequently be poor, since poverty is often a root cause of state vulnerability. But there is no precise correlation between the two. Bosnia was not a poor state in world terms before the wars of the early 1990s – indeed it was, by the standards of the region, a rather prosperous one. The result of DfID's poverty-based funding formula has been that when it gets involved in peacemaking and post-conflict reconstruction it has frequently had to rely on funds begged, borrowed or stolen from elsewhere. So if, in the British context, overall policy coordination of the three phases of peacemaking were to be given to DfID, then it should be renamed the Department for International Development and Stabilisation and its resource allocation re-balanced accordingly.

Within present-day government structures, however, logic would appear to lie more in favour of giving the overarching responsibility for this area of public policy to the MFA or equivalent, rather than to a development ministry. The British Foreign Office (FCO) supported me magnificently in vital practical ways during my mandate in Bosnia and for this I am most grateful. It is not, however, I think unfair to say that the FCO has until recently had a reputation for seeing its role more as a policy maker and can sometimes give the impression that it rather disdains implementation – a luxury not afforded to many other government departments. Equally, there is much more glamour attached to a minister who has directed and won a war than there is to one who has prevented a conflict in a country no one has heard of, or cleaned up after the fighting has ended. The FCO may also currently lack the requisite project management skills to design and implement reform and capability-building programmes in other countries. So, if it were to take on this task, it would have to realise that it was not creating another piece of exclusive Foreign Office territory, but acting purely as the leader of a cross-agency process which would bring in skills from outside where necessary. In the end the arguments between an MFA or development ministry lead are rather finely balanced and deciding between the two may depend on subjective factors such as where the right experience and culture lie.

But avoiding getting our fingers repeatedly burnt in these kinds of operations will depend on more than the restructuring of government. We also need to make sure that the wealth of expertise which has been accumulated by practitioners in the field is preserved, codified and passed on to future practitioners, so that we do not have to go on and on re-inventing the wheel with every new intervention. There is, therefore, a powerful case for the establishment of a school for conflict prevention, armed intervention and post-conflict reconstruction, which could act as a kind of high-level staff college to learn lessons, propose changes to government and develop and pass on expertise to senior service officers, civil servants and politicians. One of its tasks should be the development of curricular modules to be used in the training of all junior and middle-ranking leaders in the civil and armed services, since high-quality leadership in these enterprises is as crucial at the lower as at the higher levels. This teaching should have an international dimension too, given that one of the tasks is to spread best practice and raise capacity, not just in the developed world, but in other armed forces and government practitioners worldwide. And incidentally, if such an 'international' college were to be established, where better than in Britain, where we have more expertise in this field than any other country?

Better People

Next, we have to find a way to raise the quality of those whom governments send out to take part in post-conflict reconstruction missions. These can range from police officers in CIVPOL and training missions, to civil servants constructing a whole new civil service, to legal experts rewriting laws and setting up constitutions, to customs officers reforming customs services, to auditors, to judges and prosecutors, to water engineers. Although some really high quality people have found their way to key jobs in recent peacekeeping and reconstruction missions, it remains the case that the initial instinct of those who nominate secondees from organisations is to send not their best, but those they wish to get rid of for a few months. In consequence, the quality of those sent out to these international missions often falls very far short of what is required, damaging not just the process, but also the level of domestic trust in the whole international intervention. There is a particular problem here in respect of police secondees. Many of Britain's policemen seconded to police missions abroad have been first class. But this is not always the case. In Iraq the US has dubbed 2006 as 'the year of the police', reflecting the fact that, up to then, the Iraqi police have been inappropriately trained by the army, or by unfit retired police officers nicknamed 'the pie boys' by the British army because of the beer bellies protruding from their polo shirts. The problem lies in our own police and Whitehall structures – chief constables are, perfectly naturally, under pressure for delivery of their domestic performance targets in their own constabulary areas and not what happens in Bosnia, Basra or Baghdad. So they have no incentive to send their best people on secondment. Similarly, the Home Office, under huge pressure to improve its performance at home, is not going to spend very much time, effort, or resources on improving the capabilities of its counterparts abroad. And yet almost nothing would reduce the level of organised crime in our inner cities more quickly than improving the capacities of local police to take on the organised criminal structures in their country of origin abroad – like in the Balkans.

The fact is that secondees to missions in foreign countries need to be the best, not the worst. In practice, these missions almost always require relatively junior people to take on responsibilities far beyond those they would have borne in their parent organisations, so providing them with unique responsibility and experience which will greatly benefit their ability to do their jobs on return to their home departments. And there is no shortage of people of the right calibre and motivation. There are young diplomats in the Foreign Office who want to implement reform rather than write elegant reports and bright majors in the military who would rather prevent conflict than take part in it. But their corporate cultures have not caught up with global change and too many bright people are still allocated to the glamour posts in Europe and North America, rather than to the places that are least understood but will most affect our well-being. Service in one of these missions should not be given to those from the bottom, but should instead be viewed as a career enhancer for high-flyers. This will require a change in culture, which only governments can drive by making it clear that secondment to a peace intervention mission should be regarded as something for the best of candidates not the worst and that success on one of these missions should become a qualification for promotion.

Better Communications

Intervening governments also need to be rather more honest when it comes to explaining the realities of intervention to their publics. When intervening governments pretend to their people that the exercise they are embarking on 'will be over in a year or so' they either don't understand or are trying deliberately to deceive. Reconstructing a country takes a long time, sustained will and huge resources. Creating the expectation of a quick fix and a fast exit diminishes the chances of success because it gives the destructive forces of the country concerned an incentive to 'sit out' the interveners. It also provides a reason for public opinion in the intervening country to press for an early exit. Having been a politician, I know the difficulty of telling the public that once we are in, we will have to stay until the job is done. But it has to be done if the aim is success in the first intervention, rather than returning a second time to finish the job. Given the central importance of getting key messages across to the public domestically, internationally and in the country in which the intervention is taking place, there is even a case for institutionalising a capacity to do this in, say, a Conflict Communications Unit within the Cabinet Office's Overseas and Defence Secretariat.

International Structures

So far this chapter has concentrated on what improvements can be made to national structures in order to give them a greater chance of success in peacemaking and post-conflict reconstruction. But the essence of these operations is that they must be international in character and, as a rough rule of thumb, the more international they are, the greater their chances of success. So we need to think about what improvements can be made to international structures as well.

There are many players on the international stage working in this field, including the OSCE, the International Financial Institutions (IFIs), a number of NGOs and some new regional groupings that are becoming increasingly involved (such as the African Union). It is impossible to discuss all of these in detail here, so I will deal only with the three chief international organisations currently engaged in major peacemaking or reconstruction efforts: the United Nations, the

European Union and NATO. Each of these has their particular strengths and weaknesses in this field. And this is useful, since it enables them to complement each other and to give a degree of flexibility and a range of choices when it comes to apportioning tasks.

The UN, whose Security Council is smaller than the equivalent structures in NATO and the EU, has the most simple decision-making processes and command and control arrangements. Once the Security Council takes a decision, full control of the operation passes to the Secretary General and Troop Contributing Countries (TCCs) have only a minimal further operational voice in their actions on the ground.* The UN also has a unified civil and military command structure with clear civilian primacy and provides the best context for the widest possible burden sharing. Indeed, the burdens of troop contribution in UN operations, which used to fall mostly on Western nations, now fall chiefly on developing ones† – of the 58,000 UN troops deployed around the world in 2005, just eleven were from the US, thirteen were German, seven were Belgian and two were Dutch.[6] When it comes to deploying troops, the UN is also by far cheapest of the three. The annual cost of the entire UN force currently deployed worldwide is less than the price the US pays for its troops in Iraq in a single month. UN operations also have the advantage of being legitimised by the UNSCR process[7] and are therefore able to attract a wider coalition of international support.

But the UN suffers from some sharp disadvantages too. It is constantly subject to the veto process of the Security Council and can easily become a prisoner to the current political battles going on in the world (as in the Cold War or, more recently, the East/West divide in global affairs). The UN Security Council, moreover, was set up as a law-making and negotiating body – not as a manager of executive action. The result is that, having authorised a peacekeeping or peacemaking operation, it has a depressing tendency to lose interest in it rather quickly. The UNSC's ability to think ahead and spot conflicts before they happen is also very limited. Issues tend

---

* TCCs have regular meetings with UNDPKO and the UNSC – but they tend not to go into too much detail on operational matters.
† One of the reasons for this is because many poorer nations benefit financially from contributing troops and most of the richer ones no longer trust theirs under UN command.

to arrive on their agenda only after the fighting has started. The UN also suffers critically from a lack of the effective command, control, communications, intelligence and logistics structures which are necessary for the prosecution of a conflict in difficult circumstances.[8] There is a strong case for further strengthening UNDPKO's capacity to provide a proper headquarters capable of providing better management of operations in the field which are permissive in nature. But the UN will always remain weak in comparison to the professional armies of its most powerful member states or military alliances like NATO, when it comes to either an opposed intervention or an in-conflict reconstruction in the face of a continuing insurgency. These factors also limit the size of the troop deployments which the UN can handle in a sustained operation – it is generally accepted that the UN's maximum capacity force on the ground is around 20,000, or a reinforced division.[9]

NATO, on the other hand, has a high capacity to cope with these more difficult interventions and can deploy large-scale forces very quickly (60,000 in the dead of winter in Bosnia in a matter of weeks in 1995). Its decision-making procedures also tend to be less contaminated by global politics (though they can be severely influenced by Euro-Atlantic ones). NATO can take on any force globally and is therefore well equipped to deal with an opposed entry or an in-conflict reconstruction. But NATO troops are very expensive and subject to extreme overstretch at the moment. The Alliance can also find it more difficult to legitimise its operations through the UN process and consequently to attract the support of a wider group of nations. NATO also gives its member nations much greater influence over the operational decisions its commanders take at its Brussels headquarters and in the field – as evidenced by the number of 'red card' caveats which individual nations attach to the use of their troops in operations in Afghanistan and elsewhere. Finally, NATO, being an exclusively military organisation, does not have the easy access to the wider array of civilian assets needed for the reconstruction phase which both the UN and the EU enjoy.

The EU decision-making process, like that of NATO, is also consensus-based. But its structures are lighter and it is sometimes able to move faster to respond to events. Its soldiers are nearly as militarily capable as NATO's, but they are also nearly as expensive and frequently suffer from equivalent difficulties with overstretch and caveats imposed by contributing nations or (more often) their parliaments. The EU's advantage lies in its political influence, especially in the European theatre and (but less so) in the Middle East, where it has the potential to act as an honest broker more effectively than either the US or NATO. The EU's other great strength is in its ability to deploy fully integrated, high-capacity civilian expertise in the reconstruction phase. In this it is superior to both the UN and NATO. Bosnia provides a good example of this, with its wide range of EU assets, including the 6,000 troops of EUFOR, a heavyweight EU Police Mission, a European Union Special Representative and a European Commission Mission whose access to substantial funds through the CARDS programme* enables it to deal with issues as wide ranging as customs reform and the establishment of a VAT structure.

There are improvements that can be made to all three of these structures, which together carry the main burden of peacemaking and reconstruction around the world. But the most important improvement is that all three have to work more closely together. The greatest deficiency in all of them is that they are not yet fully institutionally capable of docking with each other in the closely coordinated manner necessary for success.

Improving the UN

The trend, post Iraq, has been to pass more to the UN and, as with UNIFIL in Lebanon, ask them to get involved in less permissive environments. There has, however, been neither a commensurate increase in resources, nor the establishment of a proper process for analysing whether the UN, or some alternative international actor (for example a coalition of the willing or regional grouping) would better deliver what is needed. Despite the increase of the UN's activity in this field, the organisation still has no formal mechanism for estimating risk, measuring their missions' progress, or deciding when it is safe to close a mission and hand over to the domestic authorities when the task is finished.

Nevertheless, the UN, perhaps more than the other two

---

* The CARDS (Community Assistance for Reconstruction, Development and Stabilisation) programme is the EU's €6.8 billion programme connected to stabilisation of the Western Balkan countries.

organisations mentioned here, has taken important strides in this area recently. In December 2005, the UN General Assembly and the UN Security Council established the Peace-Building Commission (PBC), together with its subsidiary organisations, the Peace-Building Support Office and the Peace-Building Fund. The PBC has a governing organisation committee of thirty-one members, seven of whom come from the UNSC (including the five permanent members), and the remainder are elected on a geographically distributed basis from other members of the General Assembly. Its work will be complemented by the work of the UN's Systems Wide Coherence Panel, whose aim is to improve the operation and coordination of all UN agencies in a particular country.

The PBC has not yet started its full range of work. But its role is defined as to advise and propose strategies, focus on reconstruction and provide recommendations on closer co-ordination between actors within and outside the UN. What is lacking here is an agreed definition of peacebuilding or any agreement as to how the PBC will relate to ongoing operations in the field, how it will mobilise resources and how it will ensure accountability of the actors involved. The creation of the PBC presents the UN with both dangers and an opportunity. The first danger is that the PBC proliferates a whole new series of organisations to deal with peacemaking and reconstruction and thus undermines or duplicates work already going on, both within the UN and in its member states. The second danger, given the UN's capacity for internal turf wars, is that the PBC gets itself into a conflictual relationship with UNDPKO and the Department of Political Affairs (DPA).

The opportunity which the creation of the PBC offers is to be a coordinator alongside the many national and international players already in the field in a way which enhances their output by ensuring better cohesion between them. The UN Office of Coordination of Humanitarian Affairs (OCHA), set up in the late 1990s to coordinate emergency aid delivery, is a model to be followed here. The PBC could perform the same function for peacemaking and conflict resolution. The High-Level Panel on whose recommendation the PBC was founded has recently produced a second report, entitled 'Delivering as One'[10] which makes recommendations on better coordination between UN bodies in the fields of development, humanitarian assistance and the environment. What is needed is a similar set of recommendations on how to achieve better cohesion in peacemaking and post-conflict reconstruction, which places the PBC at the centre of this effort.

The PBC should therefore avoid replicating existing multilateral and bilateral structures in the field of peacemaking and concentrate instead on integrating these better and filling in the spaces where capacity should be, but isn't. Two such areas are of particular note. The first is in encouraging, assisting and enabling the growth of regional capacity for peacemaking and reconstruction − especially in Africa, where the African Union is making real efforts to improve its abilities in this area. There is a lot of work to be done here, including raising the professionalism of troops to be used in these operations and creating capacity in the civilian aspects of reconstruction.

One other crucial role that the PBC could perform would be to provide the context in which the 'end state', which comprises the joint aim of the international community and the country involved, can be determined. The January 2006 'Afghanistan Compact'[11] drawn up between the UN, the Afghan government and the international community is an example to be built on.

Finally, the PBC should be a strategic forum for educating the international community, especially when it comes to the importance of drawing up a high-quality integrated plan, the necessity for adequate 'through life' funding for reconstruction missions, the ability to stay for the long haul and the need to build international coalitions to support individual countries in danger of failure.[12]

There is one further role which the UN can fulfil in peacemaking better than anyone else − facilitating the process of peacemaking through its specialist organisations, such as the United Nations High Commissioner for Refugees (UNHCR), the United Nations Development Programme (UNDP), the newly formed Office of the High Commissioner for Human Rights (OHCHR), and others. These organisations perform a vital role in almost all peacemaking missions, whoever is leading them. There is a case for expanding this facilitation role of the UN, either through the creation of new specialist organisations or − more likely − through widening the remit of those that already exist. Three particular cases spring to mind.

The first is the maintenance of a register of expert peacemaking practitioners in the field who can be called on to assist in the

make-up of peacemaking missions.[13] Next, there is the question of
how international mission heads are appointed. Since the UN is
ultimately the body which either appoints or ratifies the appointment of the international mission heads, the UN Security
Council should institute without delay, an open, transparent, merit-
based system for choosing mission heads, in which the country that
is the subject of the intervention should be treated in a courteous
manner and be able to have its voice heard, even if only informally.

The third is a far larger task that could either be done through an
organisation such as UNDP, or perhaps through the World Bank. It
concerns the question of foreign remittances sent by refugees back
to their home country. Although individual sums sent back home
in this way are relatively small (the average seems to be about
300 Euros), the total is enormous. A recent World Bank Report[14]
estimated that global remittances in 1995 were around 48.5 billion
Euros. By 2005, this figure had nearly tripled to 123.2 billion Euros.
Taking the single case of remittances sent home by Serbs in Germany, these amount to some 1.85 billion Euros per year, equivalent
to 12 per cent of Serbia's GDP, or 65 per cent of the total annual
exports from the country, or nearly twice the total of foreign direct
investment into Serbia (just over 1 billion Euros). Around 50 per
cent of these remittances are believed to be sent home by informal
means – that is carried personally, given to bus drivers or sent with a
friend. The primary reason for this very high percentage is said to be
the extortionate transaction costs charged by banks and remittance
organisations and lack of trust in the banking system. Studies of
remittance patterns in other countries have shown similar patterns
and percentages.[15]

Competition among formal organisations dealing with remittances is by no means strong, due to the overwhelming domination
of Western Union, whose appeal to hard-pressed families waiting
for their money to arrive from a relative abroad lies in the fact that
they have by far the most extensive network of offices worldwide
and can transfer money to any of them in fifteen minutes. The sight
of people queuing outside the Western Union office, mobile phone in
hand asking their relative abroad if the money has been sent yet, was
a very common sight in Bosnia and in almost every country under
reconstruction.

However, Western Union charges heftily for its services – for a typical sum of 300 Euros the charge is around 26 Euros or 8.7 per cent. Add to this the currency exchange charge and bank charges and the cost of remittances through formal means can amount to as much as 10 per cent of the sum transferred. This is big money indeed. If we use very rough figures and assume that 50 per cent of the total of 123.2 billion Euros of remittances transferred globally every year is sent informally, then the remaining sum transferred through organisations like Western Union and the banks amounts to some 61.6 billion Euros. Taking an average transaction charge of 10 per cent, that amounts to some 6 billion Euros every year lost in transaction charges to the poorest families and to development in some of the poorest countries.

Unfortunately, the loss to post-conflict reconstruction in some countries is not measured solely in monetary terms. The World Bank report quoted above estimates that there is a marked development loss where money is transferred informally and in liquid form, compared with transferring it through bank deposits. As the report puts it:

> The extensive use of informal channels to send money reduces the developmental impact of remittances in Serbia, because remittances through informal means do not have the same multiplier effect as bank deposits. If more remittances were received in Serbia through banks or other financial institutions, the Serbian financial system would be deeper, thus increasing the availability of resources to finance economic activities in Serbia. Moreover, the use of financial institutions to remit money would broaden the access of recipient households in Serbia to more financial services that would help them improve their living standards. As the experience of other developing countries illustrate, a larger availability of financial products specifically designed for migrants and remittance-receiving households – such as consumer loans, mortgages, life and non-life insurance, and so forth – would help maximise the developmental impact of remittances in Serbia.

There could be a real role for the UN here in overseeing these transactions, which affect some of the most vulnerable people in the world. Some have suggested the setting up of a UN Bank of Remittances, but that would be a huge undertaking. Better perhaps to use the facilities of the UN, or one of its specialised agencies, to create a set of standards, accredited systems, proper competition and transparent charges, in return for UN encouragement to refugees to use the deposit systems offered by a global network of accredited existing banks prepared to take on this huge business.

Improving NATO

NATO, the UN's partner in Afghanistan, also needs to raise its game, as a recent report on the Alliance's operations there pointed out.[16] This identified that NATO, although fully skilled in military matters, needs to ensure that it also has clear political goals for its operations and that its military missions should be more clearly defined. As the report puts it, NATO will *'have to improve its own "political map" as its missions are in essence an element of state building.'*

NATO's funding mechanisms also undermine its effectiveness in this area. At present NATO funds the operations of the NATO Response Force (NRF), on a 'costs fall where they will' basis. This means that nations which contribute to the NRF bear the cost and those that don't, don't. This naturally acts as a disincentive both to contributing nations and to follow-on forces. The effect is to undermine one of the key strategic purposes of the Alliance. NATO is a burden-sharing organisation and there is no logic why this should not apply to the funding of its NRF intervention operations as well. NATO also suffers from the fact that some of its member states have 'parliamentary armies' – that is, armies whose deployment and actions when deployed (including 'red card' caveats) are the subject of parliamentary agreement. To overcome the problems this can create (see Chapter 8 on national caveats) NATO needs much closer relations with its parliamentary assemblies than it currently has.

NATO's role has fundamentally changed in recent years. From a purely European war-fighting alliance, it has become a major peacemaking and reconstruction enabling force, worldwide. It has made great strides in altering both its structures and its ethos to account for this change – but there is further still to go.

Improving the EU

One of the areas where this will apply is in NATO's relationship with the EU which, despite progress over recent years, still remains uneven and incomplete. One of the reasons for this is that no one knows who is in charge of the EU when it comes to its peacemaking and post-conflict reconstruction efforts. As EU Special Representative in Bosnia, I was responsible to the EU's Council and its boss, Javier Solana. But the EU had a second heavyweight player in Bosnia – the Commission. No one knew which of the two of us spoke for Europe – because we both did. The proposed EU Constitution would have resolved this issue in favour of the Council – but since the Constitution did not get past the French and Dutch referendums the issue remains open. In Macedonia this lacuna was filled by a process called 'double hatting' in which the EU's Special Representative is also the head of the Commission's mission in the country. This should be the norm for all future EU peacemaking and reconstruction missions.

The EU could also afford to be much more muscular in the application of conditionality for the huge sums of aid it hands out. The United States does this far better (see Chapter 6 on 'tough love').[17] Its aid is less than that of the EU in, for instance, the Balkans, but it is often able to lever more reform than Europe for what it dispenses, because the US is much more straightforward about the conditions it attaches to its giving.

The other improvements that need to be made to EU structures and policies in order to increase its ability to conduct these kinds of operation are familiar enough. A recent study, 'Civilian Crisis Management: The EU Way',[18] listed these as the need for funding and resources to match the EU's enlarged ambitions in this field; a tendency to be behind events rather than ahead of them; lack of political will; closer coordination, especially between the civil and military elements; clearer strategies and better planning; over-ambitious targets for individual missions; lack of manpower; better coordination with other international players; strengthening communications strategies, and above all greater policy coherence within the EU's activities.

The Private Sector

There is a final set of stakeholders who are, or should be, part of the multi-disciplinary mix of peacemaking and reconstruction – the private sector. The involvement of the private sector in this arena can be divided into two categories – those actively engaged in providing 'lethal' services in the security (chiefly personal protection) sector and those involved in providing expertise in a discrete area of peacemaking and post-conflict state reconstruction.

As far as this latter category is concerned, provided there is a proper transparent contracting process, clear aims and good oversight, I can see no objection to and many advantages in the involvement of the private sector. There has been a rash of private diplomacy companies springing up in recent years and many have proved that, when it comes to preventative diplomacy, they can reach places governments cannot easily get to, for instance by enabling governments to have a dialogue at one remove with a 'terrorist' group with whom they could not formally be seen to be talking to. A number of other private sector companies are assembling teams of people with past expertise which enable them to offer subcontracted services in defined areas of post-conflict reconstruction, such as legal affairs, the security sector, press and information operations, economic reform etc. It is often the case that these providers can be cheaper, swifter of foot and lighter in footprint than government departments or in-country international bureaucracies. There is real potential, therefore, for both sides in sensible use of emerging private sector provision of this sort and it is in the interests of governments to encourage the growth of this sector which can provide choices and flexibility that governments cannot offer.

When it comes to private security companies (PSCs), however, the market place is already very developed indeed and urgently needs, not encouragement, but regulation. PSCs are now involved in the provision of 'lethal' services ranging from close protection to interrogation, landmine clearance, protection of private sector installations (such as oil terminals), and security work for NGOs. It has been estimated that there are some 20,000 PSC employees operating in this sector in Iraq alone, making the PSC contingent the second largest contributor, after the United States, to coalition forces in that country.[19] As one recent report put it: *'the scale of private involvement on today's battlefields has not been seen since mercenaries disappeared from state armies in the nineteenth century'*.[20] *Business Week* estimated the value of the services provided by PSCs in Iraq and Afghanistan in 2006 at $104 million (excluding weapons and research and development).[21] The fact is that the number of PSC companies providing 'lethal' services has grown unchecked in a climate that is almost completely unregulated. At the time of the prisoner abuse scandal, two PSC companies, CACI and Titan, provided military interrogators in Abu Ghraib prison, 35 per cent of whom lacked any formal military training. Although the US military responded to the scandal with formal investigations and courts martial for military personnel, no similar mechanism existed for bringing private contractors to account and none has been either investigated or prosecuted.[22] In Bosnia in the late 1990s Dyncorp, which provides protection services to senior US diplomats in the country, was involved in a scandal in which its employees were engaged in a prostitution ring. Although the employees were dismissed, a loophole in US law meant that they were never held to account for their actions.[23] There is also strong cause for concern about the quality of some PSC employees. One company operating in Iraq, Armor Group, employed a former Royal Marine who had previously been jailed on ten counts of soliciting murder.[24]

PSC providers of 'lethal' services in this sector operate at present in what is effectively a regulatory vacuum. Many of the more responsible PSC providers recognise that this cannot continue and that there is now an urgent need to provide proper regulation for this sector before more damage is done both to international efforts in post-conflict reconstruction and to the security industry itself. This is a task which governments and the international community cannot afford to ignore any longer.[25]

Humanitarian Raiding

If the United States had pulled out of Iraq immediately after Saddam's statue had fallen and left the Iraqis to rebuild their own state, it is arguable that we might now be marking Iraq as a successful intervention whose aims were fulfilled. In any event it is difficult to imagine that the situation would be worse than it is

today. But, of course, this would not have met the US's true
strategic goals for this action, which turned out to be much more
ambitious than just regime change, encompassing as they did the
initiation of a democratic revolution in the Middle East, probably
with a view to assuring the oil supplies in which the region is so rich.
Iraq may well be noted by history as a particularly painful example
of the hubris which attends over-ambitious aims; when it comes to
intervention and post-conflict stabilisation I suspect that, in the
post-Iraq world, enthusiasm for intervening will be significantly
diminished, especially if this means taking on the duties, cost, pain
and responsibilities of governance until a state is fully reconstructed.
Paradoxically, it has not recently been war-fighting that has carried
the risk, but building the peace afterwards.

In addition, new thinking in this area is now tending to see the
international community's role in the reconstruction phase to be
that of enabler, rather than doer, leaving the domestic authorities to
carry much more of the burden of reconstruction, with their international partners acting only as a last resort if things go really bad
(for example, if there is a threat of a return to conflict).

Post-Iraq sentiment and modern thinking on diminishing the role
of the internationals and increasing the responsibilities of domestic
forces may well now come together and, in some places at least,
offer the opportunity to conduct what General Rupert Smith has
called a 'humanitarian raid' by intervening solely to remove a rogue
regime, or defeat forces which are causing a failing state to fail,
without following on by getting actively enmeshed in the subsequent
reconstruction effort. I am strongly in favour of greater involvement
by the domestic authorities in setting their own targets and carrying
much more of the burden of decision-making in the reconstruction
phase. But I am doubtful that there will be many circumstances in
which, following an armed intervention, the international community can just withdraw and leave everything to the domestic
authorities.

Nevertheless, 'humanitarian raids' certainly merit further con-
sideration as an alternative option for the international community
to consider.

A Different Mindset

Institutional changes, though necessary, are not going to be sufficient if we want to raise our strike rate of success in peacemaking and peacekeeping. We have to change our mindset, too. Currently this whole area is perceived to be one in which 'hard power' (that is the power of the military and the security services) dominates over 'soft power' (broadly speaking diplomacy, development and governance). The peacemaking aspects of foreign policy are viewed in Western capitals as strictly a contact sport in which the military predominates. In the conflict phase the military do have a natural ascendancy. But in the other two phases, prevention and post-conflict reconstruction, success depends not on military power but on mobilising consent in both the country subject to the action and in the wider world community. This is why political, not military, considerations should predominate in these phases, in which it is the instruments of 'soft power' that will have the most crucial effect.

It is not my intention in this book to cover in detail the current 'war on terror', except insofar as it illustrates a point. The way we are conducting this struggle illustrates the mindset we currently have towards these matters very graphically. As we have discussed earlier, the strength of Al Qaeda lies in its potency as an idea, not in its military strength. It and its sister organisations are engaged in a battle, not just with the West, but also for the soul of Islam. There are many, many in Islam (including I suspect the majority of ordinary Muslims) who do not wish to see their great, tolerant, civilising religion captured by the forces of fanaticism, any more than we in the past wanted our religious fanatics to take over Christianity. And yet Western leaders persist in their language and actions to portray this as a worldwide struggle for 'our Western values', inferentially against the values of Islam and the East. This is, apart from everything else, a historically illiterate notion. It was Islam and the Arab universities (especially in Baghdad) that absorbed the very Hellenic thought which we regard as the foundation stone of 'European values' into Islam, while Europe was still sunk in the barbarism of the Dark Ages. And it was Islam's great universities that preserved these crucial texts for Europe to rediscover at the start of the Renaissance. But it is also a stupid strategy if we want to win the battle against terror, for it wrongly views the fractured, highly specific structures of modern terror as a single organisation with a central guiding intelligence whose elements were all engaged in the conduct of a coordinated, global strategic military campaign. It ignores the internal fissures in Islam instead of using them and it reinforces the terrorist view of a Manichean struggle between East and West, by confirming that that is the way we see it, too.

In fact we are not talking about 'Western values' here, but about 'fundamental values' that are common to both religions. We are not engaged in 'clash of civilisations', but a campaign *for* civilisation – a struggle for the values of tolerance and humanity that lie at the heart of all the great religions – all civilisations – against a new medievalism, whose proposals are those of darkness and ignorance (and whose followers, incidentally, are not just to be found among the religions to our East). If we are to win this battle, the language we use is going to be as important as the effectiveness of our military and security structures. Our enemies are not 'Islamic terrorists', but terrorists who happen to be Muslims. Our key friends are not our Western Allies, but that great majority in Islam who share our values and who need our help to win the struggle to prevent their religion being captured by these forces of darkness. Our battlefield is not just the deserts of Iraq and the mountains of Afghanistan. It is also the multifarious and often invisible networks of global communications. Without access to satellite broadcasting, the internet and international media, Bin Laden is just a crazy man in a cave. These viral structures are his battleground and we need to make them ours too.

Our problem is that we have chosen the wrong mindset, the wrong battlefield, the wrong weapons and the wrong strategies to win this campaign. We have chosen to fight an idea, primarily with force. We seek to control territory; they seek to capture minds. We have presumed that predominant force gives us the opportunity to impose our systems on others, when the only justification for the use of force is to assert justice and establish freedom, so that people can have the chance to choose their systems for themselves. We have embarked on a battle with a self-declared global jihad by seeking to assert a self-declared global hegemony – the hegemony of Western models – as though there were no others. We have chosen language and means which unite the moderates in Islam with the fanatics, when we should be uniting *with* the moderates in Islam against a common enemy. We have adopted methods, or connived at their adoption, which undermine the moral force of our ideas and strengthen the prejudices propagandised by our opponents. And so, in a battle of concepts, we have strengthened the concepts of our enemies and weakened our own; we have elected to fight on a battlefield of their choosing, where they are strongest and we are weakest.

Force has a part to play in this struggle – regrettably it nearly always does. But this is, at its heart, a battle of ideas and values, and unless we realise that and can win on that agenda, then no amount of force can deliver victory. And so far, we are not winning that battle. In those regions of the world where this struggle is fiercest, civilisation is losing and medievalism is winning. Modern war is fought among the people – and we are losing their support. We have to find a new way of thinking if we are to reverse this situation and give ourselves a better chance of peacebuilding in future.

Summary

The expeditionary approach to peacemaking and peacekeeping, with its emphasis on military power, has not succeeded. There is a growing realisation that this is an activity in which politics and diplomacy should have primacy, and that governments have to organise themselves differently if they are to peacemake more effectively. But they have to go further than simply creating a collection of little bureaucracies with national flags stuck on them to solve the problem. In this area, if no other, the joined-up 'seamless garment' approach is crucial, both internally and externally. This means a transformation and integration of the entire national security apparatus. In the British system, for example, it means beefing up the centre of government with a joined-up committee structure and a better-staffed Overseas and Defence Secretariat guided by a regularly updated National Engagement Strategy. In due course, it may also be necessary to consider a National Engagement Act to manage relations between the armada of departments and agencies involved in conflict and post-conflict reconstruction.

It also means matching our most talented people to the threats we face. Rather than developing diplomats, soldiers, or aid workers – or trying to teach each cadre about the other – we need to go further and develop civil servants who are equally at home in all government departments.

Britain has been rather successful in countering Islamic terrorism because the relevant agencies have rapidly refocused their efforts after 9/11, have developed ways of working together and have focused on cooperating with partner agencies in a small number of important source and transit countries for terrorism. But government departments that deal with stabilisation and reconstruction and the longer-term threats that instability spawns, of uncontrolled immigration, disease, energy security and international crime, have yet to make the same changes and remain mostly focused on out-of-date issues. The Foreign Office have the political analysis and global reach to coordinate and manage the effort, British armed forces have unrivalled expertise in managing non-conventional threats, DfID have the long-term perspective to effect real change and the British police and judiciary are respected worldwide. But the Whitehall central machinery has not set proper priorities or encouraged them to work together. We should not wait to burn our fingers again before we ask them to change.

The world is also in the process of creating new institutions or adapting old ones to address the need to peacemake more successfully. The three key players in this area, the UN, NATO and the EU, each have individual strengths to bring to the table. Each can also, however, improve their individual operations. But the key task is to ensure that these three and the other new organisations developing expertise in this area (such as the African Union) are able to work together more closely, operate more cohesively and change their mindset so as to recognise that this is an area governed primarily by politics, not the military, where the efficient deployment of 'hard power' is only half the story and unlikely to succeed, unless it is also matched with the effective use of 'soft power'

Conclusion

Nunc lento sonitu dicunt, morieris.
Now this bell tolling softly for another, says to me, Thou must die.

Perchance he for whom this bell tolls may be so ill as that he knows not it tolls for him; and perchance I may think myself so much better than I am, as that they who are about me and see my state may have caused it to toll for me, and I know not that . . . all mankind is of one author and is one volume; when one man dies, one chapter is not torn out of the book, but translated into a better language; and every chapter must be so translated . . . As therefore the bell that rings a sermon calls not upon the preacher only, but upon the congregation to come, so this bell calls us all; . . . The bell doth toll for him that thinks it doth; . . . No man is an island, entire of itself; every man is a piece of the continent, a part of the main. If a clod be washed away by the sea, Europe is the less, as well as if promontory were, as well as if a manor of thy friend's or of thine own were. Any man's death diminishes me, because I am involved in mankind; and therefore never send to know for whom the bell tolls; it tolls for thee.   JOHN DONNE 'Meditation XVII' 1624

John Donne's great precept may have been a moral instruction for his times. But it turns out to be a practical code of survival for ours. Our shrinking world has meant that now, literally as well as morally and metaphorically, no man is an island and every man's death diminishes us. The revelation of 9/11 was that our peace, too, will depend on the extent that we are willing and able to work together to prevent conflict or reconstruct peace in other parts of the world.

Sometimes it is our own greed, stupidity or short-sightedness that are the root causes of conflict. Sometimes it is the rising tide of nationalism, or the new radicals who feed on past injustices and the present mood of distrust, suspicion and ignorance. Whatever the cause, we live in turbulent and instable times and, as the world moves deeper and deeper into the era of resource scarcity and massive shifts in the tectonic plates of power, this mix is only likely to get more potent and more dangerous. At the present there are some seventy-four conflicts in progress around the world, the over-whelming majority of which have occurred inside states or between ethnicities.[1] Some believe that this tells us that the era of inter-state war is over – that these 'little' brush-fire, intra-state wars of recent years are the only wars there will be in the future – and that the age of great wars is passed. I am not one of those – partly because there is so much dry tinder lying around and far too many firebrands; partly because inter-state competition, especially in the developing world, is not diminishing, rather it is increasing. And partly because the best structures for fighting wars, the most powerful ideologies for driving wars and the most destructive weapons for using in wars still remain in the hands of nation states.

But all major conflicts are preceded by a period of instability. Indeed, one way to look at the world's present 'little' wars is that they are the 'pre-shocks' which always accompany major shifts in the established order. If we can control these better, by preventing them where we can, intervening more wisely where we have to and then reconstructing peace more successfully afterwards, we may make it easier to avoid a wider conflict.

We have shown that we are anything but good at this. Though the number of interventions has been rising since the end of the cold war, our strike rate of success is little better than it was. We seem condemned to making and remaking even the mistakes we know are mistakes, over and over again. The Iraq experience – and to an extent that of Afghanistan too – represents the triumph of hubris and amnesia over common sense. And the consequence is that, in both those countries, we are now in grave danger of snatching a peacemaking defeat from of the jaws of a military victory.

But there is a deeper reason for our failures. The 'gun boat diplomacy' approach to peacemaking isn't working. And I doubt that, following Iraq and Afghanistan, Western leaders will be quite so enthusiastic, their domestic populations quite so supportive, or the wider international community quite so biddable in providing legitimacy for these adventures in the future. If they were to lead to a greater understanding of the importance of multilateralism, rather than unilateralism in these affairs, that would be healthy. But if they were to lead to the end of all interventions, that would be a tragedy, because we are going to need more of this, not less, in an increasingly globalised and interdependent world. And it would be unnecessary, too – the fact that we have got it wrong so often should not blind us to the fact that there is a way of doing it right. The things that have to be done to increase the chances of success – and things that should not be done because they can lead to failure – are not exactly rocket science and they are definitely not new. If only we could remember them long enough to apply them.

Avoid the conflict if you can – it will be much cheaper that way. But if conflict cannot be avoided, remember that it is not over when the fighting is finished. In fact the tricky bit is probably only then just beginning. So, spend at least as much time and effort planning the peace as you do in preparing for the war that precedes it; make sure your plan is based on a proper knowledge of the country, especially its political dynamics, and leave your ideologies and prejudices at home. It is a mistake to try to fashion someone else's country in your own image; leave space for them to reconstruct the country they want, not the one you want for them. Remember that you don't get a second chance to make a first impression; so don't lose the 'golden hour' after the fighting is over – remember, too, that an army of liberation has a very short half-life before it risks becoming an army of occupation. Dominate the security space from the start; then concentrate first on the rule of law; make economic regeneration an early priority; remember the importance of articulating an 'end state' which can win and maintain local support; but leave elections as late as you decently can. When rebuilding institutions, be sensitive to local traditions and customs. Understand the importance to the international community effort of coordination, cohesion and speaking with a single voice. And then at the end, do not wait until everything is as it would be in your country, but leave when the peace is sustainable.

Another key to doing it better is foresight, which is the mother of prevention. There is no reason why the need to intervene should always take us by surprise. Of the fourteen case studies listed in Chapter 2, only two (the initial the war in Croatia and Afghanistan after 9/11) could not be said to have been predictable months, if not years, earlier. It is possible that, if the international community had, as in Macedonia, put as much effort into prevention as they did into military intervention, some could have been avoided altogether.

But this new approach will also require a new way of thinking and new kinds of national and international architecture to make it work. Cohesion here is the key. Success can come only from a joined-up, cross-agency approach which extends from the bottom to the top, is holistic in its application, international in character and views the continuum of peacemaking as a 'seamless garment' stretching from prevention right through to the final exit of the interveners when a sustainable peace has been reconstructed. Success, however, needs more than the right structures, good intentions and a warm desire to do something to help. International intervention is a very blunt instrument, whose outcomes are not always predictable.

So, intervention is not for the faint-hearted – or the easily bored. It needs steely toughness and strategic patience in equal measure – and strategic patience requires strategic vision. It also requires a willingness to commit a lot of troops at the start, a capacity to provide sustained international support to the end and an ability to endure a time frame that is measured in decades, not years. And the only reward for success, if it can be achieved, is that all that expenditure will be less than the cost of the war that was avoided, or the price of chaos which would have ensued if the international community had stayed at home. Meanwhile, leaving early, or doing it badly, may end up making things not better but worse.

What that means is that intervention should not be undertaken lightly or because something must be done and no one can think of anything better. It is important to remember the effect on the interveners, as well as on those subject to the intervention. Intervening has a tendency to make the former arrogant and the latter either angry or dependent – and often both. These can be reasonable risks to take if there is a reasonable chance of creating a sustainable peace. But, intervention is not risk-free and should not be the primary policy option. It should be considered only when all other options have been exhausted. It should be the last answer, not the first instinct. The really difficult decision to take is very often not when to intervene, but when not to.

The bad news is that intervention is expensive, tough and difficult. If it must be done, it must be done properly and that means following through all the way. If it isn't done properly, it may be better not to do it at all. The good news is that if we can learn to do it better we will get our fingers burnt less often – and in the process may make the world a much safer and less painful place than it is at present.

Appendix A
The Preparations for Bosnia

Whoever lies awake in Sar-ajevo hears the voices of the Sar-ajevo night. The clock on the Catholic cathedral strikes the hour with weighty confidence: 2 am. More than a minute passes (to be exact 75 seconds – I counted) and only then, with a rather weaker but piercing sound does the Orthodox church announce the hour and chime its own 2 am. A moment after it the tower clock on the Bey's mosque strikes the hour, in a hoarse, far away voice that strikes 11, the ghostly Turkish hour, by the strange calculation of distant and alien parts of the world. The Jews have no clock to sound their hour, so God alone knows what time it is for them by the Sephardic reckoning or the Ashkenazi. Thus at night, while everyone is sleeping, division keeps vigil in the counting of the late small hours and separates these sleeping people who, awake, rejoice and mourn, feast and fast by four different and antagonistic calendars and send all their prayers and wishes to one heaven in four different ecclesiastical languages.

IVO ANDRIC

In March 2001 Prime Minister Tony Blair asked me to put my name forward as Britain's candidate to replace the then High Representative in Bosnia and Herzegovina, Wolfgang Petritsch. It was not a difficult decision to make. I had had a long interest in and love for Bosnia, which I had visited many times during the Bosnian war, during which I had argued for international intervention to stop the fighting. And I had already been asked to do the job once before, in 2000, but had refused because I was still Member of Parliament for Yeovil and believed that I should finish one job before taking on another.

A few months later the European Union confirmed that I was their candidate for the job (which by convention has always gone to a European) and this was in due course confirmed by the UN Security Council and by the Peace Implementation Council (PIC), which oversees the Bosnian peace mission. The twenty-seventh of May 2002 was fixed as the day my mandate in Bosnia would start.

In this appendix I will describe the nature of the job, how we prepared for it, what our analysis was of the situation in Bosnia and Herzegovina at this stage and what plans we drew up for my mandate.

The Job

By the time I arrived in Bosnia there had already been three High Representatives; the ex-Swedish prime minister, Carl Bildt,[*] who set up the office in 1995, Carlos Westendorp, a Spanish diplomat, and my immediate predecessor, a diplomat from Austria, Wolfgang Petritsch. I was, however, unlike them, to be 'double hatted' as High Representative and European Union Special Representative, the latter reflecting the fact that the European Union was going to take over the leadership of the peace mission in Bosnia in the next phase of the country's development to full statehood. In effect, however, although the two jobs doubled my reporting lines, they were, for the period of my mandate at least, rolled into one.

The task of the Office of the High Representative (OHR) in Bosnia, as defined in Dayton, is to be responsible to the Peace Implementation Council (PIC) for the implementation of the civilian aspects of the Dayton Peace Agreement. In effect this means that the job of the High Representative could be as broad as he wished to make it, ranging from education, to human rights, to the conduct of government, to the operation of the economy, to the restructuring of the transport system, to the reconstruction of houses, to the reform of the media, etc, etc, etc. In this job, you could interfere in anything and get swallowed up in everything, if you wanted to.

To help him interfere in everything if he wants to, the High Representative (High Rep) had, when I arrived, a staff of approximately 800 and a budget of some €26 million. The largest

[*] Carl Bildt also carried the title of EU Special Envoy.

concentration of the staff, made up of internationals and local Bosnians, is in the headquarters of OHR in Sarajevo and the rest in field and regional offices scattered across the country. When I arrived in Sarajevo, I had one Principal Deputy, by tradition an American, and a Senior Deputy, a German. It was my good fortune to have as my Principal Deputy Don Hays, an extraordinary dynamo of a man seconded by the US State Department, who was to become not only a stout and reliable pillar on whom I could always rely, but also a close personal friend.

One of the tasks laid on the High Representative by the Dayton Agreement was the 'coordination' of the myriad international organisations in Bosnia – a veritable alphabet soup of UN and other bodies, ranging from the UN High Commission for Refugees (UNHCR), through to the UN Development Programme (UNDP), to the UN Mission in Bosnia (UNMIBH), the World Bank (WB), the International Monetary Fund (IMF), the European Commission (EC), European Union Monitoring Mission (EUMM), the Organisation for Security and Co-operation in Europe (OSCE), the International Criminal Tribunal for ex-Yugoslavia (ICTY – or as it is better known, the Hague Tribunal), the International Commission for Missing Persons (ICMP) and so on ad infinitum. The problem was that, although the 'High Rep' has a formal duty to coordinate all these bodies, he has no formal power to do so. In effect, they each have their own mandate, report directly to their own headquarters and need pay little heed to the OHR in what they do.

In addition to this source of potential confusion, there exists alongside the OHR an entirely separate parallel military structure (in most of my time, SFOR or Stabilisation Force). This was commanded by a three-star US general responsible directly to NATO for the security and military aspects of the implementation of the Dayton Peace Agreement. There was no formal structure for co-operation between OHR and SFOR and relations between the two headquarters had been at best minimal and at worst (as with my predecessor) cool to the point of hostility.

It is sometimes said that the High Representative in Bosnia is accountable to no one. The opposite is the truth. I was directly accountable to the Peace Implementation Council (PIC) through a 'Steering Board' established by the Dayton Peace Agreement, consisting of the ambassadors of the US, Russia, UK, France, Italy, the

European Commission, the European Union Presidency, Germany, the Netherlands, Canada, Turkey (representing the Organisation of Islamic Countries or OIC) and Japan, with whom I met every week and whose broad agreement I had to obtain for any major action I intended. I was also charged with reporting to the UN Security Council twice every year. And, as European Union Special Representative, my boss was the European 'Foreign Minister' in Brussels, Javier Solana. I was also constitutionally required to meet with the PSC (Political and Security Committee) which is linked to the European Council in Brussels. Then there was the European Commission, to whom I was responsible for the money allocated to my office. The Commission has the largest single financial programme of aid in Bosnia, so it was wise for me to keep the closest contact with the commissioner responsible for the Balkans, initially Chris Patten, who became an indispensable and ever-helpful colleague in what I was trying to do.

In the early days of OHR, progress in Bosnia was constantly being blocked by those political forces in the country whose aim was to use the Dayton peace process not for peace but for the continuation of their war aims. This led to complete stalemate (they could not even decide on number plates, flags or who should be represented on their currency and stamps). To overcome this, in December 1997, the High Rep was given new powers, called the 'Bonn powers'. Under these the High Rep could impose a law, which domestic parliaments were subsequently required to endorse, and remove officials and politicians who were, in his view, blocking or undermining the implementation of the Dayton Agreement. By any standards these powers, which are not subject to appeal or review, are extraordinary. However, the High Rep is in effect much more constrained in his use of them than might at first seem the case. First of all any major use of the powers required de facto, if not de jure, the agreement of the Steering Board of the PIC before they could be used. And secondly because, like any law, they rested on public consent. Any decision using the Bonn powers depended, just as any law does, on the ultimate acceptance of the people to whom it was being applied. If any of the Bonn decisions taken by myself or my predecessors had been rejected outright by the people of Bosnia, or by their politicians, there was no way the decision could have stood and the powers themselves would have de facto vanished overnight.

This made it necessary to have a very close feel for public opinion in the country and had a profound effect on the way the powers could be used and on judgements about their use.

The Analysis

Thanks to the work of my predecessors and the courage and common sense of the ordinary people of Bosnia and Herzegovina (a phrase I would not necessarily apply to all their politicians), the country had made extraordinary progress in the seven years since the war.

But this had not been properly recognised by the international community, who still regarded Bosnia as a black hole, a view often shared by many of Bosnia's political and intellectual elite who seemed to relish describing their country in the bleakest terms possible. These opinions were probably understandable, given the impatience in both the international community and the local population to see things getting better, faster. Nevertheless, measured by the time scales of peacebuilding, Bosnia's progress, especially from such a devastating war, had been miraculous. In Northern Ireland, thirty-six years after the outbreak of violence, those driven from their homes had not returned. By the time Bosnia reached the ten-year point after the war, a million of the two million driven out had returned home, even to the Golgotha of Srebrenica. Unlike the Basque country, where, nearly thirty years after the troubles started, elections continue to be marred by violence, Bosnian elections, although still monitored by the international community, are regularly and entirely peacefully held, to the highest international standards and under full control of the Bosnians themselves. Unlike Cyprus, which remains divided thirty years after the peace agreement, there is complete freedom of movement for all across Bosnia and Herzegovina.

So, peace and stability was not going to be my problem – that had been basically assured by the time I got there. My problem, rather, was going to be state-building. And here the situation was completely stalled, with less than 50 per cent of the authorised state ministries installed and the authority of those which were continually undermined by entity power and influence.

My first enemy was time. Bosnia was no longer at the top of the international priority list for aid, troops and political attention. Over the years of my mandate these would, I assessed, go down. NATO troops stood at 12,000 when I arrived in Bosnia. It seemed likely that these would halve over my time, as the pressure of other trouble spots such as Iraq and Afghanistan built up. So I concluded that we had better get the difficult things done early while the troops were at full strength. Secondly, I could sense that the mood of Europe was changing too. As the EU went through its next round of enlargement it seemed likely to me that enthusiasm for further enlargement, including the Balkans, would diminish. Bosnia could not afford to lose time. If there was one obsession that ran all through the years of my mandate it was to make the changes necessary in Bosnia to get the country through the doors and on to the European road before those doors closed further. It would be disastrous, I believed, were Bosnia to be left behind as the rest of the Western Balkans moved towards the EU.

I needed to define a common destination to work for that could unite the international community and the people of Bosnia and Herzegovina. My predecessor, Wolfgang Petritsch, had already declared that the international community's exit strategy should be to transit Bosnia into Europe, so it was clear to me that our destination should be ultimate membership of the EU and NATO – the so-called Euro-Atlantic structures. But we would have to move fast – brutally fast if Bosnia was not to be left behind. And the first enemy to moving fast was the very Dayton Agreement which it was my job to implement and protect.

The Dayton Monster

Dayton had given Bosnia peace, but in the process it had created a monster in Bosnia. This is not to criticise Dayton. I don't think peace could have been agreed with the warring parties without the compromises in the treaty and most people would, at the time, have preferred an untidy peace to a continuing war. Nevertheless, I now had to deal with the monster which Dayton created: two 'entities', the Federation (joint Bosniak and Croat) and Republika Srpska (predominantly Serb), each with many of the attributes of a state. In the Federation, ten cantons each with their own police, health structures, education ministries etc etc. When my mandate started,

Bosnia – a country of 3.5 million – had three armies, two customs services, effectively three intelligence services, five presidents, twelve prime ministers, thirteen police forces, no effective central government, no state taxation system, no single judicial structure and no single economic space. In some parts of Bosnia 70 per cent of taxation revenue was spent just on government, leaving only 30 per cent for citizens' services. Running 'Dayton' Bosnia required three times the civil service than Bosnia pre-war.

We could not change all of this during my mandate. But we could change enough of it, I believed, to create the beginnings of a light-level state structure that could qualify Bosnia for membership of NATO's Partnership for Peace and start Bosnia on the road to Europe, within the EU's Stabilisation and Association Process. So the central theme of my mandate would be to use every opportunity and leverage I had to transfer powers from the entities to the state.

The problem was that at least one of Bosnia's two entities, Republika Srpska, already saw itself as a state and had neither interest in, nor intention of, allowing any of its powers (like the control of its own army) to be passed to the state level. This would require a change of the terms of the Dayton Agreement. But, since my job was to uphold Dayton and my legal powers stopped at the limits of Dayton, I could not force them to do this. I had to persuade them – and that would be difficult. So I assessed that one of my first jobs was to persuade the Serbs in Republika Srpska that they were not a state, but part of a state and that they could have no future in Europe or NATO or anywhere else, until they recognised this. I was going to have to take some tough and controversial actions which would require being prepared to risk real confrontations, especially with Republika Srpska, and it would be better to take these early rather than late.

Corruption

But the problems of Bosnia and Herzegovina were not just structural. Endemic corruption had brought the country very close to the status of a criminally captured state. Because the international community had thought that elections were more important than the rule of law, those who had prosecuted the war and profited from it were now elected as the politicians who ran the country.

The establishment of the rule of law should have been our first priority after the war ended. It hadn't been, primarily because the international community didn't think it would stay there that long. So it would have to become my priority now. The problem here was not so much the police. The UN had invested c$150 million a year (five times the budget of OHR) in the UN Police Mission whose job it was to create a modern police force in Bosnia. But they had forgotten the equal importance of effective reform of the judiciary and the structures of law and the prosecutors and the penal system, all of which remained unreformed and, in many cases, corrupted by Communism and the war. We were going to have to vet and re-appoint all the judges, reform the prosecutorial system, create a state structure for the judiciary and rewrite the Bosnian criminal and civil codes.

We were also going to have to get into the corrupt spaces, chiefly in the public utilities and begin to clean them up. Corruption was the soft underbelly of the nationalist parties and if we wanted to attack the old nationalist structures, then the best way to do this would be through attacking corruption, not least because this would be likely to attract a higher level of public support than a direct frontal assault on the nationalist structures which had supported and protected people during the war. And the best way to tackle corruption in the utilities was to deploy teams of auditors (including internationals), set up proper criminal intelligence structures and create a court at state level, which, because it was supported by foreign judges and prosecutors, would be strong enough to try even the highest in the land, who many ordinary people in Bosnia had come to view as the 'untouchables'. I assessed that we could not clean out the Augean stables of corruption ourselves, but we could decapitate the most powerful in the criminal structures and leave the domestic courts, over time, to deal with the rest.

Next, the Bosnian economy was in a dire state. Although the Central Bank (under the guidance of a remarkable New Zealander, Peter Nicholl) had done a brilliant job getting inflation out of the system, establishing a local currency and stabilising its value, the rest of the economy was being held back by myriad old Communist business-destroying laws, punitively high taxation, the lack of a single economic space in the country and totally ineffective government regulation and enforcement. Many good Bosnian businessmen and women were forced to operate in the grey sector (estimated at 30 per cent of the overall economy), not because they were criminals, but because there was no other way of earning a living.

Like the rule of law, economic reform should have been one of the international community's first priorities in Bosnia, since giving people jobs and the prospect of prosperity is a far better way of creating stability in a country than stationing any number of troops there. But since this hadn't been a priority at the start, liberalising and reforming the economy had to be one of mine now. I was very aware that if we were to achieve the aims we had set ourselves we were going to have to be ruthless about prioritising our activities. The tricky thing would be not to get distracted by the things it would be nice to do, in order to be able to concentrate on the things that were essential to do.

The International Community

My next problem was not with Bosnia, but with the international community. This was fractured, divisive, bad-tempered and the various factions spent more of their time, I discovered, criticising each other than working together to get the job done. The problems were not just ones of personality. The mandates of the international organisations frequently duplicated each other (OSCE and OHR both had responsibility for education, human rights and democratisation; both OHR and SFOR had a duty to oversee military reform). The result was that the international voice in Bosnia was divided, the Bosnians were confused and those who wished to drive wedges in order to slow down the process of peace implementation had a field day. It would be vital, if I was to succeed, to get the international community itself to speak with a single voice and to rationalise the divisions of labour between us.

Bosnianisation

Next, I was shocked to discover that in my own organisation, OHR, there were Bosnians who were qualified and extremely gifted, working for international bosses who were frequently less qualified and gifted and always less knowledgeable about the country. One of my aims, we decided, should be to open up OHR by imposing a recruitment presumption for all posts in favour of Bosnians, unless there was a security reason for having to have an international, or we could find no Bosnians with the right qualifications. The result of this policy was that, by the time I left Bosnia nearly four years later, I found myself working with a team, mostly of young Bosnians, who were the most able and dedicated I have ever had the privilege to work with.

Public Opinion

Finally, I knew that many of the things I was going to have to do would be highly unpopular, especially with those in the political classes who had a vested interest in keeping things as they were. The only way I could hope to do this was to try to reach over the heads of the obstructive politicians to the ordinary people of Bosnia and Herzegovina. There would be times when I would have to bet my judgement about what the people of the country wanted or were prepared to put up with, against that of their elected representatives. This is a very frightening thing for a foreigner to do in any country – but even more frightening in a country as complicated as Bosnia and Herzegovina. So, the crucial battlefield that I had to win on was the battlefield of public opinion. What this meant was that I would have to behave like a politician myself and build up public support for the measures we needed to get through. I have always thought that popularity should be to the politician what cattle are to the African chief. You build up your stock when you can, so that you can sell it when you need to in order to obtain the things you want. So we would have to construct clear, simple messages for what we were trying to do which were understandable to ordinary people; we would have to have a press operation that was efficient, powerful and embedded in the policy-making process; and we would have to measure regularly, through opinion polling, the effectiveness of our messages and whether we were winning the arguments.

The Plan

The British government was prepared to assist me by funding or seconding a team of four people to help me do my job. At the end of 2001, I began to assemble my UK team in a couple of rooms in the loft of the Foreign Office. I was again exceedingly fortunate in those who came to work with me. Two came from my old Liberal Democrat Leader's office: Julian Astle, who was to handle all relations with Bosnian politicians, and Ian Patrick, who would run my office. To this team we added Julian Braithwaite, who had very wide experience of the Balkans having served in the Belgrade Embassy at the time of Kosovo and whom I poached from No. 10 Downing Street, where he had worked in Alistair Campbell's press office. He would handle all press, media reform and public affairs matters. And finally, I persuaded Edward Llewellyn, who had worked for Margaret Thatcher, John Major in the 1992 election and most recently Chris Patten both in Hong Kong and Brussels,* to join us as Head of OHR's Political Department and my Chief of Staff. A more able team it would be very difficult to assemble. The fact that our team came from across the British political spectrum was completely coincidental, but made for very good fun in our office.

We worked together to assemble a plan for the first hundred days of my mandate whose broad outline was as follows:

1 We would grab the initiative for our state-building programme at the start and try to hold it for as long as possible. This meant that I had to make a speech laying out my programme on my first day in office. This would have to contain the overall aim of my mandate (we fixed on the phrase *'to work with the Bosnian politicians and people in order to put Bosnia and Herzegovina irreversibly on to the path to statehood and on to the road to Europe'*) and lay out the vision I was asking people to subscribe to – essentially the creation of a light-level state structure with strong decentralisation of power to local communities.

2 We knew that nothing succeeds like success. So, if we were to have any hope of doing the big things we wanted to do, we would have to establish an early track record for success. We specifically planned a series of small victories we could win early in my mandate. I knew that, as soon as I arrived, I would be tested by domestic forces opposed to change and that this could lead to some early confrontations. We had to win those.

---

* Edward is now the Chief of Staff to the Conservative leader, David Cameron.

3 We also assembled a longer-term programme of specific reforms in the rule of law and economic sectors. This required visits to European capitals and to Washington to get them to buy into our programme and to promise to provide the resources (judges, prosecutors, auditors and economic experts) that we needed to make our plans a reality.

4 We assessed that one of our most difficult tasks would be to decide what *not* to get involved in, so that we could concentrate time, energy and resources on our agenda and not get distracted. One of the clear messages that had come through from PIC countries on my tour of capitals was that they expected me to begin the draw down of OHR (a temporary organisation), with a view to handing as many of its tasks as possible to the Bosnians or to permanent international organisations (such as the OSCE), during my mandate. Ed Llewellyn had spotted that the UN organisation in Bosnia, UNMIBH, had instituted a mandate completion plan. We drew up proposals to put in place a Mission Implementation Plan (MIP) for OHR which would identify the key tasks each of OHR's departments had to complete before the department could be closed and the task handed on. This plan, which was constantly reviewed and updated, proved invaluable. It acted as the 'compass' for OHR, keeping us concentrated on our agenda and preventing 'mission creep'. It also provided an invaluable framework for reporting back to our international masters, enabled us successively to reduce the size of OHR (which, in terms of numbers and budgets, was cut by half over my mandate), and drove the process of handing over our tasks to the democratic structures of Bosnia and Herzegovina.

5 My predecessor had started to try to rationalise the international organisation in Bosnia, based on the pillar structure in Kosovo. I decided that we would have to take this much further. I wanted OHR to do less and concentrate more on coordinating and giving direction to the international community – we should be more the wheel-house which steered the ship, and less the engine which drove it forward. In order to do this, we created the concept of 'lead' international organisations dealing with each main topic. This meant handing over some of the jobs which OHR had done to other international organisations better

equipped to do them, so that we could concentrate on our priorities. We would hand education, human rights and democratisation over to OSCE, military reform over to SFOR and refugee return to a structure led by UNHCR. Then we would close down the OHR departments dealing with these tasks and create in their place a whole new OHR pillar to deal with the rule of law, to be created by two US judges, Chip Erdmann and Bill Potter, under the oversight of a new French Senior Deputy High Representative, Bernard Fassier, who had been seconded to me by the French government specifically for the purpose.

6 It was very clear that the one thing I had to do if I was to be successful was to have the closest possible relationship with my fellow Dayton implementer, NATO's SFOR Commander. At the time this was US General John Sylvester, a barrel-chested mountain of a man with a capacity for blunt Texan speaking which made some wince, but I knew concealed a sharp and highly politically attuned brain. I discovered that among my staff I had, for some reason, a two-star military officer (in my case a British rear admiral) whose job was to act as my 'military adviser.' I didn't think I needed a military adviser and if I did, John Sylvester would do a better job than anyone. So I planned to move him from my office into a unit supporting the military reform process, in which NATO should now take the lead. The close relationship between OHR and SFOR under John Sylvester and, later, his most able successors became the twin pillar on which my mandate was based.

7 Next, I needed to find a mechanism through which the wider international community could buy into the central strategy we had created. The Steering Board Ambassadors* (known as the SBA) meeting, which I chaired every Friday morning, were not the problem. I had a constitutional duty to discuss my intentions with them and get their broad agreement to what I was going to do. So they were in the loop already. I did, however, have to get agreement from them that, where we had taken a collective decision within the SBA, on a consensus basis (we never took

---

* Consisting of the ambassadors of France, Germany, Russia, the United States, Italy, the United Kingdom, the European Commission, Turkey, Holland, the Presidency of the European Union, Canada and Japan.

votes), all would abide by this in public. This undertaking was readily given at my first meeting with them and only once in a very turbulent four years broken, so far as I remember. The more difficult problem was, rather, the heads of the other independent international missions in Bosnia and Herzegovina, each of whom reported only to their own headquarters who set their individual priorities and mandates, which each guarded jealously. I decided that we should adapt an existing structure and re-name it the Board of Principals. This would meet every week and would consist of the Heads or Deputies of SFOR, the UN, UNMIBH, UNDP, UNHCR, OSCE, the European Commission, the World Bank and the International Monetary Fund. The deal I proposed to them was that I would place my Bonn powers on the table and we would decide our joint priorities together on a collective basis, in the same manner as a British cabinet. I would then be prepared to use the Bonn powers where necessary, in order to push forward the priorities the Board jointly decided on. This meant that, on occasions, say, the World Bank would find it beneficial to back something which was not strictly speaking within their mandate, because in return they could count on the Bonn powers being used to back their priorities if they could get agreement for them from other members of the Board. There was much initial nervousness, especially from the International Financial Institutions (IFIs) about this. But eventually they all bought into it and the system worked throughout my mandate, without any one of the Board breaking ranks publicly over decisions with which they did not agree. We had, at last, a mechanism which enabled the international community to speak with one voice, act with a single purpose and reinforce each other's priorities where necessary. And when we did this we soon discovered that we created a force for reform in Bosnia that could not be resisted.

8 Over this period Don Hays and I drew up plans to restructure OHR so that it reflected our new priorities. I agreed with Don that he should run the OHR organisation, leaving me free to run the politics and set the strategy. He proved a brilliant and tough administrator who took a huge burden off my shoulders and enabled me to steer the organisation without being trapped in the engine room.

9 We also drew up a detailed press strategy, which concentrated not so much on the newspapers and outlets which were the favourites of the international community because they said things the international community liked to hear, but on those outlets which had the broadest readership and listenership in the country. We needed to get our messages across and that meant reaching the widest audience, which was not necessarily the same thing as the one which was either most receptive, or whose beliefs were closest to ours. I spent a lot of time with my team finding the right phrases in Bosnian (which we were all either trying to learn, or had already learnt) to get across what we were trying to do to the wider Bosnian public. We needed a single slogan which would work in the local language, which would sum up what I was trying to do and which would act as a gathering point for reformers, and help get their vote out in the forthcoming elections of October 2002. We finally fastened on 'Justice and Jobs' ('*Posao i Pravda*' in Bosnian). A lot of time and care was also spent in writing and trying out my opening speech to the Bosnian Parliament (included on pages 298–313).

10 Finally, we drew up a plan for my personal activities for the first hundred days. This quite deliberately had me out of Sarajevo for a large proportion of the time, setting the pattern for the rest of my mandate. The intellectuals and the Sarajevo circles had claimed a lot of the time of my predecessors, but I needed to build up understanding and if possible support from a much wider group of Bosnians. So I intended to spend more of my time visiting, living with and speaking to the ordinary people of Bosnia outside the capital city (especially the refugees) than I did with the Sarajevo establishment. I wanted them to believe that, when I took my decisions, I knew of the way they had to live their lives quite as well as their politicians claimed to. I paid a heavy price for this, when later, the Sarajevo *carsija** turned strongly against me. But I am convinced it was the right strategy and made it easier for me to get my agenda through, often against the strong opposition of one or other section of the political establishment.

---

* Bosnian word meaning roughly 'coffee society' – usually refers to intellectuals.

Having assembled our plan in detail, I embarked on a series of visits to the major European capitals, Brussels and Washington to get their buy-in to what I intended to do, followed by a visit to Sarajevo for discussion with the politicians of Bosnia and Herzegovina.

Finally, we organised a retreat before the start of my mandate, attended by all members of the Board of Principals at Leeds Castle in Kent on two glorious days in April 2002 to talk them through our plans and get their support and agreement. Part of the programme included a meeting between the Board and Tony Blair in Downing Street. We were now ready to go.

Appendix B
The Savage War of Peace[1] – Bosnia 2002–2003

'Lako je tudzim kurcem gloginje mlatati'[*]

MONDAY 31 MARCH 2003

A glorious day today. Azure blue skies and the day is going to be very hot.

We had a magnificent flight from Sarajevo to Srebrenica over Romanija mountain and then skimming over successively descending ridges east towards the Drina. Then suddenly there was the little town of Srebrenica crouched below us in the valley. We spiralled down to land on the football field, where so much of the terrible killing took place.

We made our way down to the burial ground to join the fifteen to twenty thousand people who had come, most to mourn and remember, but many to bury their loved ones. The quiet agony of some as they carried the mortal remains of their loved ones, killed eight years ago, was almost unbearable. The bodies were lined up in little coffins, covered in green cloth (though goodness knows what filled them. In most cases no more, I suspect, than shards of bones and tufts of hair – the dried bundles of body parts which I had seen a few weeks earlier, each in its white plastic bag, at the Tuzla salt mines where they were gathered, sorted, and identified).

I found myself close to tears, not at the thought of the desiccated human remains of the dead in the coffins, but at the quiet dignity and solemn grief of the living. Here they were, on the very site where they had last seen their loved ones, in a Serb majority area,

---

[*] A very rude Balkan saying which, roughly translated, means, 'It is easy to beat thorn bushes with other people's pricks'. It was first quoted to me by a Bosnian friend when I asked him why his politicians left me and the international community to do the things in Bosnia which they should be doing.

surrounded by RS police, still wearing the hated Serb double eagle of the soldiers who had killed their husbands and sons. Yet there was, as far as I could see, neither anger nor insult nor recrimination. Just dumb, silent, terrible grief.

I could not help comparing and contrasting Belfast's sectarian funerals in the early 70s when I had been there as a soldier.

Then in due course, under the boiling sun, we gathered on a small plinth, the muftis* and the ambassadors and the politicians. The Mufti of Tuzla led the *Dzenaza*.† Rather short. Then the *Reis*‡ said his *Dzenaza* in a wonderful deep sonorous voice, the Arabic words of the prayer magnified by the loudspeakers and echoing back at us from the surrounding hills.

My imagination fled back to those terrible scenes on the day of the slaughter, when fathers were made to shout up into the very forests from which the *Reis*'s voice was now echoing, calling their sons down and telling them that, if they did not come, the Serbs would kill them. Many came down in trust or desperation to keep their fathers alive, only to be rounded up and killed, father and son alike.

Then the Bosnian President, Sulejman Tihić, spoke. His speech was bitter and full of politics. It struck a jarring, ugly note among all this quiet grief. There was much embarrassment and shuffling of feet.

Then it was my turn. I heard my sentences rolling back to me in echo from the forested hills, seeming somehow to mock me, that I should dare to believe that any words of mine could be sufficient to the horrors which they had witnessed. Then, perhaps most moving of all, a young girl, both of whose parents had been killed in the slaughter, made a speech and read a poem she had written.

And finally the *Reis* again, this time with a speech. He talked about Cain and Abel but said the Bosnians should not be for revenge. Justice would do. And if we could forgive the killers, then this would create the basis for peace.

Then the ceremony finished with a final prayer and with every-body saying the Muslim *Amin*, their words rising up as a rumbling murmur among the dust into the still air above the valley. And I

---

* Local Muslim preachers.
† The Muslim prayer of burial.
‡ *Reis Ul Ulema* – the head of the Bosnian Muslim community.

thought that, on just such a day as this eight years ago, this horror happened with the sun burning down and the international community looking on, as they were today, and doing nothing.

Afterwards, I wandered off to help some of the families fill in their graves.*

From my diary.

2002

I spent the first evening of my mandate in Bosnia and Herzegovina at the home of a Serb refugee in the capital of Republika Srpska (the predominantly Serb entity), Banja Luka. This was not a haphazard choice. I was conscious that, because of my wartime lobbying for intervention, I was regarded, in a country where every foreigner is presumed to have a prejudice in favour of one or other of the three peoples of Bosnia, as pro-Bosnian Muslim, disinterested in the Croats and anti-Serb. Spending the night with a Bosnian Serb refugee was intended to send the message that I understood that ordinary people of all sides had suffered during the war and that I had no favourites. But this visit turned out to be much more than purely symbolic.

My host, Uros Makić, a teacher, taught me something none of my advisers could have told me. That his own Republika Srpska government was ripping off their own Serb refugees, diverting international aid given to them to help refugees like Uros return to their homes, and using it instead to support Serb refugees from Bosnian Muslim areas to stay where they were in Republika Srpska. Uros said to me: 'You foreigners – you are very well-meaning giving our politicians all this money, but you do not know this country well enough to see what happens to the money afterwards. And so it ends up doing exactly the opposite of what you intended – helping refugees stay where they are, when you are trying to help them to return home, preserving ethnic cleansing, when you are trying to reverse it. Instead of employing lots of foreigners who do not know enough about what is happening here to check up on where the money is

---

* It is Muslim tradition that men who attend a funeral help the family fill in the grave.

going, why don't you give the job to us? We refugees have our own NGO. It is in our interests to see that the money which should come to us does come to us. We know what our politicians are up to. Let us act as your watchdogs.'

It was an early and chastening lesson in the complexities of Bosnia and of the importance of listening to the views of the ordinary people we were here to help, rather than just their politicians and the international bureaucracy.

Earlier in that first day I had given my speech to the Bosnian parliament, outlining the aims of my mandate and had already begun to face the anticipated challenges designed to test me out. The first came from the Serb side. In a meeting with the leaders of Republika Srpska (RS) that afternoon, the prime minister, Mladen Ivanić, flatly refused, with threats, to enact a law passed by my predecessor just before he left, which established a national structure for the oversight of the judiciary. I made it explicitly clear that I backed my predecessor's actions as if I had taken them myself.

The second test came the following day – this time from the Bosnian Muslim side. The Bosnian Muslim-led Federation government were attempting illegally to sack a local Croat police chief whose investigations, it was believed, were getting too close for comfort. To make matters more complicated the minister who was doing the sacking was himself a Croat. I passed a message to the Federation prime minister[*] that if he acted illegally, I would have to intervene and he would have to go – on my second day in Bosnia! At this, the entire Croat contingent threatened to withdraw from the government, leading to a political crisis. I said that was their business not mine. My business was to uphold the law and I would do so, whatever the threats. The crisis quickly passed. I was beginning to understand just how frightening it is to have so much executive authority in a country about whose complexities I knew so little.

It was at this time that I also learnt a crucial lesson about interpreters and interpreting, which merits a few words of explanation. In my first days I did a number of interviews on Bosnian television and radio. One of these was especially combative. I thought I did rather well, giving as good as I got. But when I got out of the studio, my interpreters told me that I spoke so fast that they couldn't

[*] Alija Behmnen.

translate me. I didn't think I spoke like an idiot, but to my audience I must have sounded like one. I have been an interpreter so I ought to have known better – but I didn't. Foreigners trying to get political messages across need to remember that their interpreter is their most important friend. For it is the interpreter's words which will be heard, not theirs. And, by the way, there is a world of difference between translating the dry text of a diplomatic communiqué and a carefully nuanced political speech or quick-fire interview.

Before I had arrived, we had spent a great deal of time crafting my opening speech to the Bosnian parliament, so that we got it just right – especially the central slogan 'Jobs and justice through reform' But when it was finished, I had it translated into Bosnian and then back into English and it was the English translation of the Bosnian which I delivered, not the English original.[*] I very soon realised that I had to learn a whole new way of speaking, thinking about the words I used to ensure there was a proper local translation, trying to warn my interpreters (not always successfully, I confess) if, in a conversation, I was going to use a particularly colourful phrase or English idiom so they could think about how to translate it before-hand. And paying attention to the physical needs of the interpreter and the physical layout of the speaking venue so that the interpreter could not only be heard by the audience, but also hear the speaker they were interpreting. In OHR we had the best collection of inter-preters I have ever had the privilege to work with – they could translate with astonishing speed and fluency in and out of their own mother tongue for hour after exhausting hour. But all this amounted to nothing if they could neither hear the speaker or be heard by the audience: which is what happened when Bill Clinton came to open the Srebrenica memorial grave site in 2004. One of our brilliant OHR interpreters was given the task of translating his speech to an audience of 25,000. But he was positioned behind Clinton and behind the loudspeakers and so could not hear what

---

[*] Failure to consider how words are translated can lead to very damaging consequences. Before the decision was taken to disband the Iraqi army, the United States was considering the possibility of converting the existing Iraqi armed forces into a new force – the New Iraqi Corps – or NIC as it was referred to in acronym by US officials, who were, it appears, completely oblivious to the fact that 'nic' is the Arabic word for 'fuck'. The title was quickly changed to New Iraqi Army, or NIA. But by then the damage was done.

Clinton said. Disaster was only partially averted by an excellent piece of extemporisation.

About two weeks after my arrival, following a dinner with the Board of Principals, General John Sylvester* took me to a private corner and said in a low voice: 'Some of the guys from your old unit will be active tonight.' I knew what he meant. British Special Forces were about to mount an operation to catch Karadžić. My heart rose. It shouldn't have done. They drew a blank. This was the first of many similar operations over the next few years – all with the same result. In due course we would realise that if we were serious about catching war criminals, we would need more than a single piece of intelligence and a lightning commando raid.

Over the next month or so we remained firmly on the back foot responding to crises, rather than pushing our own agenda. In mid June, however, two major scandals broke, both involving high-level government corruption and illegality – one in the RS and the other in the Federation. This gave me the opportunity I was looking for to shift the agenda on to the rule of law and justice.

I had two aims – the first was to begin to put in place the instruments which the State would need to tackle high-level crime and the second was to begin to clean up the political space in Bosnia. I used the scandals to accelerate the creation of a Special Chamber capable of trying even the highest in the land, on which, for the first years, would serve international judges promised to me for this purpose on the tour of capitals I had done before taking up my mandate.

We also made it clear that, since huge sums of government money had been lost in the scandals, the relevant government ministers must be held responsible. After much pressure, and some superb work by Julian Astle in Banja Luka, the Serb minister in due course resigned (but not before RS Prime Minister Mladen Ivanić had again threatened to withdraw from government). The Croat, however, refused to do so and was again strenuously supported, with threats, by his fellow Croats. I had to use the Bonn powers for the first time in order to show we were serious about the establishment of the principle of ministerial responsibility – a battle which continued throughout the years of my mandate.

* SFOR Commander.

Shortly after this, my staff brought me another case on which they wanted me to use the Bonn powers in order to remove a Bosnian Muslim local mayor who had been obstructing refugees from returning and intimidating local and international officials. He was clearly acting in a way which undermined the Dayton Peace Agreement and this therefore was an appropriate case on which to use the Bonn powers. But the approach we were taking to the use of these powers left me with grave concerns. We had become far too used to relying on the Bonn powers, instead of seeing them as the avenue of last resort. It is frequently said that the Bonn powers in Bosnia have created a culture of dependency among the Bosnians, who rely on the international community to do things they should be doing themselves. While there is truth in this, it is also true that the international community itself had become dependent on the use of the powers as a short cut around the necessity for long-term persuasion and proper courteous procedures. I set a policy in OHR that we should regard the use of the Bonn powers as a mark of failure – not success; that I should never be presented with a decision with only one option: to use the powers. And that, before the powers of removal could be applied, a rigid procedure had to be followed to exhaust all other avenues to alter the behaviour of the recalcitrant official whose actions were obstructing the Dayton agreement.

Meanwhile Don Hays, my Principal Deputy, was restructuring OHR to meet our new priorities. I called together the senior staff and told them Don would run the organisation and I would do the politics. There was some grumbling to start with, but it soon settled down. At the same time we opened the front gates of our Sarajevo headquarters to make the place look a little less like a fort in hostile territory, flew the Bosnian flag alongside the OHR flag and initiated the Bosnianisation policy which we had planned, opening up almost all international posts in the organisation to Bosnians.

In early June the governor of the Bosnian Central Bank, Peter Nicholl, and I formulated a secret plan to take Bosnia and Herzegovina into the Euro by the end of the year. It had to be kept very secret because any word of this in public would have initiated an unstoppable flight from the Bosnian currency into the Euro, unbalancing the fragile Bosnian economy in the process.

The Bosnian currency (the KM) was originally based on a one to one ratio with the Deutschmark. Our plan was to replicate what had happened in Montenegro by simply changing that base to the Euro and adopting this as the new national currency. It did not mean that Bosnia would be part of the Euro zone – merely that it would use the Euro as its legal tender. This was a big throw. But the advantages to Bosnia and its stabilisation were clear and over-whelming. The process of Europeanisation of the country – the centrepiece of my mandate – would have been hugely boosted; the currency would have been permanently protected against manipulation by local politicians; transaction costs to the country's main potential markets would have been reduced and it would encourage investment.

Our plan was to announce this in late July, and make it subject to a referendum – with a majority required not just at the state, but also at the entity levels – to be held at the same time as the October 2002 elections. This, we believed, would add political advantage to economic gain. By now we were having worries that the pro-reform-minded Alliance government could be vulnerable at the elections. If the Alliance lost, the nationalist wartime parties would get back, with serious consequences for the reform agenda. A referendum on the Euro (which we judged would have over-whelming support) would have raised turnout, identified European reform as the key subject of the elections and helped the Alliance.

On 26 June, Peter Nicholl and I flew secretly to Frankfurt to try to persuade the governor of the European Central Bank, Wim Duisenberg, to back the plan. Somewhat to our surprise he did so immediately and with enthusiasm. The following day I briefed Javier Solana by phone and agreed to see him and Chris Patten in Brussels on 3 July to discuss the issue further. At that meeting, Patten and Solana gave us their backing.

The day before I had called in to No. 10 to brief Tony Blair's senior foreign policy adviser, who said that he would brief Blair, but that he thought this would be 'welcome in Downing Street and with Jack Straw'. The inference was obvious. Gordon Brown might not be so enthusiastic. So I asked him to do what he could to 'keep it out of treasury ministers' boxes for as long as possible' while I built up wider support. Meanwhile, back in Sarajevo, we were briefing first the British ambassador,[*] then the American,[†] the Danish,[‡] the French[§] and the German[¶] ambassadors and finally the World Bank and the IMF. All agreed to report back to their capitals and let me know later.

The IMF's response was swift and negative. For reasons which did not make sense to Peter Nicoll and I, the IMF believed that moving to the Euro would lock Bosnia into an exchange rate which would prove uncompetitive in time. We pointed out that the things which made Bosnia uncompetitive were supply side rigidities in the economy, not the currency, and that leaving the currency vulnerable to political manipulation would undermine competitiveness, not improve it. The IMF were unconvinced however, so we decided we would have to fly to Washington to see if we could change their minds. We would stand a better chance of doing this if we had the support of some of the key IMF board members, especially the UK and the US. On 12 July, Tony Blair rang to say he strongly backed the plan and a day later the US rang to say they did too and would do what they could to change the IMF's position.

We now had the ammunition we needed to go to Washington and try to persuade the IMF to change its position (we had already got the support of the World Bank). We had two meetings in the IMF's headquarters on 18 July, the first with more junior officials who maintained their opposition. But at the second meeting, with Anne Kreuger, First Deputy Managing Director of the IMF, the position changed and they promised to support the project – our lobbying of their board members had worked! Elated, Peter and I prepared to fly back to Sarajevo, believing we had it in the bag. Once again, our elation was premature. Even before we left Washington, we started to hear stories about reservations from Berlin, backed by Paris. By the time we got back to Sarajevo it was clear that we had a problem.

A highly embarrassed French ambassador came to see me (the German was out of town) to say that Paris was backing Berlin in opposing the plan. A number of unconvincing reasons were given – but I knew the real one. Germany was in the middle of elections; the

[*] Ian Cliff.
[†] Clifford Bond.
[‡] Johannes Dahl-Hansen. The Danes at this time held the European Presidency.
[§] Bernard Bajolet.
[¶] Hans-Jochen Peters.

German Chancellor, Schroeder, was in difficulty and one of his problems was that Germans believed that they had lost their much-valued currency because it had been swallowed up in a Euro which was proving much more volatile than everyone had hoped. The Chancellor, fighting for his political life, simply could not take the risk of trying to explain to the German people in the middle of an election campaign that the Euro, regarded by many as less 'strong' than the Deutchmark it had swallowed up, should now be further contaminated by association with a failing Balkan state.

I rang London and Solana saying that I intended to go to Berlin and Paris to see if I could rescue the plan, even though I knew the chances were small. I considered asking Blair to try to convince Schroeder, but decided against because I knew that, although we had London's backing, this was too far down London's priorities to justify the expenditure of the political capital necessary to persuade the German Chancellor to take a hit in an election campaign which he was showing all the signs of losing. Paris came back saying de Villepin, the new French foreign minister, would see me, but there was no chance of him changing his mind: the Berlin–Paris axis was proving stronger than the merits of the argument. Nevertheless we flew to Berlin on 23 July in a last ditch attempt to rescue the plan. We met with a brick wall.

In London the following day I learnt that the plan had apparently fallen foul of 'tensions between No. 10 and No. 11', presumably Gordon objecting that Tony was playing fast and loose with the Euro. On 26 July in the Quai D'Orsay, de Villepin, courteous and complimentary, nevertheless confirmed that they were sticking with Berlin.

I returned to Sarajevo dejected and despondent. Not for the first time a good idea and the one thing which might have saved us from the eventual election of nationalist governments in October was lost on the happenstance of the international electoral cycle.

On the same day, the US dropped a bombshell on us. As part of their campaign to obtain immunity for their servicemen from the decisions of the International Criminal Court, the US had threatened to withdraw from all UN bodies. This meant that they would withdraw their involvement in the UN Mission in Bosnia and, most worrying of all, from its police reform mission. Jacques Klein, head of the Mission told me that it could not survive this and he had to start to draw up plans for its immediate closure – which would have been a devastating blow to our whole operation. Although this looked to me like brinkmanship, I could not afford not to take it seriously. I arranged for London to put what pressure they could on Washington and placed a telephone call to Colin Powell, then US Secretary of State. At our meeting in Washington before I took my post, Powell said I could call him any time if I needed help. This was not a promise to call in lightly – but this seemed an appropriate occasion.

I spoke to Powell on 1 July, reminding him that he had agreed with me that the rule of law should be our first priority in Bosnia. If the US pulled the plug on the UN police mission that would fatally damage any chance we had to establish the rule of law. Powell was, as always, courteous and very straightforward. He said that he realised this of course, but I also would understand that this was a big issue for the US and Bosnia was only one of the factors that they had to bear in mind.

Fortunately the issue resolved itself about a week later. Once again, I was learning that any international operation can become prey to anything that happens on the wider international scene. Before I started my mandate I had been told that managing Bosnia was like herding cats. What I hadn't appreciated was that this applied to the international community, too. In fact, during my mandate I spent more time overall managing the international community than I did trying to manage the situation in Bosnia, a tendency which appears to apply to all those whose job it is to lead international operations of this sort.

Meanwhile Bosnia's own electoral cycle was beginning to have its effect. The long shadow of the forthcoming October elections was starting to fall across the whole political scene. The incumbent Alliance government was a coalition of several uncomfortable bedfellows, put together in a shotgun wedding, presided over by the international community (especially the British and Americans). It was designed primarily as a vehicle for the international community's favourite Bosnian politician, Zlatko Lagumdzia, the leader of the SDP, which was at that time Bosnia's only genuinely multi-ethnic reformist, pro-European party. The problem was that, by the time the Alliance had been formed, there was too little time to get much done before the next elections and the Alliance government's record of introducing reforms in the time they had fell far short of their promises. Moreover, Lagumdzia, a genuinely charismatic politician, was also a highly egocentric one, given to arrogance from time to time. This had made him deeply personally unpopular with many Bosnian voters. In the Balkans (and in quite a number of post-conflict situations) there is a long-standing tradition of 'boutique' political parties formed round a single person, rather than a set of ideas. The SDP, though genuine in its convictions, was not immune from the trend.

In late July, with the election campaign in full swing, I had to speak to Lagumdzia and tell him that I knew his Bosnian Muslim intelligence chief* was using intelligence, or allowing it to be used, against his (Lagumdzia's) political enemies for electoral purposes. I warned him that if this continued, I would have no option but to act – so please would he send the appropriate warning to the appropriate place? On 9 August the US ambassador and I repeated the message to Lagumdzia when we met with him jointly to say that this would have to stop, or I would be forced to remove the intelligence chief from his job. Meanwhile, we watched the trends moving in the polls during June with increasing nervousness. They started hopefully enough, with the Alliance comfortably ahead. But by the end of the month, it was clear there was a strong shift to the nationalists under way.

We needed to create some insurance for ourselves that the reform agenda would survive a change of government by getting buy-in from all parties for the reform programme. To do this we drew up a document called 'Jobs and Justice' which listed the reforms that were needed for BiH to start the journey to Europe. The document was the first to be drawn up jointly by the OHR and the government and became, during the campaign, more or less the manifesto for the re-election of the Alliance government. Before the campaign started, however, we were able to gain the formal acceptance of all parties to the 'Justice and Jobs' package, who declared publicly that this would be their programme in government, if elected.

By July we began actively to plan for the less than welcome

---

* There were effectively three intelligence structures in Bosnia at the time, a Serb one in the RS, and, in the Federation, a formal one dominated by the Bosnian Muslims and an informal one serving the Croats. The intelligence chief in question was Munir Alibabić, the head of the Federation intelligence service.

possibility that the elections would bring a sharp swing to the right and give me nationalist governments to work with for the rest of my mandate. We started to put together a package of measures which I would bring in straight after election day, taking advantage of the post-election hiatus. There is always a period of calm after an election, while the government forms and takes over the wheel. Normally this lasts days or weeks. But in Bosnia it can often last up to three months, as the complex dance to put together the cross-party and cross-ethnicity coalitions required by the constitution plays itself out. I simply could not afford to have the reform agenda held up for three months, if we were to meet the timelines we had set ourselves for getting Bosnia through the gates and on to the road to Europe.

Our plan was to announce an ambitious package of reforms, on which we had previously secured agreement from Solana and Patten and the PIC countries, straight after the elections. These were designed as a continuation of the 'Justice and Jobs' agenda agreed by all Bosnian political parties before the election. The overall title was to be 'Making Bosnia and Herzegovina work' and it contained a number of major changes to the way BiH was run, aimed at cleaning up politics, strengthening the state and reforming the economy in order to help create jobs.

The state government of Bosnia had so far been run by a council of ministers whose prime minister (or chairman) rotated between the different ethnicities, every eight months. Needless to say this reduced the whole process to one oscillating between tragedy and farce. Our most controversial proposal was to end this immediately and establish a single 'prime minister' with a full four-year mandate. Secondly, Bosnia had no conflict of interest law governing the behaviour of officials and politicians. We planned to introduce one modelled on modern European standards and take steps to protect the civil service from political interference, which was rampant in Bosnia, with incoming governments regularly kicking out the previous administrations' civil servants and bringing in their friends – especially in the security and intelligence sectors.

More worryingly, politicians in Bosnia were protected from prosecution by a blanket system of immunity that covered actions which they had committed while in elected or executive office, even when they had left that office and even when these actions had no direct link with their public duties. Under these provisions, it became positively advantageous for criminals to get themselves elected in order to evade prosecution. In a speech at the time I said that Bosnia's politics, which should have been a crime-free space, had become instead a criminal sanctuary. As part of our post-election package of measures, I planned to narrow significantly the scope of immunity provisions and replace them with provisions in line with the standards in other democratic countries.

Though this was not announced publicly, we also took steps massively to strengthen our capacity to carry out audits, especially in the public utilities, where high-level political corruption was rife. Thanks in large measure to support from the US government, we were able to put together a team of Bosnian and international auditors housed within the Organisation for Security and Co-operation in Europe (OSCE). This was to prove one of the best decisions we took and the unit became a key element in the long (and still continuing) battle to re-establish the rule of law and clean up the public space in Bosnia.

In the package we intended to introduce there were also a number of measures aimed at liberalising the Bosnian economy and creating a single economic space in the country. The centrepiece was to be the abolition of the complex, inefficient, corruption-generating sales tax system in Bosnia and replacing it with a single state-wide VAT that would give central government an assured revenue stream and cut back massively on the scope for corruption. We also set out measures to abolish the country's two customs services and combine them into one. Both these measures would, we knew, be strenuously resisted by the Republika Srpska.

The final and arguably least contentious element of the package was the one which caused me most trouble – not with the Bosnians but with the international community. We intended to regularise the government in two 'special regime' cantons which were regarded as the most difficult in Bosnia because of hostile relations between Croats and Bosnian Muslims. I could see no further purpose in maintaining these and intended to place the government of these cantons on exactly the same basis as that of every other canton in the country. However, on 4 October, the day before the election and my announcement of the package of measures, I received an urgent delegation of senior internationals led by Jacques Klein, the head of the UN Mission in Bosnia, saying if I did this, Herzegovina would blow up. A number of the PIC ambassadors, especially the Turk and German, supported this view and were predicting an uprising among the Croats if I went ahead. Even the British were worried. It was a nerve-racking moment, but I decided that we should back our own judgement and go ahead nevertheless.

There was one more element that I wanted to add to the package – the disbandment of Bosnia's two entity-based armies and the creation of a single army, under the control of the state. This was an essential requirement for membership of NATO. But it would be furiously resisted by the Republika Srpska, who regarded their army as the badge of their 'statehood'. It would also require a change in Dayton, which I could not effect, and so could only be achieved by consent, including from the RS. I decided in the end that this would be overloading the apple cart at this stage. We would have to digest the rest of our already very heavyweight package first and then wait for the right political moment to undertake defence reform.

While we would take many other contentious decisions in the years ahead, it was this package of measures and their ultimate acceptance by Bosnia's local parliaments that laid the groundwork for the rest of my mandate. What they set in train was a new dynamic in Bosnia – a dynamic of reform, rather than a dynamic of obstructionism. We were now running on our agenda.

The elections, when they came, confirmed our worst fears, but more so. The nationalists swept back to power as the SDP and most of its partners lost around 15 per cent of their vote. Even though some of us had sensed this coming, it still came as a shock. I lay awake all night wondering whether this was not the end of what I had hoped to do and, effectively, of my mandate. The following morning I found the whole international community in even worse disarray and the papers, local and international, saying that Bosnia had turned back to the past and the international intervention had failed. As I hoped, the papers and the politicians were far more concerned with the election results than with my package of reform measures which, at the time, passed off rather quietly – though it was not long before their full impact was realised.

Meanwhile I had a new problem. We quickly understood that it was now up to us in OHR to shepherd the international community back together again and to develop a new strategy for handling governments across Bosnia that were now in the hands of the nationalists who had fought the war. During the morning Julian Braithwaite developed a press line, pointing out that all European countries transitioning from Communism had swung to the right after their first reformist government; that actually, most of the nationalist parties had lost votes even if in combination they had gained power; and that, anyway, all the parties, including the nationalists, had committed themselves to our 'Justice and Jobs' reform agenda in the elections. Slowly we began to move the story on to something more positive.

But I still had my international community colleagues to deal with. The first meeting with the PIC ambassadors was a shambles, with the Americans determined not to accept nationalist governments no matter what happened. Others were keen to join them in attempting to set up another reformist coalition (despite the fact that, as I pointed out, this would require a coalition of twelve extremely disparate and mostly mutually hostile parties who at the best were doubtful reformers, all in order to give it a majority of just one over the nationalists). The Russians took the opposite view and were in favour of accepting the verdict of the ballot box and working with the government that emerged.

I thought the Russians were right and suggested that our policy should be to judge the government that would emerge not by who they were, but by what they did (incidentally this seems to be a far better policy than picking winners – which we nearly always get wrong anyway). We had our reform agenda. The nationalist parties had said they agreed with it. We should require them to implement it. I had detected some internal divisions in each of the nationalist parties between the old recidivists, who just wanted to return to the past and the new realists who realised that they had to start to build a European future. If we were to insist on the reform agenda as the price for joining Europe and NATO (which every party supported), the effect over the next few years would be to split the nationalist parties and perhaps open the way to a more sensible re-alignment of politics in the country. In the end, the PIC ambassadors agreed to give this a try – but I was left in no doubt that if it failed they would want to go back to the good old days of electoral engineering with their friends, even though they agreed that, on this occasion, the mathematics for this were far from helpful.

There were few decisions I took in these early days which opened me up to more criticism in Bosnia and outside than my willingness at this time to work with the nationalists. The defeated SDP virulently attacked me for the next four years for 'working with the nationalists' – somehow believing that since they had (roundly) lost the election, I should have somehow put them back into power anyway. As it happens the electoral outcome was not conducive to this, but even if it had been, I believed that the days of the international community engineering to put their friends back into power ought to be over. It was one thing to seek to influence the politics of the country – but quite another to seek to reverse-engineer the outcome of an election. If we wanted Bosnia to be a democracy we had to respect the result of the ballot box, not manipulate events to overturn its verdict – which on this occasion, though unwelcome, had been very clear.

Two days after the elections, on 7 October, the new US general in charge of SFOR told me confidentially that his soldiers were about to raid an armaments firm called *Orao* (it means Eagle) in the RS, which was suspected of supplying arms and spare parts to Iraq, in breach of the UN arms embargo (and of course Dayton). The raid took place the following day but the information from it took some time to be analysed. When it did it fully confirmed our suspicions – *Orao*, a state firm controlled by the RS government, was supplying aircraft spare parts and technical assistance to the Iraqi air force in direct contravention of the UN arms embargo in force at the time. In the worst case, this breach of international law by the RS could have opened up Bosnia to the possibility of UN action. We knew at once that this would give us the opportunity I had been looking for to try to push through defence reform in order to abolish the two opposing entity armies and create a single Bosnian army under state control.

Meanwhile, however, opposition was beginning to build up to the reforms I had introduced. The earliest came from the newly elected Bosnian Muslim president (there are three state presidents in Bosnia, one from each of the ethnicities), Sulejman Tihić, who insisted that the new incoming governments should be able to appoint their own civil servants. This was followed by some pretty blatant attempts by the Bosnian Muslim nationalist party, the SDA, to influence the appointment of police chiefs and judges. Shortly afterwards the Serbs expressed their outright opposition to VAT.

Much of the immediate post-election period was spent fire-fighting these attacks and keeping our agenda on track. I rang Chris Patten in late October and asked him if he would weigh in as Commissioner and say that these reforms were required if BiH wanted to join Europe. As always he agreed, and we drafted a letter for him to send to the presidents along these lines, which received a lot of press and gave us crucial support at a key time. But squabbling was not confined to the Bosnians. Before my arrival a team mostly made up of internationals, largely from the US, had been hired to rewrite Bosnia's criminal and other legal codes. The product in my view was a mess and paid little attention to local Bosnian traditions. So I had brought in a former Bosnian law professor, Zoran Pajić, who had been working in London, to assemble and coordinate a team of local lawyers to rewrite Bosnia's legal codes, starting with the criminal code. They were an exceedingly gifted team and completed the process in record time. The product was a legal code which had its roots in local law, but also drew, where appropriate, on the Anglo-Saxon and continental European traditions. In the French view, however, the outcome was too Anglo-Saxon and insufficiently Napoleonic. I had quite a strenuous time insisting to the French ambassador that the balance was right and that it was necessary to get it into operation as soon as possible so we could start catching and prosecuting criminals.

Earlier in the year, on 11 March 2002, the decision had been taken to hand over the UN's responsibilities for the reform of the police service to a European Mission on 1 January 2003. The new EU Mission was to be responsible to Brussels through my chain of command. But there was much tension between the two organisations, culminating in a refusal by the UN, on bureaucratic grounds, to hand over their files to the incoming EU Mission. We never did solve that one and paid heavily for it later.[*]

It was during this period that I also decided that I would allow myself one personal project outside our Mission Implementation Plan in Bosnia and Herzegovina and my first one would be to help those engaged in designing and building a fitting cemetery and

---

[*] Bosnian policemen dismissed by the UN subsequently challenged their dismissal on the grounds that the proper procedures had not been followed and we could not check these against the UN documents which were held in New York.

memorial for the more than 7,000 slaughtered in Srebrenica, including raising the 5 million Euros necessary to fund it.

In late October, the situation concerning the Bosnian Muslim intelligence chief came to a head. The warnings we had given about his intelligence service not being used for political purposes had gone unheeded. I had no alternative to but act and removed him from his post. He had been appointed by the previous SDP-led Alliance government. This produced a furious reaction from the SDP and its supporters in the Bosnian Muslim press. One of their weeklies published a vitriolic attack on me which replayed earlier UK press headlines from my days in politics, under the headline 'How our idiot will destroy us through reform'. I am rather thin-skinned and for a short time this got through to me. But Julian Braithwaite persuaded me that the best response was no response. The attacks on me mounted, and even on my staff and their families from this quarter of the Bosnian press, and continued throughout my mandate, becoming more and more shrill and based on outright lies – even to the extent of claiming, on one occasion, that I was a secret Karadžić supporter! But we stuck to our policy of not responding and I am convinced that was right.

One good aspect of these events was that they opened the way later for the creation of a single state-wide intelligence service in Bosnia, established on European standards. A more worrying aspect, however, was that it became clear that both my house and my office were bugged. When I arrived I had insisted on purchasing a 'secure room' for OHR in which we could hold all our private discussions. This had just arrived from Britain. From now on all our most important discussions were held in what subsequently became known as known as the 'fish tank'.

On 29 October I flew to Brussels to see George Robertson, then Secretary General of NATO, to brief him on the *Orao* affair. I wanted to tell him that I intended to use this scandal to initiate a complete reform of the defence structures in Bosnia – would NATO take the lead in this? I warned him at the time that when the full enquiry I had instituted was complete, it would be likely to show some high-level political culpability for the scandal and that might require me to take some tough decisions that would be politically contentious. I would handle that, if NATO would handle the defence reform process that would follow. He agreed and issued some strong statements about the seriousness of the *Orao* affair.

A week later, meeting with the Serb leadership in Banja Luka, the capital of Republika Srpska, I made it clear that they now had to carry out a full investigation into the *Orao* affair, produce a report within a month establishing who was responsible for this breach of the UN embargo (which had opened up the possibility of UN sanctions against Bosnia) and then a further report within three months identifying the measures they were proposing to take in order to ensure that this didn't happen again. NATO, who were responsible for arms sales under the Dayton Agreement, would oversee the process.

As November proceeded it became increasingly clear that political responsibility for the *Orao* scandal was most likely to centre on the then Serb member of the State Presidency, Mirko Šarović, who had been directly elected to this position only a month previously with 70 per cent of the vote. At the time the UN sanctions-busting deal had been set up with Iraq, Šarović had been not only president of Republika Srpska and thus the person constitutionally responsible for the RS army, but also the chairman of the RS Supreme Defence Council who oversaw the deal. It seemed very likely that when the full facts of this affair came to light I would be left with no option but to remove him from his office if he didn't resign. I started to discuss this possibility with the ambassadors of the Contact Group nations (essentially the most powerful nations of the PIC – Russia, Germany, the United States, France, Italy and Great Britain) at a dinner in the middle of November. The Russians backed by the French and the Germans were opposed to any removal of Šarović, the other three in favour. This left me with a huge dilemma. My moral authority would be broken if I failed to be consistent with the previous actions I had taken insisting on ministerial responsibility. Moreover, a failure to act in the face of such a grievous breach of not just Dayton, but also international law, would have been impossible for the other two peoples in Bosnia – the Croats and the Bosnian Muslims – to understand. I decided to play for time in order to give me space to build up international support for the action I knew it was likely I would have to take. So when General Kip Ward, the SFOR commander overseeing the *Orao* enquiry came to see me on 17 December to say that the report was progressing well and there was now strong evidence that Šarović was in the frame, I asked him to delay the report well into the early months of the following year. Apart from anything else, I was fighting the Republika Srpska on enough fronts and needed to get over these battles before engaging in others. In these kinds of operation, I said to him, it is important to programme your crises if you can.

And I had more than enough to handle for the moment. The Serbs (Mladen Ivanić again) strongly objected to having a VAT system established for the state. However, with strong support from Chris Patten, who made it clear this would be necessary if the country was to join Europe, we persuaded them to join a technical commission to be established in the New Year. This would look at the possibility of establishing a state-wide collection structure which would then disburse funds, according to an agreed formula, to the state and the two entities. The sticking point for the Serbs was that their revenues should be treated as theirs by right and not depend on state disbursement.

Next, the Serb leaders flatly refused to give passage through the state parliament to the reforms I had introduced to improve the operation of the state government. I had made it clear that if these were not passed through parliament, I would be prepared to impose them. The Russians, again, but this time with instructions from Moscow, strongly opposed this, but did so privately. I spent some time trying to persuade them to change their view, but without success. On 2 December I had a polite but difficult meeting with the Russian ambassador, who I both liked and respected, and said to him that despite Moscow's objection I felt I had to go ahead. To his great credit he said that though Moscow was strongly opposed to me using my powers on this, they would not make that opposition known publicly. Indeed, despite this difference of opinion, I visited Moscow in mid December for a very constructive series of meetings with Foreign Minister Ivanov, in which the Russians gave me generous moral and practical support for our agreed agenda of reforms, while still insisting that I should not have used the Bonn powers on this.

Meanwhile the Serbs threatened to walk out if I imposed the law reforming the state government structures. But we judged that this would not be more than a token walk-out and they would soon return, so we went ahead. When they walked out the next day, I gave instructions to our press people that we should not make a great fuss about this. Three days later they were back again, having made their point.

But our crises in the last months of 2002 were by no means confined to political ones. On 13 November, the IMF came to see me to report on their three-day study into the economic situation in the country. It was dire. The economy was static; we had a huge internal debt overhang as a result of war damage claims. The Fund's officials estimated that the last country to face a post-war debt problem on this scale was the Weimar Republic in Germany in the 1920s. This situation was exacerbated by the Bosnian courts which were handing out huge and unrealistic settlements. If this continued, the IMF explained, it would bankrupt BiH's governments. They went on to point out that the country was also carrying a large balance of payments deficit, amounting to some 20 per cent of GDP, similar to that in Argentina before the collapse. Up to now this had been covered by international aid, but this aid was being withdrawn, exposing a massive black hole. Unless we could swiftly get the economy going, we would have either to block imports, which would cause terrible problems, or the economy would default, which would be even worse. Peter Nicholl, the governor of the Central Bank, who knew the economy very well, told me privately that he thought that the IMF were exaggerating – though he admitted that the situation was pretty dire.

Since the end of the Bosnian war, a huge amount had been done to reconstruct the entire Bosnian infrastructure and reform the macroeconomic structures of the country's economy, led in large measure by the World Bank and Bosnia's own Central Bank. In the briefings I had received before the start of my mandate, the International Financial Institutions (IFIs)[*] had stressed that the need now was to press ahead with an aggressive programme of supply side reform aimed at liberalising the economy and attacking rigidities in the economic system, as little progress had been made on this front in recent years. Bosnia had lost time, so we would have to be even more aggressive now.

Meeting with the IFIs and Don Hays, we concluded that the Bosnian economy could only be rebuilt on the basis of small

[*] In Bosnia these consisted of the World Bank, the IMF and the European Commission.

businesses and individual enterprise. There was no chance of re-establishing the old heavy industries of the Tito era – though this is what most Bosnians wanted. We had instead aggressively to strip away the myriad business-destroying laws, push down taxes and do what we could to stimulate Bosnia's four key potential growth sectors: tourism, forestry and wood products, organic agriculture and electricity generation.

The World Bank and the IMF, in partnership with key people in the Bosnian governments and with OHR in support, drew up a national development strategy* with short, medium and long term priorities for economic reform, part of which was to establish a committee of businessmen called the 'Bulldozer Committee' from a phrase I had used in a speech outlining our economic reform pro-gramme. The aim was first to identify and then remove the leftover laws of Communism which prevented business growth; our target was to get rid of 150 laws in 150 days and then another 50 laws in the next 6 months. Don, with the indispensable help of the IFIs, applied his formidable energies to this and to tackling (successfully – but after a very long battle) the internal debt problem. He achieved miracles. The targets of the Bulldozer Committee were met and this body was eventually handed over to the Bosnians.

As part of this programme of encouraging enterprise, I also encouraged the floating off of small businesses from inside my own organisation, the OHR. I was very conscious that, in time, the OHR would close and many of its talented employees would lose their jobs. So we set up a system by which our employees could start their own businesses, initially supplying services to OHR. The first group to do this were our catering staff, followed two years later by our maintenance department. Both companies survived on the open market and still operate successfully.

We took one other decision at this time which was to have a huge impact on the rest of my mandate. On 7 November, I met with Kip Ward, the NATO commander, and senior Western intelligence representatives in Bosnia to discuss progress on catching Karadžić and Mladić. We concluded that we were pursuing the policy of the

---

* This creation of this 'Poverty Reduction Support Programme' involved very wide consultation with governments and representatives of civil society, amount-ing to some 537 meetings over 18 months.

lucky break: the intercepted phone call, the piece of intelligence which said he was here, or there, or there. We were then depending on the avenging angel of justice in the form of an SFOR helicopter descending on a mountain forest glade and, in some dramatic *coup de théâtre*, snatching him off to the Hague. And it wasn't working. What we needed was not so much a commando raid as a campaign. Karadžić's strength lay in the fact that he was still regarded as a hero among the Serbs. We had to attack that support, by changing Serb opinion about the crimes he and Mladić had committed. His vulnerability lay in the fact that he had a huge network of support which required a lot of money, almost all of it gained from corrupt and criminal sources. He was not some romantic *hajduk*,* but the tip of a criminal network that covered the Serb part of Bosnia and neighbouring Serbia and Montenegro. If we wanted to get him we would have to attack that network first – which meant first attacking the criminal businessmen and corrupt politicians who supported him by closing down their illegal businesses, freezing their bank accounts and assets and bringing them to justice. We agreed to widen our policy. The United States would look at how they could use US legislation to freeze assets abroad and I would look at how I could back this up with action in Bosnia and also seek out opportunities to expose the true nature of Karadžić and Mladić's deeds in ways which would be understood by ordinary Serbs.

There were other key international decisions also being made at this rather busy time. On 7 November NATO told me that, because of pressures elsewhere in the world, they had decided to halve troop numbers in Bosnia to 6,000 in 2004. So if I wanted to get tough things done, I had better get them done in 2003. At the Copenhagen Summit of 12 and 13 December it emerged that a decision had been taken to complete a transition from SFOR (the NATO-led stabilisation force) to the first ever EU force (EUFOR), by the end of 2003. The plan was devised by Prime Minister Blair, who had secured Washington's informal agreement beforehand. But we knew nothing of it. The decision took not only us in Sarajevo but also most of Brussels by surprise. However, we manfully pretended that we had known about it all along and issued statements welcoming

* Balkan Robin Hood.

this as an important step towards Europe for Bosnia. In the end, as the Iraq war put increasing strain on transatlantic relations, the planned transition was delayed and the transfer of authority was not in fact completed until December 2004.

Earlier, on 19 November, Carla Del Ponte[*] visited Sarajevo and we took the historic decision (private for the moment) that we would take on the task of establishing a domestic war crimes chamber in Bosnia. This $25 million project would give Bosnia a mini-Hague court and make it the first country in the Balkans to be able to try its own war criminals in its own specialised court, on its own territory. A month later I was in the Hague giving evidence against the camp commandant of one of the Serb concentration camps I had been the first to visit in 1992, at the time when the death camps of Bosnia were just coming to light.

Kofi Annan visited us, too, and (at our request) reinforced the united international community message that the future for Bosnia lay in 'justice and jobs through reform.' I found him, naturally, very pre-occupied with Iraq, on which he confided to me he credited Tony Blair, pretty well single-handedly, with reconnecting the US with the UN at this tricky moment. I also received a visit from the much respected ex-mayor of Mostar, a Croat named Neven Tomić, begging me to take action to reunite this divided city, where, more than anywhere else in Bosnia, the old wartime suspicions and hatreds had remained largely undiminished. I told him that I recognised that this was something I had to do on my watch, but I had just too much on my plate to do it now. I promised I would turn my attention to Mostar before the end of 2003, when we had digested the highly contentious reforms which we were trying to deal with at the moment.

Finally and in great secrecy, on 15 November I received a visit from Tomislav Jokić, Croatian President Mesić's personal adviser, with the following private message from the President; he was strongly in favour of what I was doing and if ever I needed his help, especially with the Croats, I should call on him and he would do what he could. This was welcome indeed. I had admired Mesić as one of the very few politicians in the Balkans with real moral force,

---

[*] The Chief Prosecutor at the ICTY Hague Tribunal.

since we first met when giving evidence against a Croat general involved in Operation Storm in the Hague in March 1998.* His promise of help, especially with the Croats, was one I called in on several occasions.

By the end of November my French Deputy Bernard Fassier had completed the setting up of OHR's rule of law pillar. Meanwhile, we were well advanced on the long task of reviewing all the judges in Bosnia and replacing all the bad apples† and OHR's newly established Anti-Crime and Corruption and Criminal Intelligence Units were also, at this time, beginning to work with local Bosnian prosecutors in uncovering high-level corruption in the country.

On 20 December, two and a half months after the elections and after long and tortuous local negotiations, the governments of Bosnia in the two entities and at the state level were finally assembled. On that day I met with the Bosnia's first non-rotating 'Prime Minister' Adnan Terzić (his actual title was 'Chairman of the Council of Ministers' but I insisted on calling him Prime Minister and the title has largely stuck). His first words when he walked in to see me were: 'Look, I am only interested in one thing. Getting this country into Europe and improving the lot of its people so my son, Tarik, can have a good life.' No Bosnian politician had said such a thing to me before. I took to him immediately and over the next three years we became close partners and firm friends.

Over these months we were also putting into practice our plan for visits outside Sarajevo. Here are two extracts from my diary for these months:

---

* At this point Tudjman was still in power; Mesić was living in Croatia and was a secret witness due to the fact that there had been death threats against him in Zagreb to stop him from giving evidence. My evidence centred on the map Tudjman had drawn out for me on the back of a menu at the Guildhall dinner of 6 May 1995.

† We considered two ways to review and replace judges. We could have followed the practice of 'lustration', which was the approach followed in East Germany after unification. This entailed sacking all judges and getting them all to apply to join a new bench. We concluded that it might have been possible to follow the 'lustration' approach immediately after the Bosnian war. But it was too late to pursue such a brutal approach now. So we opted for the longer and more exhausting but, in our view, fairer approach of reviewing each judge individually. Later, when we came to combining the intelligence services we faced the same choice and made the same decision.

TUESDAY 12 NOVEMBER 2002

Off to the Podrinje Identification Centre[*] near Tuzla.

They took me first into the tunnels running into the salt mines[†] and here, stacked row on row, in white plastic bags, were the remains of some of the seven or eight thousand young men and boys who were killed in Srebrenica. The smell of putrefaction everywhere. I opened one of the bags, dreading to see what was inside but feeling that I had to. It was just a collection of bones, some hair and some putrefied flesh.

We then went off to the place where they were doing DNA identification. Here a woman was working on some rather dusty bones, extracting samples for analysis. Next door was the room where they stored the personal effects of the so far unclaimed and unidentified.

This proved far more harrowing than the shards of bones and tufts of hair. For here was evidence of the living. Each body's possessions had been meticulously collected from the mass graves, the clothes washed and the possessions carefully cleaned and neatly assembled in little piles, like some ghostly left luggage office. A blue and white striped t-shirt, a pair of blood-stained underpants and shorts, some socks and some gym shoes that had been decayed by decomposition in the soil, a letter from a wife, a tobacco pouch, a decayed and unreadable identity card and a couple of photographs showing a woman and some children sitting round a dinner table. All that was left of a life. I couldn't stop the tears springing into my eyes.

In another room, filled with more body bags, lay the remains of the identified, each carefully labelled with the name and the details of the mass grave in which they had been found, and each with their possessions in brown paper parcels neatly stacked at the side, waiting to start their last journey back to the Srebrenica battery factory from where they had started that fateful sunny July day back in 1995.

Almost all of these, I was told, had been dug up and then reburied when the Serbs tried to cover up the evidence of this horror. The smell of putrefaction stayed with me all day.

---

[*] The centre is run by the International Commission for Missing Persons (ICMP) and is tasked with trying to identify those killed at Srebrenica from their remains.
[†] The Tuzla district of Bosnia is built on salt and peppered with salt mines.

Later we went to the collective centre where many of the widows of Srebrenica are still housed, living in indescribably awful conditions, four and five to a single room. Women, children, men, the old and the young all bundled together. These people have lived like this for six or seven years! Desperate, hopeless and without a future. But there is no longer the international aid to find them homes and they do not want to go back to Srebrenica like so many of the others have – and who can blame them?

As usual the problem is a bureaucratic one. The local Municipality has the duty to look after them, but no money. The Canton has the money, but not the duty. Which means that everybody dodges responsibility.

What a dreadful day. The bereaved, the decomposed and the desperate all in a single afternoon.

FRIDAY 29 NOVEMBER 2002

Up at 6 and to Drvar,[*] where Jane and I had breakfast with a Serb refugee, Milorad Srdić, and his wife. They were the first two returnees to Drvar after the war and suffered terribly from intimidation by the Croat population.

Drvar used to have a Serb majority but all were driven out by the Croats during Operation Storm. But now, slowly over time and as a result of Milorad's courage, the Serb population has re-established itself and now outnumber the Croats again.

Drvar remains, however, a most depressing town. It is still full of recently destroyed buildings, every wall pock marked with bullet and shell holes and a general air of depression. There were terrible acts committed here during the war.

Wealth and jobs in Drvar come from its forests. But these remain in Croat hands and are being plundered on a daily basis by illegal loggers taking the timber over to Croatia. All the community's wealth is being passed over into criminal hands. There is still tension between the two sides, although things, Milorad told me, are getting slowly better. But there are still few jobs for the Serbs except in the municipality, where the first Serb mayor after the war was recently

---

[*] Drvar is at the western edge of Bosnia and Herzegovina, where, in Operation Storm, the Croat Army drove all the Serbs out in 1994.

elected. But 99 per cent of the jobs in Drvar are in logging firms which employ only Croats.

Milorad has one of those wonderful sturdy Balkan faces. Deep-lined, with startling blue eyes and a very self-possessed aspect. His wife was delightful too. They live from hand to mouth, making a bit of money by breeding hunting dogs. He also heads up a little local NGO which tries to help Serb refugees.

Of course the first thing we had to do, even at this early hour, was to join him in a glass of Šlivovića,[*] downing it in one. It made my head swim. Then his wife brought out some little cakes, some kaymak[†] and some of his own cured ham. I spent an hour with them before leaving for Livno.

As we drew towards Christmas, our children and grandchildren came out to stay with us. I was looking forward to a quiet Christmas with them.

Some hope! Just before we sat down to our joint family/staff Christmas dinner, Edward Llewellyn whispered to me that there had been some terrible murders the night before in a village in northern Herzegovina, some twenty miles south of Sarajevo. A young Muslim had burst in on a Croat family sitting down to their Christmas eve meal, shot dead the father and two of his daughters and seriously injuring one of their brothers. In any country this would have been shocking. In Bosnia it was likely to be explosive. Shortly afterwards I heard that the young Muslim was mentally unstable – this was not a killing with ethnic or religious motive, just a gun crime by some-one with an unbalanced mind, as can happen in any country (c.f. Dunblane and Hungerford, in Britain). But how to explain this in the supercharged atmosphere of Bosnia amid the emotions of the Christians' main holiday of the year? I rang Prime Minister Terzić (who is a Muslim) and suggested we should go to the scene of the crime and see the family together the following day. He immediately agreed. Then I rang the head of the Muslim religious community, the Reis Ul Ulema, Mustafa Ceric, and asked him to put out a statement condemning this crime. He had already done so in the strongest terms.

[*] Plum brandy.
[†] A kind of cottage cheese.

After some days of nervous tension the situation gradually came back on an even keel. But not before a grenade incident at a mosque in Republika Srpska required another visit in early January, this time with the new European Police Commissioner, Sven Frederiksen, whose European Union Police Mission (EUPM) had taken over responsibility for police reform in Bosnia from the UN Police Mission on 1 January 2003.

My diary records, however, that I was far from optimistic at the end of the year:

MONDAY 30 DECEMBER 2002

I think things are going to get far worse in Bosnia, before they start getting better.

I anticipate a year of social unrest as a result of the economic reforms, particularly from the trade unions. There is some evidence that they are going to organise opposition on the streets. There will inevitably be substantial bankruptcies as the old inefficient firms go and privatisation takes hold. And then there is the spectre of economic crisis. It is the Serbs that I will have to battle with in the first part of the year ahead, and probably the Bosnian Muslims in the second. The Republika Srpska will find it very difficult to accept customs unification and VAT. But in the latter part of the year it is the change in the status of Mostar and the privatisation, especially of the energy companies, which is going to cause trouble among the Bosnian Muslims.

And behind it all the gloomy spectre of a war (in Iraq). This worries more than anything else – not just for the instabilities it will create, but for the tensions in the Atlantic alliance and its effect on the international coalition that I have to hold together to get the job done here in Bosnia.

2003

Three issues dominated the first months of 2003: VAT, customs unification and the consequences of the *Orao* scandal.

It was becoming increasingly clear that I was probably going to have to act against the Serb president, Mirko Šarović, because of his complicity in the *Orao* affair – and that this was going to cause real difficulties, not just in the Republika Srpska, but also with the international community. My diary for 6 January records a conversation with my closest staff, which I opened with the following words:

> We are now moving into the second part of my mandate. Whether or not we can keep up the pace of reform depends on the next two months and on three key issues: the linked issue of VAT and customs; pressing forward with economic reforms; and ensuring that we take the right steps on *Orao*. On the latter, we do not know what the outcome of the enquiries will be. But it looks very likely that I will have to act against Šarović. If this is what emerges, it will be very tough. So we will have to start preparing for the contingency now. We will have to do a lot of preparation with some of our international colleagues to keep them on board. If I reach the conclusion that I have to remove Šarović then I will have to be very clear about this if we are to persuade them. We will need to ensure that we first get the UK and then the United States behind us, then try to persuade the rest of the ambassadors [of the Steering Board of the PIC] to agree. My powers here in Bosnia rest on my moral credibility and this depends on being seen to act consistently – I cannot insist on ministers taking responsibility in the case of [the Croat finance minister] Grabovac and not apply the same standard to Šarović just because he happens to be the Serb president and directly elected. I may have to stake my mandate on this, because if I don't then the authority of my mandate will be broken.

The following day, NATO gave me a first, private sight of the latest Republika Srpska government report on the *Orao* affair, which they had just received. The RS government's previous, very skimpy report, published in October, had placed all the blame on the local managers of *Orao* and sacked two of them, thus conveniently bypassing the political responsibility in all of this. NATO, backed by the PIC ambassadors and the UN, had said that this was unacceptable – there had to be a further report identifying where the political responsibility lay for breaching the UN arms embargo – and the Dayton Peace Agreement – if UN sanctions were to be avoided against Bosnia.

This latest RS report was 1,600 pages long and a deliberate

attempt to provide a snowstorm of paper which would obscure the issue of political responsibility. It did, however, accept that there had to be political responsibility and concluded that this should be placed on Biljana Plavšić, a previous Republika Srpska president and a sworn enemy of the current RS administration, who was, very conveniently, already in jail, having been convicted by the Hague Tribunal. The conclusion of the RS report was that since a culprit had already been found and was already in jail, no further action on the political front need be taken!

I asked NATO to spend a very long time indeed looking into this voluminous report. I didn't want this issue on my desk until late February as I needed time, first to prepare the international community for the action it looked as though I was going to take and second in order to deal with the other pressing issue of the moment, getting Serb agreement on VAT and customs unification.

Serb opposition to VAT and customs unification was spearheaded, once again, by Mladen Ivanić, who, in the new government, had moved from prime minister of Republika Srpska to state foreign minister. The Serbs were wholly opposed to unifying the customs and, though in agreement with VAT as a principle, wanted it exclusively raised and spent by the entities, not the state (so, of course, strengthening the former and weakening the latter). Since the introduction of VAT required an amendment to the Dayton distribution of competencies, it could be achieved only by persuasion, not imposition using the Bonn powers. At my request, the international community, led by the EC, made it clear that the Serb position was unacceptable if Bosnia wanted to get on to the path to Europe. The World Bank and the IMF supported this – though the latter had to be strenuously persuaded to the position, since their practice to that date had been to deal with the entities, not the state.

In mid January, just after Greece had assumed the European presidency, Greek Foreign Minister George Papandreou (an old friend) and Javier Solana paid a joint visit to Bosnia. Ivanić took advantage of the visit to complain to both of them about VAT and insist it must be entity-based. Ivanić approached Papandreou after the meeting to say how much he was looking forward to coming to Athens to see him. Papandreou responded: 'Not until you have agreed with Paddy on VAT and customs. Come then – not before.'

Shortly after this visit, Don Hays went to Banja Luka to see if he could negotiate a deal with the Serbs. He rang me that evening to say he thought he had secured a deal on customs. I was delighted at the breakthrough. But when we looked at the Serb translation of the deal Don had secured we immediately saw it had a flaw. Don had, as we agreed, conceded that the entities should have the right to audit the operation of the state customs service. But because the Serb language uses the same word for 'audit' and 'control', what their version of the agreement meant was that they retained control of state customs. I sent a swift message back thanking them for their movement on this, but insisting that we still had to go further to meet the EU's requirements. It was not the last time that an issue of great importance was nearly lost on a matter of translation.

By the third week in January, the momentum on VAT was building up and I felt that we were at last getting somewhere, when suddenly the IMF dropped a bombshell. Their Washington-based desk officer – an ex-employee of the Bank of England – suddenly announced that they had changed their policy – they wanted VAT at entity level after all! This spelled disaster for the whole project, especially if the Serbs got to hear of it.

I rang IMF headquarters in Washington to see if I could shift them and when I found I couldn't, arranged for a high-level démarche to be made at the most senior IMF level by the US, the UK, the Greek EU presidency and the European Commission. At first this didn't work, with the IMF desk officer taking an even more obdurate position. To my horror, the European Commission local representatives also then started to wobble – not, I think, wishing to be isolated if the IMF took a contrary position. I had a series of extremely stormy meetings with the local IMF representative, Valeria Ficchera, a remarkable lady for whom I had a high regard, but whose job, of course, was to defend the policy of her head-quarters. Her fiery Sicilian temperament and my equally fiery Irish one did not mix well when, as on this occasion, we disagreed. After further high-level lobbying in Brussels and Washington, we held a local meeting which Don Hays shooed me out of, so he could take down the temperature and get the discussion from one of high politics to one of detail, in an attempt to find a way round the IMF's objections. With the help of the local EC expert, Renzo Daviddi, they managed to find a technical fix that enabled the IMF to change its position back again. A very tricky moment passed.

There were tensions elsewhere in the international community, too. The United States, operating through NATO, took into custody a Bosnian Muslim called Sabahudin Fijuljanin, with suspected connections with Al Qaeda. Prior to my arrival, in January 2002, six Bosnians residents had been whisked away to Guantanamo in circumstances which I thought very questionable under Bosnian law. I had made it clear to the US administration before I arrived in Bosnia that if this had happened on my watch, I would not have stayed silent. US assistance and support for my mandate was extremely generous and one of the pillars on which I built most of my actions in Bosnia. But my job was to enforce the law of Bosnia and Herzegovina, and however much I needed US support, that had to come first. The situation now seemed to be repeating itself.

I was shown the information linking this man to Al Qaeda and told that US Secretary of Defense Donald Rumsfeld wanted him in Guantanamo. I replied that that could only happen if it happened according to the law of Bosnia and if it didn't I would be very publicly opposed to it. In the end, I conceded, since I wasn't in charge of the NATO troops in the country and there was nothing I could do to stop it if the US simply flew him out. After being held briefly in Tuzla, Fijuljanin was released. I am glad to say that my US colleagues were generous enough not to allow this plain speaking and the tensions it caused to do damage to my long-term relationship with, or the value I put on the help of, Washington.

In the middle of January, Carla Del Ponte paid us another visit, which we used to start the public process of establishing a war crimes chamber in Bosnia. For the first time we also talked in detail about the support network that was helping keep Karadžić on the run. Huge sums of money were being illegally funnelled through a complex network that included private businesses, banks and politicians. To break down the network, the domestic authorities would need help from the international community and we talked about what it would take to shine a bright light on the institutions involved to expose their activities. I began to consider appointing international administrators for the banks, securing wide-scale audits of the businesses involved and removing politicians and officials who continued to obstruct efforts to bring Hague-indicted war criminals to justice.

At about the same time, the president of Republika Srpska, Dragan Čavić, came to see me to threaten that I would have outright revolt from the Serb leadership and widespread disturbances in Republika Srpska if I removed President Šarović. I listened politely and said that I hadn't yet decided what it might be right to do. But he needed to understand that there was a very serious question which could not be dodged, about who was politically responsible for a scandal that had opened up Bosnia and Herzegovina to the possibility of UN sanctions.

Meanwhile at a dinner in Brussels with Patten and Solana they gave me their backing for going ahead on Šarović, if I had to. The following day I met with George Robertson at NATO headquarters, to brief him about our change of policy on catching Karadžić and about the possible instabilities that we might have to cope with after the Šarović removal, if it came to that. He seemed quite relaxed.

But Sir Michael Jay, the head of the UK Foreign Office, whom I saw the day after in London, was much more nervous and urged caution – he was visibly relieved when I reassured him that I was not going to rush into this. Apart from anything else, I needed time to bring the other key nations on board. The following day I got backing from Jack Straw for widening the attack on Karadžić and we agreed to explore the idea of placing members of the Karadžić network on the European visa ban list. He promised that Britain would take the operational lead in this new campaign to catch the world's most wanted war criminal, though Defence Secretary Geoff Hoon told me that if this meant more UK Special Forces, there weren't any since they were fully occupied already. I knew what he meant without asking – the impending war against Iraq was beginning to throw a long shadow across the path of all those with whom I met on these late January visits.

Back in Sarajevo, other events were also stirring during January. The initial results of the first audits on the Bosnian Muslim, Croat and Serb electricity generating companies were shown to me privately in mid January. What they revealed was a network of corruption even wider and deeper than I had imagined. The politicians, the political parties and their friends were syphoning off huge sums of money from these public utilities and the poor citizens of Bosnia were paying the price. But I wanted to drop this bombshell at the best time for maximum effect in the context of our struggles with the Republika Srpska on VAT and customs. So I held back on publishing the results for a few weeks, until the third of the three audits – into the Serb generating company – was completed. If anything, the pace of events increased in February.

Prime Minister Terzić was now engaged in the deals necessary to form his government from among the five, largely nationalist, parties from which his parliamentary majority would be drawn. The Bosnian constitution requires all ethnicities in Bosnia to be represented at every level of government and in the civil service. So he had some delicate and tricky compromises to make. In the course of these, my staff told me in early February, he did a deal with the Serb representatives which slightly weakened some of the provisions I had brought in to increase the effectiveness of the state government. I was under some pressure to use my powers to reverse these. But it was clear to me that to do so would only add to Terzić's difficulties in trying to assemble a government. As a politician, I sympathised with his plight. He was, I thought, doing the best he could and I would probably have done the same in his position. So I made it clear that, since this deal was done locally and did not fundamentally undermine the reforms, we would not interfere.

Meanwhile, Serb opposition to VAT was increasing and at a dinner with the Russian ambassador on 3 February he made it clear that he agreed with the Serb proposal that there should be two VAT rates, one for each entity, and two collection systems. I became very nervous that international support for a single state-level VAT system was slipping away and decided that we had to go for a deal with the Serbs, before the situation unravelled further. So I asked Don Hays to go back to the RS capital Banja Luka and see if he could negotiate a deal with the leaders of the Serb nationalist SDS Party.

The deal we designed was based on a single rate and collection system, but a distribution formula for the revenue, based on a fixed percentage going to each of the entities and the state, calculated according to population and economic activity factors. There would also be an all-party commission established to decide on the technical details. On 5 February after long hours of negotiation, Don pulled off a breakthrough deal along these lines.

Later in the month I announced the formation of the VAT Commission, but not before a further determined attempt by Foreign Minister Mladen Ivanić to undermine the whole delicate edifice.

Ivanić, a Serb who was regarded as a reformer by the international community and headed one of the smaller Serb parties, had not been present at Don's meetings in Banja Luka. He knew there would be political advantage in outflanking the Serb nationalist SDS Party by opposing VAT. Ivanić conducted a series of lunches with Western ambassadors, some of whom he convinced that a two-system VAT was better. The Belgrade government,* who had a legitimate role under Dayton to protect the interests of the Bosnian Serbs, also visited Sarajevo in the person of Foreign Minister Svilanović who lobbied me hard to alter the plans for VAT. Svilanović, a friend, was reassured, however, when I told him that I would not impose this using the Bonn powers, so it all had, in the end, to be agreed by the parliament of Republika Srpsk.

On the day before I announced the formation of the VAT Commission, I met with Ivanić who told me that, since he had not been part of the Banja Luka deal, he did not consider himself bound by it, would oppose VAT to the end, and that if I sought to go ahead there would be widespread public opposition in Republika Srpska. In an attempt to find the Serbs' leaders a face-saving device to cover their domestic difficulties with this reform, I arranged for the Bosnian Muslims to attack me viciously for having given too much to the Serbs in the negotiations – and then went ahead as planned.

For the rest of the month we waited for the reaction, but, beyond a little more complaining from the Serb leadership, everything remained, by Bosnian standards, very quiet. The VAT Commission, under the chairmanship of an expert supplied by the European Commission,† swiftly took the political steam out of the debate by turning it to technical matters.‡

Meanwhile, I was having a pretty torrid time with the Bosnian Muslims as well – this time over appointments to civil service positions in the new governments. In Bosnia, the old Communist system still applied. Politicians appointed the civil service and one of the perks of being in government was that you could kick out all the

---

* Probably at Ivanić's prompting.

† Joly Dixon, who had set up the taxation systems in Kosovo and who went on to lead the Board established to bring VAT into operation through Bosnia's Indirect Taxation Authority.

‡ There were many battles yet to come on VAT. But this was the crucial moment in introducing what I believe was our biggest reform. VAT came into operation in Bosnia in record time on 1 January 2006.

friends of the last government and put in your own. I had some difficulty explaining that modern democratic standards required an impartial and professional civil service. I tried to do this by persuasion in the first days of the new government, but no one listened. I was suddenly faced with a swathe of political removals from the civil service and an army of new appointees. I had to close the door quickly by freezing all appointments and setting up a Civil Service Commission which would make all new appointments on merit. The Bosnian Muslim president, Sulejman Tihić, complained bitterly about the removal of his patronage, saying, with some justification, that the civil service was full of appointees from the last government, why should they put up with them? I replied rather lamely that I recognised the unfairness – but we had to start somewhere with the new standards the country would need to get into Europe and that this was the time to do it.

My new-found relationship with Prime Minister Terzić was under strain as well. Bosnia had recently introduced a single state-wide identity card. This was vital for security and for any chance the country had of getting easier access to visas for Europe. But this too had caused some difficulties, again with the Serbs in Republika Srpska, who saw it (rightly) as a state thing and wanted nothing of it. There had been much toing and froing before a negotiated deal was done. And even as late as February, with the cards being issued, I was confronted with a deliberate go-slow on handing out the cards in the RS, which was overcome only when I threatened to remove the RS minister of the interior if the law was not obeyed.

Potentially more worrying, however, was the fact that Prime Minister Terzić was fighting a widespread public revolt against the price of the cards themselves. These had been set at around 14 KM (just under £5) – rather a lot of money for citizens of a country where the old-age pension was sometimes less than £30 per month. My advisers told me that any lower price would undermine the financial viability of the cards and could bring down the whole system, so damaging both the economy and external investors' confidence in Bosnia (the scheme was supported by an Austrian bank). However, at one of his first Council of Ministers sessions Terzić, responding to pressure from outside and inside his government, agreed to lower the price to 10 KM. My advisers told me that this was a completely unsustainable price and this view was backed up by the local IMF and the Austrian bank supporting the scheme – the unanimous advice, both from my experts and from the PIC Steering Board ambassadors, was that I should immediately use my powers to overrule the Council of Ministers, abolish the Commission overseeing the introduction of the cards and set a price of 14.5 KM. I was extremely reluctant to do this as it would have undermined the new prime minister, reversed the first major decision taken by his new government, and overturned a decision taken through a genuine cross-party and cross-ethnic consensus, painfully put together by Terzić.

I was, however, concerned that Terzić may not have been fully aware of the potential economic consequences of this decision, so I eventually passed a temporary decision (extremely unpopular at the time) to hold the price of the cards at their original level in order to give the Council of Ministers time to hear the views of the international experts. I made it clear to the new prime minister, however, that this was his decision not mine and that if, having heard the view of the experts, he decided to stick with the lower price, I would not change this. The consequences would be his. To Terzić's great credit, he heard the experts and stuck to his guns. Eventually he was proved right and we were proved wrong – but that did not become evident until a few months later.

Meanwhile, at about the same time, the IMF was meeting with me privately, once again predicting disaster. They were very worried about the uncompetitive nature of the Bosnian currency and believed that a devaluation was going to be necessary, perhaps around September, adding that if this happened the only solution would be to go straight into the Euro in order to prevent any further flight from the Bosnian currency with disastrous effects on the economy. Later, in March, I was to have a meeting with the local banks who reinforced the message that the Bosnian economy, hard hit by the withdrawal of the UN Police Mission which had spent millions a year locally, was in a downwards spiral. Once again, Peter Nicholl from the Central Bank believed they were exaggerating and this was my hunch too – provided we pushed ahead fast enough with economic reform.* One of the IMF's messages at this

---

* No such devaluation proved necessary, either then or later and the KM is now one of the strongest currencies in the Balkans.

time was that the Bosnian banking system – one of the real success stories of Bosnia's post-war reconstruction – had grievously broken its credit limits. Action was urgently needed to pull back bank credit. This would lead to a slow-down of consumption and reduce taxation for the government. The outcome would be either a reduction in public spending or an increase in taxes, both of which would be disastrous for an economy as weak as Bosnia's.*

On the international front, things were little quieter. The Atlantic tensions brought about by the impending Iraq war were beginning to affect us, too. It was, on occasions, all I could do to keep my ambassador colleagues focused on Bosnia, rather than arguing about the relative positions of their capitals on the situation in the Middle East. I refused to comment at all on Iraq, either in Bosnia or abroad. My duties were confined to Bosnia and Herzegovina and taking a position on Iraq would have made it much more difficult to hold together the already fractious international coalition on which my capacity to do my job depended. And anyway there was more than enough going on in Bosnia for us to disagree about.

In early February, the British ambassador came to see me to express his strong concern about the possibility that I might remove President Šarović over the *Orao* affair (though my diary records that I didn't think that London was as concerned about this as he was). A little later at a meeting with all the Steering Board ambassadors, I concluded that they were coming round. But by the end of the month, opinion had swung back again and almost all were opposed to any thought of a removal. Clearly there was much more work to do here and time was running out.

We were also beginning to think about how to handle the unification of Mostar. The French ambassador complained bitterly to me in February that we were sweeping this problem under the carpet. I told him that the carpet was already overloaded. The one thing I did not want was to be fighting on two fronts – with the Serbs on VAT and with the Croats over Mostar. Mostar would have to wait, I said, until we had made progress on our other reforms. Privately, however, I was beginning to look at how we could tackle Mostar and had concluded that we would have to abolish the six municipalities (three Croat and three Bosnian Muslim) who ran a divided Mostar

---

* This, too, didn't happen.

and create a single multi-ethnic sixty- or seventy-member-strong city council. This would require checks and balances for each side and entail making a large number of politicians and even more civil servants who ran the municipalities redundant. I set a private date of September to begin getting personally involved in the long process of unifying Mostar. However, we recognised that we could not keep Mostar completely off the agenda for that long, so we formulated a plan to launch a Commission on the future of Mostar in the spring with a reporting deadline of the end of the summer. This Commission would be made up exclusively of local politicians. OHR would specifically *not* be politically involved. I knew that it was extremely unlikely to succeed, but it would give me time to get our other issues resolved before getting too deeply involved in Mostar. If, as I anticipated, the local Mostar commission failed, then in September I would have more of a case to propose a Commission chaired by an international which would then do the heavy lifting to unify the city. My hope was that in this way the main structures of the new unified city council would be agreed, leaving me to impose the last bit at the end of the process, if I had to. We estimated that this whole process would probably take at least a year to complete.

In the middle of February I had three secret meetings which were to have a profound effect on the future. The first was with representatives of the Bosnian Human Rights Chamber, who were considering a claim by some of the families of those massacred in Srebrenica that their human rights had been violated because the government of the Republika Srpska had knowledge of how their loved ones had died and of the whereabouts of their mortal remains, which they were refusing to divulge. The Chamber's representatives explained that they had reached a decision in favour of the bereaved in this case and were about to hand down a very large fine on the government of the RS. Furthermore, they would require the RS government to provide this information with a deadline in September. The Chamber said that they would like the fine, amounting to £1.3 million, to be put into a fund which we had set up for the construction of a suitable memorial site and graveyard for the Srebrenica dead – did I believe that the fund could deal with this sum of money safely? I assured them that it could and undertook to use my powers, if necessary, in order to see that the decision of the Chamber to insist on the provision of the missing information was fulfilled.

The second meeting was with the Swiss and Norwegian ambassadors to whom I explained that if we were able to make the reforms necessary to get Bosnia on to the road to Europe, then the next task we would have to tackle was constitutional reform. As European nations who had real experience in these matters, could their governments help pave the way for this by setting up private seminars with Bosnian politicians to discuss constitutional reform, outside the country? Both readily agreed.

The third secret meeting followed the decision Carla Del Ponte and I had taken during her January visit to target the Karadžić network. This planning meeting involved NATO, senior Western intelligence representatives, the UK and US ambassadors and representatives of the Office of Foreign Assets Control (OFAC) of the US Treasury. We reviewed the information we had on the Karadžić support network of businessmen, banks and corrupt officials and started to plan a complex and substantial operation against them, with the codename Balkan Vice, setting March as the deadline for action.

Meanwhile, the new crime-fighting institutions we had set up were beginning to score their first successes, with the arrest, in the market town of Prijedor, of the family running Bosnia's biggest women-trafficking ring. It was at this time also that the auditors completed their first phase of work into the electricity generating companies of Bosnia. I had, of course, known for some weeks of the widespread corruption and mismanagement they had found in the Croat and Bosnian Muslim generating companies. But even these revelations had not prepared me for the scandalous network of corruption brought to light in the auditors' report on the Serb-controlled generating company. This was based in the south-eastern town of Trebinje in Herzegovina. The Serb generating company here had been operated as little more than a cash cow for the corrupt and the criminal in the area, feeding huge sums of money into the hands especially of the Serb nationalist ruling party structure. There were also suspicions that some of the money had been used to support the Karadžić network – this being the mountainous area where he was said to have almost complete freedom of movement. We used this report and the others to insist on the removal of corrupt managers and the cleaning-up of the system, so weakening the nationalist political structures in the area, accelerating the process of creating a single state framework for electricity generation in Bosnia and moving this towards privatisation. Indeed, these audits gave us crucial leverage to push forward the whole process of economic reform at a faster pace, with emphasis on three key fronts – reforming the sales tax system, introducing modern bankruptcy laws and pushing privatisation across the whole economy.

Internally, our Mission Implementation Plan was also having an effect. It was already clear that by the end of the year we would reach our targets in assisting with refugee returns in Bosnia. This task, one of the most politically sensitive of all in the early days, could now be handed over to the Bosnians and OHR's forty-one-strong Refugee and Return Task Force could be closed down. This sent something of a shockwave through the OHR as our employees suddenly realised that, instead of always growing, the organisation was now shrinking and would one day close altogether. It is always hardest to keep morale up in an organisation which is going out of business. But, thanks to some superb personnel work inside the OHR and our highly dedicated and committed staff, this problem did not become as severe as I had feared.

I was also planning one other major change in OHR. In July 2003, my Senior German Deputy, Enver Schroembgens, was going to leave us at the end of his tour. I conceived the idea of asking a Bosnian to replace him. I reasoned that this would show that I was serious about the Bosnianisation of OHR even up to the highest levels and would also help in creating a spirit of true partnership between the internationals and the new government, so paving the way for our exit and their takeover. I chose a Bosnian Muslim called Beriz Belkic for the task, a man of simple tastes, patent honesty, and without a nationalist bone in his body, who was widely respected across all communities in Bosnia.

My staff were somewhat shocked when I first put the idea to them, but they soon saw the advantages. I then approached Belkic himself, being careful to explain that this was just an exploratory approach and to outline the dangers of accepting. He was equally shocked and asked for time to think. He came back to me a few days later saying that he would do it and would resign from parliament and party to take up the post if I wished to go ahead. My German Deputy was, however, visibly shaken by the proposal and made it clear that he thought it a very bad idea – but he would consult Berlin. I then approached key ambassadors; the British were in favour, as were the Americans. The Russians expressed concerns (I think on the grounds that he was a Bosnian Muslim rather than a Serb), but said they would go along with it – pointing out, however, that this being a post reserved for the Germans, we should not go ahead if Berlin was opposed. The Italians said they were in favour, as did the French in principle, adding that, whatever their personal opinion, they would follow Berlin. Berlin took a little time to come back to me, but when they did, they made it very clear that this was an important international post for them and they were not pre-pared to give it up. The British and the US then made it clear that if a key colleague (the German ambassador) was opposed, then they would support him.

It would have been difficult but not impossible for me to go ahead against this opposition, this issue being about my own office staff. But it would have cost me large amounts of political capital and I knew I was going to need this for the battles ahead – especially on the actions I was going to have to take on the *Orao* scandal. So I called Belkic in and explained to him in detail why I had to con-clude, with bitter regret, that we couldn't go ahead. To his huge credit he saw the point immediately and made my retreat easier for me.[*] I remain convinced that an opportunity was missed here to make a reality of the principle of partnership with the Bosnians, which we were always better at talking about than doing.

There were also meetings in February with the Islamic ambassa-dors who I kept regularly informed on events (a lot on Iraq here) and with ex-British Tory Minister of Defence Malcolm Rifkind who came to Bosnia representing a private British consultancy firm bid-ding for business on Bosnian privatisation projects. I had to explain to him that I was not a British official, charged with helping British

[*] To his even greater credit, he has never let these events be known publicly – though it would have been greatly to his advantage to do so.

business, but an international civil servant who could have no part in this process.

In early March, with tension rising over impending war in Iraq, the leader of my Close Protection Team (CPT)* told me privately that the security people had received information that there was now a serious threat on my life and they would have to change my routines. According to this information a team connected with foreign Islamic extremists and stay-behind mujahidin elements from the Bosnian war had been targeted to do the job. The Balkans are always full of threats and rumours of threats and I was pretty sure that this was just another of these. But it was their job to assess risks and mine to conform to their professional judgement. They said that I could continue the habit I had started when I came to Sarajevo, of walking into work – but we should alter our schedules and routes from time to time. Later in the month, things got more serious and they estimated that the threat could now extend to my wife, Jane, so she too had to start having protection. This raised threat level lasted on this occasion for two or three months, before we could relax back to our old routines again.†

On 7 March we launched Operation Balkan Vice against the Karadžić network. I passed a law modelled on European statutes, to enable the freezing of assets and bank accounts of individuals and companies and immediately froze the assets of two prominent Serb businessmen/politicians identified by the Hague Tribunal and others as having used their business networks to assist war criminals evade justice. This included closing a bank and freezing a network of petrol stations. My decision also froze the individual bank accounts of fourteen individuals, including Karadžić himself. The United States took parallel action through OFAC to freeze these assets

---

* The British government decided that I should have close protection while in Bosnia. This was provided through a team consisting of eight members of the armed forces – mostly from the Royal Military Police – who rotated every six months and provided protection for me around the clock, including living in our house. They were outstandingly professional and mostly became personal friends – and for my wife, a new team of sons and daughters every six months.
† There were two other threats on my life during my four years in Bosnia, which the security people took seriously, including one which reportedly incorporated a 2 million Euro price tag. Of these, one was believed to originate from a corrupt Bosnian businessman/politician with connections to the Chechens and the other from a group of Serb criminals believed to be close with those who assassinated Serb Prime Minister Zoran Džindžic.

and accounts on a global basis; and the European Union in due course placed some of these individuals on the European Union visa ban list. At the same time SFOR raided a number of the individuals' houses, searching for documents, and also a part of the building occupied by the RS parliament – Republika Srpska National Assembly (RSNA) – which was believed to house an army intelligence unit being used for espionage purposes against the international community and local politicians, specifically contrary to the Dayton Agreement.

This last raid yielded a huge cornucopia of intelligence. The army unit was found to be intercepting international telephone calls, targeting internationals and running agents as far afield as NATO headquarters in Brussels. Among the documents recovered was a plan for an invasion by the Republika Srpska army, with the aim of capturing territory up to the line agreed between Tudjman and Milošević at their secret meeting at one of Tito's old hunting lodges in March 1991, which was revealed to me on the 'map on the menu' in that now infamous dinner I had with Tudjman on 6 May 1995.

This last information was almost certainly not as bad as it looked, and was probably contingency planning in the case of an attack on the RS, rather than evidence of intention. It was, however, so explosive that we could not, at the time, let it be known publicly. Indeed, one of our problems was that, precisely because this was such a valuable haul for the intelligence people to exploit, we could use very little of the information publicly for political purposes, or even privately with non-NATO members of the PIC Steering Board. What made the matter worse was that this Serb intelligence unit was actually operating from within the parliament building and regularly briefing the Serb politicians to whom we were speaking, including Serb President Šarović, whose position was already highly vulnerable because of his involvement in the *Orao* affair.

On 12 March we heard the shocking news that Zoran Džindžic, who I had known quite well and who was a genuine force for reform in Serbia, had been assassinated in Belgrade, almost certainly by organised crime elements. I attended his very moving funeral a few days later.

During March there was a series of meetings in Sarajevo, London and Brussels about what to do on the now combined issues of *Orao* and the espionage affair. Opinion amongst the PIC Steering Board wavered back and forth. I had decided that the espionage affair had now given us exceptional political leverage to do something much bigger than I had intended and that this leverage, which was unlikely to come again, should not be wasted. So I put forward a plan, not only to remove Šarović, but also to institute a series of reforms that would, in effect, begin the process of abolishing the two entity armies and combining them into one state-controlled army.

To remove a directly elected president was itself something which caused considerable nervousness in some capitals – but to add to this a series of reforms that would lead over time to the abolition of the Republika Srpska army was a considerable escalation that caused a lot of consternation. I embarked on a round of consultations aimed at getting support for my plans. It did not start well.

At a Sarajevo meeting in mid March the Russian ambassador, backed by the German, said this was going far too far and the French, while promising their ultimate backing, also expressed the need for caution. At a Contact Group* meeting at more senior political director level in Brussels ten days later, the position shifted somewhat in our favour, with only the Russians holding out. They, not being members of NATO, were the only nation present who did not have access to the information from the NATO raid on the intelligence unit, so I arranged with the US ambassador to show them excerpts from it. But it didn't change their opposition. I noted during this meeting that some capitals seemed to be much more prepared to take tough actions on this than some of their local ambassadors.

At a later meeting of the PIC Steering Board countries, also at senior political director level, all agreed with the package of measures I proposed, with the exception of the Russians who maintained their strong opposition and the French who, while backing the removal of Šarović, thought the defence reforms were going too far. The British and the US were solidly for it, however, and other members of the PIC were also supportive in varying degrees of enthusiasm. The US even undertook to démarche Moscow at a senior level in an attempt to bring the Russians on board. This was real progress and I congratulated my staff that night on the fact that

---

* A core group of nations comprising the US, the UK, France, Germany, Italy and Russia.

their hard work to shift opinion had paid off. As I was shortly to discover, it was a premature judgement.

Back in Sarajevo, I engaged in a programme of local consultation about my impending decision to remove Šarović. To my huge surprise, Bosnian Muslim President Sulejman Tihić, backed by his Croat colleague, warned me that I should not remove the Serb president as this would destabilise the whole country. Shortly afterwards the Serb leadership in Banja Luka issued a threatening statement echoing the same sentiment. I sent Julian Braithwaite to Belgrade to brief Foreign Minister Goran Svilanović and he returned with the same message. A day later the head of the OSCE mission in Bosnia came to see me privately with the same warning.

On 28 March, I met with my staff and announced that I had decided that we should, nevertheless, press ahead with the removal of Šarović and the full package of defence reforms and set Wednesday 1 April as the day we would do this. This was the best opportunity we would ever get to undertake defence reform and I was not going to miss it. As for Šarović, I would give him the opportunity to resign on Tuesday, making it clear that if he didn't I would have to remove him on the following day, Wednesday. I asked Julian Braithwaite to leak some of the information to the press over the weekend, so as to prepare public opinion for what I was going to do over the following week. I also gave instructions that my decision was not, for the moment, to be known by anyone else in the international community in order to give me the maximum room for manoeuvre.

The next day I briefed Chris Patten, George Robertson and Javier Solana of my intentions and of the possibility of trouble. Two days later, on 31 March, the French ambassador, no doubt sensing that something was afoot, asked me to call a meeting of all the ambassadors of the Steering Board of the PIC. This proved to be a most difficult meeting which seemed to me to bear no resemblance to the earlier, more senior meeting in Brussels. The Russian ambassador, quoting instructions from Moscow, repeated their total opposition to the whole package and insisted that I was mandated by the PIC and couldn't go ahead unless I had their unanimous backing. I said I was not mandated. I was chosen by the PIC to do this job, using my judgement. If they wanted someone who could do no more than voice the unanimous opinion of the PIC Steering Board whenever they happened to agree, they had better get someone else to do the job. The French ambassador again said they backed the removal of Šarović, but thought the defence reforms were going too far. The German said I was going too far on all fronts and would blow the whole place up, for which I would take full responsibility.

I said that I noted the differences between this meeting and the opinions I had heard from their bosses in Brussels a few days earlier and retired for a disturbed night to consider the options. By the morning I had decided that we had, nevertheless, to go ahead.

TUESDAY 1 APRIL 2003

This is the big day . . .

After the morning meeting I told my Senior Deputies of my decision on Šarović. Enver Schroembgens[*] said I would have trouble over this but that I was right and I should push ahead. Useful support given the German opposition of last night . . .

At 12 a meeting to brief the IMF, World Bank and European Commission. I said to them that if we were to get ourselves into difficulties we would need them to say that they couldn't continue to support the country financially in order to get the Serbs back to the negotiating tables if they decide to obstruct. My big fear is not riots or instability as predicted by the French and the Germans yesterday, but a Serb withdrawal from the whole reform process. Then at 12.30 I rang Goran Svilanović[†] in Belgrade. I took him through my reasoning. He said that he thought this was the wrong decision but that they would not create a fuss.[‡] And he would do everything he could to persuade Šarović to resign when I saw him. Then at 1.30 the Steering Board ambassadors again. I said that we weren't going to discuss the packet of measures since we did that yesterday. Overnight I had carefully considered the points made at yesterday's meeting and concluded that the best course was to go ahead as I had originally planned. Glum faces. The French and Germans were quiet and the rest supported me, but the Russians were furious and said that they would oppose it bitterly. I think they have told Šarović they could save him. So this is a double slap in the face for them.

---

[*] My German Deputy High Representative.
[†] The foreign minister of Serbia Montenegro.
[‡] I knew that there was no love lost between Svilanović and Šarović.

Once again they played the line that I was not mandated to do this and Sasha [the Russian ambassador] claimed that he had Moscow's explicit instructions that they should oppose this bitterly and, if necessary would make their opposition known publicly. I thanked them in what I hoped was a courteous manner and said that, on the question of being mandated, my comments of last night still stood. I was not obliged to agree with them, though I was obliged to listen to their views and I had done so. Above all I could not be in a position where I could move forward only if we had unanimity. This would mean that we would have to go at the pace of the slowest and the country could not afford that. I then left after about fifteen minutes leaving it to Don Hays to chair the meeting, while I went up to see Šarović at my house.

Julian [Astle] came with me . . . Šarović was there when I arrived and we sat out on the balcony in the sun while Jane brought us a cup of tea. He seemed genuinely shocked when I told him that I had decided that the right thing to do was for him to resign and if he didn't by midday tomorrow I would have to act to remove him. But he recovered and took it with great dignity. As we parted I shook him by the hand and said (genuinely enough) that I had enjoyed working with him and I was sorry that it had to come to this. I hoped that we would be able to continue our good relations in the future. I was impressed by his dignity in what must have been a very difficult moment.

Then down to brief the other leaders of Republika Srpska,* who I had asked to come to a meeting in my office. There followed a long and very tough discussion. I said Šarović was not being sacked because there was proof of his personal involvement, but because he had the political responsibility for what had happened, which amounted to gross violations, not just of the Dayton Peace Agreement, upon which the peace of Bosnia depended, but also of Security Council Resolutions. The latter could have opened up Bosnia to UN sanctions. I pointed out that I would not be understood in this country if I were to sack others for political responsibility, but wouldn't do the same for Šarović, just because he was a Serb and an elected president. I had to be consistent. I then briefed the other

* Dragan Kalinić, the speaker of the RS Parliament, Dragan Čavić, the president of the RS, Dragan Mikerević the RS prime minister and State Foreign Minister Mladen Ivanić.

presidents and Prime Minister Terzić. Tihic of course said that I hadn't gone far enough, that I should have gone further . . .

Later in the evening the Serb leaders came back to see me to tell me that they had had a long discussion with Šarović and he was pretty determined to be kicked out, rather than resign. But they just wanted to double check that if he resigned there was nothing I would do to stop him from continuing in political life or returning after the next election. I said there was absolutely nothing to stop him from continuing in public life and even being the president of the SDS.[*]

The word from Banja Luka is that things are quiet, but the storm will break tomorrow.

WEDNESDAY 2 APRIL 2003

At 11.30 Šarović gave me a call. He said: 'Look, I don't change my mind often. But I spent much of last night discussing this with my political friends and my family. So I am going to change my mind on this occasion. I am going to resign.' It was a very measured, decent conversation in which, once again, he showed great dignity. He said that he hoped the vacuum after his resignation would be filled quickly . . . He wants the Serbs to continue to work on the political agenda.

I am hugely relieved. The moment of greatest danger is passed. Apparently there have been fiery denunciations in the Serb parliament, but apart from that all is quiet in Banja Luka.

Next morning at a specially scheduled ambassadors' meeting I was asked what was happening. I said I wasn't sure – I felt like one of those characters in a 'Beau Geste' film of the 1930s who is made to pace the fort battlements saying things like 'I don't like it Carruthers – it's just too quiet out there.' In the event, tension quickly subsided after the Šarović affair and April proved to be rather a quiet month.

On 3 April, in one of my regular weekly meetings with Prime Minister Terzić, he suggested that we should press the advantage won in the *Orao* affair and announce that the next task should be to unify Bosnia's two and a half intelligence services into a single one under state control (the half was the Croat intelligence service which

---

[*] The Serb nationalist party.

existed as a de facto separate spy service within the Federation one, which was nominally under the control of a Bosnian Muslim). I thought this was a great idea and we arranged that he would suggest it in the near future I would then weigh in with support and we would set up a Commission charged with the task.[*]

Meanwhile, the defence reform process initiated by the *Orao* affair was beginning to move forward. I had established a Commission to unify the two armies under state control, a process in which NATO would take the lead. What we now needed was a good international chair. I asked the US if they could provide one, as they had special leverage in the area, and to my delight Secretary Rumsfeld readily agreed. We had a bit of a struggle finding the right chairman because of the near open warfare which was raging at this time between the US Defense and State Departments – another backwash from the war in Iraq, which had started on 20 March. We eventually settled on a former US Assistant Secretary of Defense called James Locher.[†] It was an inspired choice by the Americans. Locher proved a brilliant chair with that combination of subtlety, quiet persuasive power and toughness where necessary, which made things happen in the Balkans.

Following the successes of the *Orao* affair I became a little over-exuberant about what thought was possible. I began to cast eyes on trying to resolve the problem of property restitution during my mandate. Property restitution after war is always a problem. But in Bosnia this issue was a complete nightmare. The already complex issues of restitution were overlaid by the special difficulties of religious property holdings (in three dimensions of course), and further complicated by the nationalisation of all property in the Tito years. We had long, strenuous meetings in which my staff sought to persuade me that this was a giant we should not take on, if we wanted to slay the other giants we had already engaged in combat.

---

[*] This Commission consisted of members from all 'three' intelligence services under the chairmanship of Kalman Kocsis, seconded by the Hungarian government. Kocsis had reformed the Hungarian intelligence service after the fall of Communism. He did a brilliant job and by 1 June 2004 Bosnia had the Balkans' first modern, European-standard state-level intelligence service, accountable to parliament, in the Balkans.
[†] Locher had been the managing hand behind the seminal Goldwater–Nichols Act, which restructured the US armed forces in the 1980s, and led the development of the Pentagon's special operations capabilities.

They warned me that if we opened this issue, it would swallow up all our energies for the rest of my mandate. Eventually, the IMF and World Bank came to see me to tell me that, if I really wanted to pursue this, I should look at East Germany. Here restitution had soaked up all the early capital in property re-purchase which would otherwise have been invested in productive industry and commerce. This had slowed down the economic recovery of East Germany in the early years. We couldn't afford this in Bosnia.

Eventually I had to admit defeat. Restitution was indeed a bridge too far. In these kinds of operation deciding what you will not do is sometimes just as important as deciding what you will.

Apart from a very annoying struggle we had with the European Commission to pay their budget contributions on time, which nearly caused me to have to start sacking staff, April closed on a high note. We held the first ever joint planning meeting between the international community and the new governments of Bosnia and Herzegovina, made real progress on VAT and customs unification and benefited from a raid on the bank whose assets I had frozen in the *Orao* affair, which again yielded a treasure trove of intelligence on corruption in the RS and on links to Karadžić.

In early May we were already beginning to plan Operation Balkan Vice II, using the intelligence gathered from the Balkan Vice I raids and our initial audits on the electricity generating companies, which had revealed the extent of Bosnia's organised and war crimes networks in, especially, the RS. What this showed was that one of the key areas used by Karadžić and his network was centered on Trebinje, a beautiful little Balkan town with many buildings from the Venetian Republic, which is situated just a stone's throw from both the Montenegrin and the Croatian border above Dubrovnik. Since the Bosnian war, the area had suffered from isolation and economic deprivation, having been ignored by the RS capital, Banja Luka and, in large measure, the international community too. The only exception was a scheme run by the Spanish government which had launched a project growing fruit in the highly fertile Popova Polje valley close by. I paid a visit to the area on 7 May and went to the border crossing with Dubrovnik, where I discovered that, despite investment by the European Union in the customs post, the flow of agricultural goods to Trebinje's natural market in Dubrovnik was being blocked by the hardline

Croat nationalist mayor of Dubrovnik, backed by the Croat fruit and vegetable traders in the Dubrovnik area. The former was determined to pay back Trebinje for the part played by nationalist Serbs from that area in the bombardment of Dubrovnik and the latter were equally determined to protect their virtual monopoly on the supply of vegetables and fruit to the city.

Next I visited the Republika Srpska customs post with Montenegro. This is positioned in some of the wildest mountains I have ever seen, with towering crags and vertiginous valleys all covered by thick, almost primeval forest. It was not difficult to see why this border has always been a key avenue for smugglers and for Karadžić, who seemed to be able to move at will between Bosnia and Montenegro.

On my return to Sarajevo we put together an international task force whose aim was to tackle police and customs corruption, accelerate economic development in the Trebinje area and put pressure on Zagreb to free up the border crossing near Dubrovnik in order to provide a market for Trebinje's agricultural produce.

It was on this trip, too, that having taken a journey on a local bus, I arrived at the local bus terminal and was unknowingly photographed by an enterprising cameraman against a background of a calendar carrying Karadžić's picture. This was subsequently used by some in the Bosnian Muslim press when they wanted to put pressure on me, by inferring that I was a secret Karadžić supporter.

A few days later I went to see the head of the Federation customs in Sarajevo, Zelimir Rebac, a Croat, who was under strong pressure because he had begun uncovering very high-level corruption amongst Croatian elements at the top of the Bosnian state. He had received death threats, the most recent being a threat to murder his daughter and send her body back to him piece by piece if he didn't stop. He told me that whatever they did to him, he was determined to continue. Beyond arranging for him to have protection and offering him moral support there was depressingly little I could do to protect this very brave man. [*]

---

[*] Rebac's investigations were in part instrumental in an indictment against the then Croat president of the Bosnian state Dragan Čović, together with the president of the Constitutional Court and a number of high-level Croat politicans and businessmen. This trial, recently concluded, has resulted in a guilty verdict being handed down on Čović. Rebac has subsequently, at the second attempt, committed suicide.

In the middle of May I took my first holiday out of the country since the start of my mandate. But before leaving I met with my staff to discuss the plans for the next year. We were all concerned that, having gained the initiative, we were now losing momentum. Julian Braithwaite particularly expressed his worry that we had lost focus in our public messages. I asked them to come up with a plan for the next year, together with core public messages, by the time I got back from my ten days away.

Before I left I had one important piece of diplomacy to attend to. My relations with the Russian ambassador had been very strained since the Šarović affair. We agreed to mend these, in true Russian style, over a bottle of vodka one evening. Unfortunately, the only evening I could do was one on which I had already agreed to attend a dinner at the British ambassador's residence. The only way out was to meet the Russian ambassador earlier and then go to the British ambassador's later. What I hadn't bargained for was that Russians wouldn't dream of drinking vodka unless accompanied by food. So when I arrived I found a full-scale Russian dinner. A very great deal of vodka was drunk very fast, followed by liberal quantities of Georgian cognac accompanied by Georgian gypsy songs – the Russian ambassador was a Georgian. I am unable to say what state the British ambassador found me in by the time I got to his house for my second full-scale diplomatic dinner of the evening, since he was too polite ever to mention it again. But the thick head and extremely bloated stomach I had next morning seemed a reasonable price to pay for rebuilding relations with Moscow.

The month, and my first year in Bosnia, ended a with huge haul of intelligence from the bank raid carried out as a consequence of Operation Balkan Vice II. This showed the tentacles of organised crime, often linked to war criminals, extending from Republika Srpska across the whole Bosnian community, including Bosnian Muslims and Croats (the same people who, when acting as politicians, found it impossible to work together, found no such difficulties when pursuing their criminal links) and as far abroad as the Ukraine and Chechnya.

My first year ended as it had begun, with a visit to some refugees.

TUESDAY 10 JUNE 2003

At 3 o'clock in the middle of a crashing thunderstorm I left for Visegrad, with Jane. It took us a good two hours to drive to our destination, with much lightning and rain as we passed over Roma-nija mountain. But we burst into the Drina valley in glorious sun-shine having followed the old Austrian railway line that runs down through the tight little gorge from Rogatica. Here the road skirts the Drina, plunging through cliffs in a series of dramatic tunnels on its way to the little, ancient Bosnian town of Visegrad (made famous by Nobel Prize-winning writer Ivo Andric's book *Na Drina Cuprija*).* Then sharply left and dizzily up the mountain rampart, skirting along the edge of a steep slope, with the Drina thousands of feet below us as we climbed and climbed. Finally we arrived at the little hamlet of Rogrohica, with barely half a dozen houses, all but one of them burnt out.

We stopped by one blackened and roofless ruin, alongside which was placed an extremely decrepit and disintegrating tent with the faded letters 'UNHCR' still clearly visible across it. This was the home of our hosts, Ahmet and Sebiša Sitkić who had lived in this tent on this spot, fierce Bosnian winter and boiling summer alike, for the last two years. Ahmet brown as a berry with a nose as sharp as a hawk's beak and eyes to match, is seventy-seven and Sebiša seventy-four. They have lived here since the war, eking a living by growing vegetables, chiefly potatoes, paprika and onions, on the little patch of land by their house and waiting for a foreign donation to help them rebuild their house.

We sat round a rough table outside the tent and chatted, as I idly watched some clouds beginning to gather in the distance and silently marvelled at the Drina sparkling in the sunlight thousands of feet below us and the tumbling cliffs pouring down the moun-tains into the valley below. This, of course, is one of the most important border lines of history. Along this valley ran the line drawn by the Emperor Diocletian in the third century to separate the Eastern and the Western Roman Empire. Since then this river has marked the border between Byzantium and Rome, the end of ancient Christendom, the sometime Western frontier of the

---

* *Bridge on the Drina.*

Orthodox faith and for many centuries, one of the main battle lines of the Ottoman Empire.

Ahmet's life story, as he told it to me in the slanting sunlight on his little patch of land on the mountainside, was just a modern version of the fate of so many particles of human dust, caught up in the conflicts spawned by this great fault line down the march of the centuries. A Muslim, he had been born in this house, as had his father and his grandfather before him. His grandfather had lived to a hundred and twenty-five and his father to over a hundred. The land round here and the special air of the Drina valley was the best in Bosnia, he said.[*] Everybody here lived to a ripe old age – unless they were killed in the mindless storms of war which generation after generation swept over them for unknowable reasons from faraway places.

Then, their lot was not peace and the quiet enjoyment of simple lives, but burnt houses and blood and the swift exodus to the hidden, traditional places, in the caves and forests where father and grandfather had hidden before. And then always the sly return when the madness had passed and the back-breaking job of rebuilding their houses, re-clearing their land and re-planting their crops.

It had happened to Ahmet three times in his seventy-seven years. First the Germans burnt his house in 1941. Then the Partisans in 1943. Then, in 1992, Arkan. He had been the worst. He killed everything, father, son, mother, daughter, sheep, cats, dogs – nothing was left alive. As Ahmet told his story a small crowd of his neighbours materialised around us. One, Šemso, from a neighbouring village, showed me the wound in his jaw where he had taken a bullet fleeing from Arkan's troops when they had swept through the mountains to his village. Ahmet told us many had died. Every house had been burnt. He had stayed behind with his son to try to defend their homes. They had held Arkan up for a couple of days, but he had heavy weapons, they had only hunting rifles. In the end they had been forced to flee. He and his family had spent the war in besieged Sarajevo.

But three years after the war ended he decided to try to return. At

[*] I found this was the eternal claim wherever you go in Bosnia and Herzegovina. Everyone in this country, for whom an obsession with health is a national pastime, believes they have the best air, the best grass and, above all, the best plums and slivovica.

first they had just come back for the weekend, braving hostility from the local Serbs. Then, two years ago, they had received a tent from UNHCR, which they had put up alongside their burnt-out house and come back for good – except if the winter got really bad, when they returned to Sarajevo to stay with relatives until the better weather came.

At about 6 o'clock the skies suddenly opened and it started to rain fiercely. We took shelter in a nearby empty house. Soon the rain changed to hailstones which got progressively larger and larger, until they were the size of gobstopper marbles, dancing in wild profusion on the grass and rattling off the corrugated roof of a nearby shed. We watched as showers of unripe plums were knocked off the trees and Ahmet's vegetables took a severe battering. After about twenty minutes it stopped and we wandered out to inspect the damage. To my horror I saw that the hailstones had gone right through the rotten fabric of Ahmet's tent, in which Jane and I were to spend the night. The tent now looked as though a host of shotguns had been fired at it and there were large puddles of mud where we were to sleep.

We decided to go off for a walk while the ground dried, picking our way along the mountainside on an old track, until we came to an ancient graveyard of stecaks* positioned on a prominent saddle overlooking the Drina valley. Ahmet told me that he thought that the stecaks were left by the Romans but I told him that historians believe them to be from the Bogomils who were originally heretic Christians who had fled the Cathar religious persecution in France and come to Bosnia in the thirteenth century. He told me that there are other, older graves nearby and pointed out a collection of broken stone sarcophaguses poking out of the ground about fifty metres away. These appeared to my uneducated eye to be much older, perhaps even Neolithic.

We then wandered back along the track, chatting about history, the ancient settlement of this land, of life, of war, of our children,

---

* Stecaks are a kind of gravestone or marker peculiar to this area of the Balkans. They consist of huge blocks of often intricately carved limestone. Their origin is disputed, but one theory is that they were the gravestones of the Bogomil Christians. Originally followers of the Albigensian heresy in the thirteenth century the Bogomils had been driven out of Europe by the Inquisition and had found refuge in Bosnia.

of women and of the countryside. By the time we got back to the tent, a large fire had been lit and the *sac*[*] was steaming away on the fire, smelling delicious. We all sat down under the gathering twilight, drank beer, ate lamb and chatted by the glow of the fire until it grew dark and the stars came out and the moon shone in a watery sky above us. At around ten o'clock everyone started to drift off.

It had been agreed that Jane and I should sleep in the tent, so Ahmet and Sebiša went off to a neighbouring house, which had recently been rebuilt, while we settled down for the night.

Before we went to bed Ahmet told us to watch out for snakes. When they had first moved back they had lived in a nearby stable and had been constantly plagued by snakes. Several had come in each night and they used to hear them hissing and fighting with Ahmet's dog, a stocky little terrier of an animal of uncertain breed but courageous enough. He had apparently been out seeing off a wild boar which had come to forage in Ahmet's vegetables last night. Neither of these stories was especially conducive to settling down for a good night's sleep. Nevertheless, dog tired, we fell asleep fairly quickly, lulled by the sounds of the night and the drip of the wet canvas above us.

WEDNESDAY 11 JUNE 2003

Up at 5.30 and a wash at a tap fed from a nearby mountain stream. Everything damp and musty. This morning the clouds are lying in the valley below, covering the Drina. But as the sun came up they gradually cleared to reveal an astonishing view down the valley of the river sparkling in the early morning sunshine below us.

In due course we all gathered around the embers of last night's fire, which Ahmet fanned into a roaring flame and on which he soon had a pot of strong Bosnian coffee bubbling away, waiting for us. By now last night's crowd had mysteriously regathered and we all sat

---

[*] Pronounced 'satch', this is the traditional form of Bosnian cooking vessel – it consists of a circular metal dish, into which the meat – usually lamb – is put with water, potatoes, onions and vegetables. This is then covered with a metal hood and placed on the embers of a fire, with embers also piled over the hood so that the whole cooks very slowly from the top and the bottom.

down, some ten of us, to a breakfast of cold lamb, kajmak[*] pura[†] and boiled eggs. Afterwards we grabbed some tools and set to, helping clear out Ahmet's house so that it would be ready for reconstruction if he received a foreign donation to rebuild it.[‡] It took us about two hours to clear away the broken tiles and burnt beams which filled the shell of the house.

When we were finished someone suggested that we should go up the mountain to another hamlet, where refugees were also living in tents, so I could see their conditions too. We gathered up our spades and tools and set off up the mountain. After some forty minutes skirting the valley with glorious views of the Drina and its towering cliffs below us, we emerged from the forest into a beautiful little pasture where an alpine village had been, until the Serbs burnt it down. Here we found another tent in no better condition than Ahmet's and some twenty people sitting out on the grass drinking coffee.

We helped them clear a couple of the village houses before walking back around midday to Ahmet's house, to say our farewells to him and Sebiša and dropping down the valley to Visegrad.

---

[*] Bosnian cottage cheese from the mountains.
[†] A kind of polenta, much favoured by the poor in the Balkans.
[‡] When I arrived back in Sarajevo I managed to get him the donation he was waiting for and he and Sebiša are now, I hear, back in their home.

Postscript

The next nearly three years until the end of my mandate on 31 January 2006 were no less turbulent as we pushed forward the reforms we had started in this first year and widened the scope of our state-building agenda.

On my return from holiday in May, we agreed that our two next big tasks should be, firstly, to reform Bosnia's thirteen fractured police forces so as to put them under a single state structure and secondly to break the eight years of obstructionism in the RS on arresting war criminals, especially Karadžić, so that Bosnia would be able to join NATO's Partnership for Peace (PfP).

On 21 June, at the Thessaloniki summit, the European Union made what has become known in the Balkans as the 'Thessaloniki promise', that the Western Balkans could join the Union provided that they could bring themselves up to European standards. The declaration listed, among the other reforms required to start the EU's Stabilisation and Accession Process (SAP), a requirement to reform the 'security structures' – in Bosnia's case, the police. This declaration was central to our next three years' work. It gave us both the destination to head for (beginning the Stabilisation and Accession Process) and the leverage to get there.

Following the judgement from the Bosnian Human Rights Chamber on the case submitted by the bereaved of Srebrenica to know what had happened to their loved ones, I contacted the Chamber to suggest that the best way to ensure that the RS government obeyed the court's ruling was to establish an RS government Commission charged with finding and submitting the relevant information on what had happened at Srebrenica. They agreed and I passed the decision requiring the RS government to set up a Srebrenica Commission with foreign observers and a representative of the bereaved as members.

Over the next year and a half and after much bruising persuasion, the relevant information was painfully extracted from those who held it (chiefly the RS army and police). The resulting Srebrenica Commission Report, written by the Serbs themselves, was a brave and extraordinary document which not only led to the discovery of many mass graves, but lifted the veil on what had actually happened at Srebrenica – especially for the Serbs themselves. President Boris Tadić of Serbia/Montenegro told me later that the publication of this report had done more than anything else in Serbia to change opinion, especially on Mladić, making it easier for the Serb authorities to arrest him. We were at last making some progress in separating the Hague-indicted war criminals from their public support. Later the terrible video showing Srebrenica victims being shot reinforced the effect. In a remarkable and most courageous statement at the time of the publication of the final Srebrenica report, the RS president Dragan Čavić acknowledged that the event had taken place and that it would constitute a terrible stain on the Serb people for all time. Even more remarkably, Tadić and Čavić had the courage to attend the tenth anniversary commemoration of the massacre at Srebrenica. I had hoped that these events might have initiated a more general acknowledgement by the Bosnian Muslims and Croats of their atrocities, too (which, though they did not include anything on the scale of Srebrenica, also needed to be acknowledged). Although there is now an initiative to start a Truth Commission in Bosnia there has been, so far, no such reciprocal movement from either of the other ethnicities in Bosnia.

Defence reform also made good progress, though not without many mini-crises. By mid 2004 it was clear that Bosnia could make the reforms necessary to join NATO's PfP, with one exception. The RS had still completely failed to fulfil its international and Dayton Treaty obligations to cooperate with the Hague Tribunal in the arrest of indicted war criminals. By the middle of 2004 the RS had not, in the nine years since Dayton, arrested a single Hague-indicted war criminal. Some fourteen had been arrested on RS territory – but all of these had been arrested by NATO's troops and none by the RS. In 2004 we started to build up a campaign of pressure to persuade the RS to fulfil their duties of cooperation with the Hague. On 30 June that year, in a single decision, I removed fifty-nine Serb officials and politicians in relation to non-cooperation with ICTY. This was a very tense moment in which again wide-spread and violent reaction from the RS was predicted. But the intelligence we were now operating on, largely as a result of the Balkan Vice operations (which had continued), was now much better than before – and we were able to target people who, though they had high-profile positions, did not, in the main, enjoy much public support among the Serb population. I was assisted in this exercise with information provided by a number of international bodies, including, on this occasion, the Russian government.

The Russians did not, however, take the same view when, in December 2004, I removed another, smaller tranche of nine Serb officials and froze the funds of the 'ruling'* Serb nationalist party, the SDS, because of information that they had had illegal contact with Karadžić or his network. On this occasion the Russians stated their opposition publicly (the only time during my mandate that there had been public opposition from within the Steering Board Ambassadors' group) and to show their displeasure ostentatiously cancelled a trip I was due to make to Moscow. Neither this, nor the 'crisis' caused by the brief boycott by the Serbs lasted long, however. And very shortly afterwards the nine-year dam of obstructionism by the RS authorities on cooperation with the Hague broke. By the time I left, a steady stream of ICTY indictees had been transferred to the Hague by the Serb authorities in Belgrade and Banja Luka, and Bosnia was declared by Carla Del Ponte to be in cooperation with the ICTY. To my eternal regret, the two primary architects of the Bosnian tragedy, Karadžić and Mladić, were not among them, a matter which I regard as the biggest failure of my mandate.

In December 2004, the European Union took over from NATO with EUFOR (European Union Force) replacing SFOR as the military force charged with maintaining security in Bosnia. Shortly afterwards, in a raid on one of Mladić's old underground head-quarters, information came to light which led us to believe that the RS army had been providing support to Mladić. We used this to further strengthen and accelerate state control of the armed services.

Our attempts to progress police reform, however, ran into far more trouble. We were now hitting the core sensitivities of the RS.

---

* The SDS, founded by Karadžić, was not formally in government at this time, as they had left this to a smaller Serb party. But they had the overwhelming majority in the RS parliament and pulled the strings from behind.

Having acceded to state control over taxation, the intelligence services, the army, the judiciary and the customs services, the RS was now down to those bedrock competencies which it regarded as essential to its de facto claim to mini-statehood. The Serbs in the RS also regarded exclusive control of their own police as being even more important than the continued existence of their own army or intelligence service.

We had a very long and bruising battle over this throughout the whole of 2005. At one stage we reached a political agreement with the Serb leaders, only to see it fall apart when they took it to their parliament. Eventually, a deal was done at a secret late-night meeting in my house, attended by the US, British and European Commission ambassadors, the leader of the Serb nationalist party and president of the RS, Dragan Čović, and the leader of the Serb main opposition party in the RS, Milorad Dodik.

As a result of this, the required resolutions were passed through the RS parliament and the European Union was able to agree that Bosnia should start on the European road by beginning negotiations on the Stabilisation and Association Process on 21 October 2005.

Our battles were not, however, only with the Serbs. In early 2005, it was clear that the Bosnian courts were about to indict the then Croat president of the state, Dragan Čović, for corruption while in public office. A principle had been established in the previous years that a politician who was indicted should stand aside from their public office in order to clear their name as a private citizen. There was again very great concern in the international community whether this ought to apply to a directly elected state president and there was much discussion and differing opinion on this. In the end, and despite very strong opposition from the Croats, I went to see President Čović and told him that, since he had been indicted,[*] he should resign and if he didn't I would have no alternative but to remove him, which, the following day, I had to do.

I made myself similarly unpopular with the Bosnian Muslims in the autumn of 2005. Sarajevo International Airport, though in Bosnian Muslim-run territory, is bordered on one side by the territory of the RS and the Serb part of Sarajevo city. In the autumn

---

[*] He has subsequently been found guilty.

of 2005, the Bosnian Muslims unilaterally decided to rename the airport after their wartime president, Alija Izetbegović, and had even started to put up the letters of his name on the airport building. I had known Izetbegović well and admired him as the person who, more than anyone else, ensured the survival of the Bosnian Muslims in a war of genocide, in which the international community had abandoned him. I had visited Izetbegović many times during the war, was at his death bed in October 2003 and had spoken at his funeral. Nevertheless, he was for many non-Bosnian Muslims a controversial figure during the war and afterwards. So naming the international airport after him was a deliberately provocative act, which would have been immediately followed by the renaming of the other airports, train stations and goodness knows what else, after the heroes of the other ethnicities of Bosnia. Again I had to act, overturning the decision and putting a law to parliament requiring wide consultation before the renaming of any facility in Bosnia which was of international character.

During 2003 and 2004 the first and second Mostar Commissions, the latter one under international chairmanship, assembled 90 per cent of the statutes for unifying the city under a single city council.[*] In January 2005, I passed a decision putting in place the final pieces of the statutes and the first city-wide elections for the city council were held in October 2005, although progress towards an efficiently functioning unified city council has been – and continues to be – slower than many hoped for. In July of that year the famous Old Bridge in Mostar was reopened.

By the time I left Bosnia at the end of January 2006, VAT was up and running, the customs services had been unified into a single state-wide service, the Bosnian judiciary was working under a single state-wide framework of law, the courts were beginning to try even the highest in the land for corruption, the economy was growing at 5 per cent, foreign direct investment and manufacturing production were up 25 per cent (albeit from a very low base), a single army was operating under state control, a single state intelligence service, accountable to parliament, had been created and the country had entered on to the long road that, hopefully, will lead it to Europe.

[†] This Commission was set up in September 2004 under the chairmanship of Norbert Winterstein, an ex-mayor of Rüsselsheim in Germany.

Providing that Europe holds to the Thessaloniki promise, I am sure that this remarkable and beautiful country with its extraordinary, courageous people will make it to Europe and when it does it will be regarded as one of Europe's little jewels.

Inaugural Speech
*by Paddy Ashdown, the new High Representative
for Bosnia & Herzegovina*

MONDAY, 27 MAY 2002

Introduction

It's great to be back.

And a great honour to be taking over from my distinguished predecessor, Wolfgang Petritsch. He has left us with a foundation to build on and, with your help, I intend to build on it.

My wife Jane and I are really looking forward to making our home here for the next few years, and I am looking forward to working with you as you travel on the next stage of your journey towards statehood and Europe.

But that destination is not yet assured, for there is a fork in the road ahead of us.

One road leads back to division and instability.

If we take this road, then this country will become an island of squabbling refuseniks left behind by its neighbours who are already moving ahead to their European future. A place that the international community cannot leave because of instability. But in which they have lost patience and interest.

The other road leads to a different kind of future.

The one most people here want.

The one the international community supports.

And the one I remain confident we can – together – achieve.

This road is the road of reform. If we have the courage to take it, it will lead us to statehood, prosperity and ultimately to membership of the European Union itself.

For BiH, our European destination is not some abstract idea – some piece of meaningless political jargon.

It means a better future for you and your children. It means providing new jobs, giving the young a better education, and giving every citizen confidence and security.

That is the choice ahead of us. Stay as we are and be left behind. Or push forward with reform, and create a new future for this country.

So my aim is simply stated:

It is to work with the people of Bosnia and Herzegovina to put this country irreversibly on to the road to statehood and membership of Europe.

Please note. I do not say this will be either easy or quick.

But if I didn't believe it could be done, I would not have accepted this job. I have grown to love this country very much. I believe in Bosnia and Herzegovina. And I believe in you.

The Past Six Years

Now, I am a rather open person. And I will tell you honestly what problems lie ahead.

But first, let us recognise how far you have come already.

You know, some complain that Bosnia and Herzegovina has been making progress too slowly. And it's true that we must now go faster.

But building peace after war is no easy thing.

If my home of Northern Ireland had made as much progress in thirty years as BiH has made in six, the conflict there would have been over much sooner.

Bosnia and Herzegovina is at peace.

Refugees are returning in huge numbers.

Freedom of movement has been restored.

You have joined the Council of Europe.

And the ethnic tapestry of Bosnia and Herzegovina's proud past is slowly being mended and restored.

There are now mosques in Prijedor, Bosniak businessmen in Doboj, Bosnian Serb communities in the Neretva valley and a Bosnian Croat community in Bugojno. A Bosnian Serb has been appointed chief of police in Drvar, a Bosniac, as deputy police chief in Srebrenica.

You are entitled to feel proud of these achievements.

But we are still far from our destination. There is much – and especially much that is difficult – yet to do.

But I cannot do it for you. You have to look to yourselves.

So a good motto for Bosnia and Herzegovina on the next stage of the journey would be, to paraphrase John F Kennedy, '**Do not ask what the international community can do for you. Ask first what you can do for yourselves.**'

'*Ne pitajte šta medjunarodna zajednica može uraditi za vas. Pitajte prvo šta vi možete uraditi za sebe.*'

Do that, and I am confident we can succeed.

Priorities for the Future

But huge problems confront us.

Next year, BiH's debt will leap from KM160 million to more than 235 million.

At the same time, foreign aid, on which we have become far too dependent, is going to fall year after year.

Rising debt, falling aid, and, because we have not reformed fast enough, little prospect of attracting inward investment to close the gap.

The pressure on government expenditure will be severe.

So we have no option but to take a long hard look at how Bosnia and Herzegovina is governed.

You have 1,200 judges and prosecutors, 760 legislators, 180 Ministers, four separate levels of government and three armies – for a country of less than four million people! You have 13 Prime Ministers! That's a Prime Minister for every 300,000 citizens!

The cost of government in BiH is a staggering KM1.8bn – and that's just for the government machine itself, it doesn't include the cost of services such as health, education and pensions. That means that just paying for politicians and bureaucrats costs every citizen of working age in BiH KM900 every year – that's almost three months' wages for the average worker!

The truth is Bosnia and Herzegovina spends far too much money on its politicians, and far too little on its people.

And we have no option but to change that.

And the same is true for defence.

Proportionately, BiH spends twice as much on defence as the United States, and four times more than the European average.

Why? Who do we think we are defending ourselves against? Serbia? Croatia? Today, these countries are focused on European integration, not territorial expansion.

A great American statesman once said:

'Every gun that is fired, every rocket made, signifies a theft from those who hunger and are not fed – from those who are cold and are not clothed. The world in arms is not spending money alone – it is spending the sweat of its labours, the genius of its scientists, the hopes of its children.'

There is probably no place on earth to which that applies more than Bosnia and Herzegovina – except, perhaps, North Korea!

This is nothing short of madness when many people here are struggling just to feed their families.

So there is no alternative to reform and to setting clear priorities.

Here are mine:

First Justice. Then Jobs. Through Reform.

Prvo Zakonitost. Zatim Zaposlenost. Kroz Reformu.

Justice, because the rule of law is the starting point – the essential requirement for a decent life for the people of BiH and for progress in everything we do.

Jobs, because employment is the key to human dignity and to a decent future for our children.

And reform, because we cannot have either justice or jobs if we don't first change the system that has denied both to far too many, for far too long.

I shall return to these priorities in detail, with some specific proposals, later in this speech.

Dayton and the Future of BiH

But first a word on Dayton.

The peace agreement that was drawn up in Ohio in 1995 was designed to end a war, not to build a country.

Dayton is vital. Without it there would be no peace.

But Dayton is the floor, not the ceiling.

It is the foundation for the state we are trying to construct. And like all foundations, it must be built on.

Now, I know there are those who believe that the letter of Dayton is all that protects their identity and safety.

To them I say this:

I will never permit any constitutional change that fundamentally threatens the identity or security of any of Bosnia and Herzegovina's constituent peoples.

It is a characteristic of modern, successful European states that they see diversity not as a threat but a positive advantage.

That's why governments right across Europe are becoming increasingly decentralised and power is being increasingly devolved.

But there is a world of difference between a diverse society and a divided society.

Between a decentralised state, and a fractured state.

Those who oppose any moves to build state institutions seem not to understand that. They believe that we can be accepted into Europe as two, or, as some even say, three failed statelets within a failed state. That the status quo is a viable option for the future.

This is just nonsense. And those who propose it, openly or secretly, jeopardise our children's future and perpetrate a cruel illusion on the people they claim to represent.

More extreme, and more detached still from the new political reality, is the idea that the old, destructive wartime dreams of a Greater Croatia and Greater Serbia can still be revived.

This is not going to happen.

The international community will not let it happen.

And both Zagreb and now, increasingly, Belgrade, have made it clear that they do not want it to happen either. They know that their future, as part of Europe, is linked, quite as much as ours, to BiH's success and the region's stability.

So we have only one realistic future – to make Bosnia and Herzegovina work.

But how?

Some argue that the answer lies in a single great event, a second Dayton, or something similar. I disagree.

What we are involved in here is not an event but a process.

Our task is not to submerge or destroy ethnic identities. It is, patiently, to build a state that protects those identities, celebrates them and harnesses them for everyone's benefit. A state that enables people to value their Bosnian identity, at the same time as valuing their ethnic identity.

But ultimately, it isn't constitutions that make a state, it is people. And it is the people – *all* the people – of Bosnia and Herzegovina, who will determine the success or failure of this country in the

future. The different peoples of BiH are the pillars that support the state – that give it its strength. Remove any one of these, and the whole thing will collapse.

We succeed together, or we fail together.

It's as simple as that.

If this country cannot find the humanity to put aside its hate, it cannot have a future for its children.

My vision of Bosnia and Herzegovina is of a modern country whose state level institutions do only what is necessary, but do it effectively.

A country whose democratic decisions are made at the lowest level consistent with efficiency.

A country whose citizens' rights are protected individually by powerful human rights laws and a strong system of justice.

A country whose governments at all levels, though established through the will of the majority, cannot endanger the rights, traditions or identities of individual citizens or groups, however small.

And, incidentally, one indispensable ingredient of that kind of modern European state is that its judiciary, its central bank and its public broadcasting service must be independent and *absolutely* free from political interference. There can be *no compromise* on that if BiH's route to Europe is to remain open.

But Bosnia and Herzegovina's route to statehood isn't just about structural reform. It is also about political leadership.

No state has ever been built – no people has ever prospered – unless they can produce from amongst themselves leaders who have a vision that transcends faction, who have the ability to put the interest of the country first and who have the courage to take the risks necessary to lead.

Bosnia and Herzegovina has not so far produced enough leaders of this sort.

Perhaps part of the reason is because we, the international

community, have intervened too frequently, interfered too much and not given enough space for others to act.

I shall also have to use the High Representative's powers from time to time. But I regard these powers as acceptable only if they are used on behalf of the people of Bosnia and Herzegovina as a whole.

I have concluded that there are two ways I can make my decisions. One is with a tape measure, measuring the precise equidistant position between three sides. The other is by doing what I think is right for the country as a whole. I prefer the second of these.

So when I act, I shall seek to do so in defence of the interests of all the people of Bosnia and Herzegovina, putting their priorities first.

And time after time the people have told us what their priorities are: Justice and Jobs.

And they are mine too.

Justice

Firstly, justice.

We do not have effective justice in this country.

Bosnian justice works too often for the powerful and the politically connected, not for ordinary people.

It may well be that the grip of nationalism in Bosnia and Herzegovina is, slowly – too slowly – weakening. But the grip of criminality and corruption is strengthening. And this poses a direct threat to every single one of us.

For ordinary people, the rule of law is vital – and not just for their security.

Businessmen need the law to start their businesses, to get investment and to trade.

Victims need the law to get protection and justice.

Voters need the law to hold their politicians to account.

And, perhaps more than anyone else, refugees need the law to return to their homes – something that remains as central for me as it was for my predecessors.

You see, the failure of law in BiH today imperils human rights, impedes economic recovery, deters investors and separates Bosnia and Herzegovina from Europe.

We must put this right.

That is why working with you to establish the rule of law will be my first, and my top, priority.

There must be nobody above the law, and no place beyond the law, in Bosnia and Herzegovina.

Thanks to the UN mission we have now created a cadre of well trained and, in the main, reliable and committed policemen. But our police all too frequently cannot rely on other parts of the justice system.

BiH has twice as many judges per head of population as Germany, which itself has more judges than any other country in Europe. Yet each German judge deals with four times as many cases per year as each Bosnian judge.

That's too many judges for too little justice.

And the consequence? Tens of thousands of innocent people are left waiting to have their cases heard, while criminals continue to operate with impunity.

That is why I will press ahead with comprehensive reform of our judges, prosecutors and courts, until we have a judicial system that ordinary Bosnians can trust.

But the rule of law isn't just about the courts. It means having clean government too.

Bosnia and Herzegovina needs a non-politicised civil service that is accountable to its people, accessible to its people and committed to serving its people.

Being in government must be about helping the public, not helping yourself. And to make sure that it is, we must shine the bright light of public scrutiny into every corner of government in BiH.

And our laws will have to be looked at too.

That is why I am setting up a new legal reform unit, consisting mainly of Bosnians, to look at our laws and to recommend reforms that make it easier to get justice and jobs for the ordinary citizen.

But if we are really serious about justice, we must go further still. We must cut out the cancer at the heart of Bosnian society: organised crime.

It is time to take on the high-level criminals – the war profiteers who have now turned to smuggling weapons, fuel, drugs and even people. And it is time to confront their friends and accomplices in positions of power – those who have ruthlessly exploited Bosnia and Herzegovina's national wealth for their personal profit.

So here is a 5-point crime action plan I shall be proposing to your government:

First. Set up a special court-chamber to take on sensitive, high-profile cases.

Second. Complete the establishment of the State Court.

Third. Complete the process of creating a comprehensive legal framework so the police, prosecutors and courts have the legal tools needed to bring criminals to justice.

Fourth. Get the High Judicial Council operational by the autumn, so that BiH can have the high-quality judges and prosecutors it deserves.

And fifth. Strengthen the systems that scrutinise government and prevent abuses of power in the public sector.

Jobs and the Economy

My second priority will be to create the conditions for jobs.

But creating jobs does not mean reverting to old style, top-down, government-subsidised work schemes. Because they don't work.

The challenge for us is not to try to revive failing public companies. It is, instead, to stimulate growth in the new private sector, and especially among small businesses, which are already becoming the engine that will drive BiH's economy.

None of this will be easy or painless. Things may have to get worse before they get better. It's tough making the transition from a centrally planned economy to an open market one. From a divided economy to a single economic space.

And yet at present, BiH makes that transition even more painful by actively discouraging investment.

If you want to invest in Bosnia and Herzegovina, just look at what you are faced with.

An unpredictable, inconsistent and often contradictory labyrinth of regulations and rules. Some formal, some informal. Some at state level, some at entity level, some at cantonal level and some at municipal level.

No wonder foreign investment amounts to a tiny KM85 per person here, compared to over KM640 per head in Croatia.

You know it takes almost 100 days on average to register a business here – ten times longer than in most other countries in the region.

Let me tell you a story. A true story.

I met a man recently who wanted to open a restaurant in Sarajevo – a pretty simple task you might think. But not, he soon discovered, in Bosnia and Herzegovina.

He required numerous forms and multiple permissions from almost everyone, including, if you please, the Ministry of Defence. The Ministry of Defence! To open a restaurant!

Months later, having got permission from the military, amongst others, he went to the Canton to get the final form. But the Canton informed him that he would first have to get hold of a municipal form. So off he went to the Municipality, who told him that they couldn't give him a municipal form if he didn't first have a cantonal one. So he took his money to Slovenia instead.

We might as well hang a sign on our front door saying, 'Go home. We don't want your money here.'

We have to change that. We have to transform BiH's image and its ways of doing business.

The only reason why the economy of this country is failing is because we have refused to reform the system that dooms it to failure.

This country has huge potential. Just last year, Bosnia and Herzegovina carried away the largest number of medals at the Inventors' Fair in Paris, winning no fewer than eleven prizes.

And this year, Bosnia and Herzegovina won the Oscar for the Best Foreign Film.

For that one night in Los Angeles, the whole world saw Bosnia and Herzegovina, not as a source of conflict, but of creativity. Not as a problem to solve, but as a success to celebrate.

This is a country situated at the heart of a region poised for real growth. But if we are to take advantage of this, we must reform and invest – and the key investment is in our young people.

Because we have failed to do this, Bosnia and Herzegovina's biggest export today is its youth – its future.

This haemorrhage of the young and the talented poses perhaps the greatest long-term threat to this country. We will not succeed, unless we succeed in stemming or reversing this.

That means two things. First, providing our young with education and training, inside Bosnia, that equips them for success. And second, creating the environment in which education, talent and hard work can translate into jobs and prosperity.

The separate system of education along ethnic lines is one of the major things that holds us back. I have seen the corrosive effects of such division in education in Northern Ireland. I detested it there – and I like it no better here.

Education is not a luxury, it is a right. And reforming our school and education system is not an optional extra, it is a core task.

If we don't bring our children together, to live and to learn, your country will never escape its past. If we don't look long and hard at the quality of teaching in schools and bring them up to European standards, your children will never have a future.

But education reform, like education itself, cannot be confined to schools. We must also make a priority of higher and further education.

We have seven universities in BiH, but not one offers an internationally recognised degree!

Our university system needs to be overhauled so students can get a first-class education without having to leave the country. And we need better training too.

In the public sector, we need the speedy implementation of the Civil Service law. We can then get down to the real work of training officials and driving up standards in the public service.

But I have a wider vision, of a public service college – a centre of excellence – through which all senior servants of the state will pass, giving BiH a public service rooted in the values of integrity and professionalism.

But crucial though these initiatives to increase the capacities of the people of BiH are, they will not, in themselves, lead to jobs.

So here is a five-point action plan for employment:

First. Sweep away the unnecessary red tape and bureaucracy that makes it so difficult to run an honest business and drives so many into the grey economy.

Second. Develop laws that will help small businesses borrow and expand.

Third. Create a single, user-friendly system for registering new businesses.

Fourth. Push forward the reforms on property and land ownership law, so that people can invest and plan with confidence.

And fifth. Establish accelerated procedures for dealing with business disputes.

Five specific, practical, achievable steps that we could start on now to attract new investment and jobs in the future.

Partnership

I turn now to the question of partnership.

To me, partnership means a more open relationship between the international organisations here and the people of Bosnia and Herzegovina.

I see myself not just as a representative of the international community. I am also a servant of Bosnia and Herzegovina. And that applies to all my colleagues as well.

I have therefore asked that the BiH flag will be flown on all OHR buildings – and I hope that other international organisations will follow suit.

And when I have to travel abroad I shall wish to do so as a representative, not just of the international community, but of Bosnia and Herzegovina, under the BiH flag.

I want the Office of the High Representative to be open and accessible to the people of Bosnia and Herzegovina. So, starting today, I will be spending more time out of Sarajevo, meeting people from across the country, and listening to their views.

And I have given instructions today, that the iron gates at the front of OHR Sarajevo will be opened, and left open, except when a specific security threat requires otherwise.

I will also be increasing the number of Bosnians working within the OHR – including at senior level – as part of a broader drive to create a cadre of young professionals who will serve Bosnia and Herzegovina and push forward the reform agenda.

The Elections

Finally, let me turn to the elections. You wouldn't expect me to ignore this issue completely. After all, I am a politician!

The elections are now very close. Polling day may not be until 5 October, but the deadline for registering is 18 June – less than a month away.

It is not my job to interfere in elections. I will support actions and reforms, not personalities or parties. It is up to the people of BiH to choose their government. And it will be my duty to work with whatever government they choose.

So, from the people of Bosnia and Herzegovina, I ask only two things.

First, please vote.

Your votes are the building blocks which we shall need to create the new Bosnia and Herzegovina.

We have some very difficult decisions to take together in the next few years. A failure to vote will only make it more likely that those decisions will be made by a small minority more interested in defending the past than in building the future.

My second plea is that you consider, very carefully, what it is you want before you vote.

Consider what you want for yourself.

Consider what you want for your family, for your children and for your country's future.

And then vote for that.

Too many people in all countries vote unthinkingly, because they have always voted that way.

Too many politicians use fear, rather than hope, to get votes.

Now is the time to vote for this country's future, not its past.

Now is the time to vote for hope, not for fear.

Peroration

I have tried in this speech to tell you of my hopes, the obstacles we will face together and what I will try to do, with your help.

You have come a long, long way. But we have a lot further to go, and we have to move faster.

Our task will be tough. Success will not come easy. But it can be achieved if we have the courage to work together, and the determination to reform.

For if Bosnia and Herzegovina doesn't reform, you will fail. And I will fail with you.

But if we make the changes that must be made, if we can reform Bosnia and Herzegovina and put her irreversibly on the road to statehood within Europe, then the future we all want can become a reality.

Real jobs. Real justice. A modern country with a new future.

Now I know that, for some, this must feel a long way off. And I am very aware that, in this speech, I have outlined a highly ambitious programme.

But to all those who share this vision, and who believe Bosnia and Herzegovina can once again be a great place to raise your children, I say this:

You're right. This is a beautiful country. It is as rich in talent and potential as any in Europe.

I believe in Bosnia and Herzegovina.

But what really matters is that you believe in yourselves.

Because if you do, I promise you, no matter how long it takes, you will succeed.

Notes

Preface (pp. xi–xiii)

1 Francis Fukuyama, *State-Building: Governance and World Order in the 21st Century*, Cornell University Press, 2005, p. 58.

Introduction (pp. 1–7)

1 Alan Leaman.
2 Arkan's real name was Željko Ražnatović. He was the most infamous of the Serbian warlords, who founded the nationalist paramilitary group the Serbian Voluntary Guard (SDG), set up in 1990. He personally commanded the most feared unit, known as Arkan's Tigers. The Tigers brought systematic terror to Croatia in 1991 and Bosnia from 1992–95. In June 1992, Arkan founded the Party of Serbian Unity in Belgrade, but it did not prosper and his political career was short. In 2000 he was assassinated in Belgrade. He was therefore never tried as a war criminal, despite his indictment by the Hague in 1997.

Chapter 1: Why intervene? (pp. 11–20)

1 Quoted in Michael R. Gordon, 'Bush Would Stop US Peacekeeping in Balkan Fights', *New York Times*, 21 October 2000, p. 1a.
2 George W. Bush, *The National Security Strategy of the United States of America* (Washington: White House, 17 September 2002), pp. 21, 31 and 1 respectively.
3 Boutros Boutros-Ghali, 'An Agenda for Peace: Preventive Diplomacy, Peacemaking, and Peace-keeping', Report of the Secretary General pursuant to the statement adopted by the Summit Meeting of the Security Council on 31 January 1992.
4 Dobbins et al., 'The Beginner's Guide to Nation Building,' Rand Corporation, August 2006.
5 P. Collier, V. L. Elliot, H. Hegre, A. Hoeffler, M. Reynal-Querol and N. Sambanis, *Breaking the Conflict Trap: Civil War and Development Policy*, A World Bank Policy Research Report, Oxford University Press, 2000, p. 1.

6 Academy for Educational Development, American Baptist Church World Relief Office – Hunger note 3 August 2006.

7 Human Security Centre, *Human Security Report 2005*, Oxford University Press, 2005.

8 David Kilcullen quoted in George Packer, 'Knowing the Enemy', *The New Yorker*, 18 December 2006.

9 Office of the Director of National Intelligence, *The National Intelligence Strategy of the United States of America*, p. 8, October 2005.

10 *State Failure Task Force Report: Phase III Findings*, 30 September 2000. The criteria used here are somewhat questionable since they lead the CIA to include states such as Egypt, India and Israel amongst these.

11 Paul Collier and Anke Hoeffler, 'Civil War', Chapter 23 (pp. 711–39) in Todd Sandler and Keith Hartley (eds), *Handbook of Defense Economics, Vol. 2, Defense in a Globalized World*, Elsevier, 2001.

12 Department of Defense Directive 3000.05 which defines peacemaking and stabilisation operations as '*core US military mission . . . [which] . . . shall be given priority comparable to combat operations*'.

Chapter 2: A short history of peacemaking (pp. 21–42)

1 I have referred to this Conference throughout this chapter by its more popular name, as the 'Versailles Conference'. In fact only the treaty with Germany was signed in Versailles. The other treaties were signed in or named after other Paris suburbs or landmarks.

2 See also Robert H. Jackson, *Quasi States: Sovereignty, International Relations and the Third World*, Cambridge, 1990.

3 See Chapter 3 for the precise wording.

4 Declaration on Granting Independence to Colonial Countries and Peoples, General Assembly Resolution 1514 (XV), 14 December 1960.

5 Paul Collier and Anke Hoeffler, *Greed and Grievance in Civil War*, Oxford Economic Papers 56, 2004, 663–595.

6 For more details, see *The Ashdown Diaries*, Vol. I pp. 321–2.

Chapter 3: What is legal? (pp. 43–64)

1 Excerpts from 'The Harvest of Justice is Sown in Peace', Office of Social Development and World Peace, United States Conference of Catholic Bishops, 1993.

2 Vitoria was a Dominican who taught at Salamanca University at the beginning of the sixteenth century, and who was one of the first people to evolve reflection on human rights, faced with the conquest of the Americas. He argued for the rights of the indigenous people, regardless of their religion, and so opposed any notion of a 'holy war'.

3 See also S. Chesterman, *Just War or Just Peace?*, Oxford University Press, 2001.

4 *Ibid.*

5 See Chapter 2 on the UN Assembly Declaration on Colonialism of 1960.

6 Declaration on the Inadmissibility of Intervention in the Domestic Affairs of States and the Protection of their Independence and Sovereignty, General Assembly Resolution 2131 (XX), 21 December 1965.

7 Declaration on Principles of International Law Concerning Friendly Relations and Cooperation among States in Accordance with the Charter of the United Nations, General Assembly Resolution 2625 (XXV), 24 October 1970.

8 Military and Paramilitary Activities in and against Nicaragua (Nicaragua v USA), Merits, ICJ Reports (1986) 14.

9 Academy for Educational Development, American Baptist Church World Relief Office – Hunger note, 3 August 2006.

10 An Agenda for Peace: Preventive diplomacy, peacemaking and peace-keeping', Report of the Secretary General, A/47/277.

11 Kofi Annan, 'Two Concepts of Sovereignty', The Economist, 18 September 1999.

12 French participation ended in 1998.

13 Security Council Resolution 1160 of 31 March 1998, Security Council Resolution 1199 of 23 September 1998 and Security Council Resolution 1203 of 4 October 1998.

14 In the case of Liberia Security Council Resolution 788, which was passed in 1992 after the intervention had taken place, commended 'ECOWAS for its efforts to restore peace, security and stability in Liberia.' In relation to Sierra Leone, Security Council Resolution 1132 (1997) authorised ECOWAS under Chapter VIII to impose an arms embargo.

15 Security Council Resolution 841.

16 Security Council Resolution 940.

17 Burma (1990), Algeria (1991), Nigeria (1993), Niger (1996), Pakistan (1999), Cote D'Ivoire (1999), Fiji (2000), Central African Republic (2003).

18 Gray, C., International Law and the Use of Force, 2nd ed., New York: Oxford University Press, 2004.

19 The Commission's full title is 'The European Commission for Democracy through Law'. It is the Council of Europe's advisory body on constitutional matters and has become an internationally recognised independent legal think-tank. Members are senior academics, particularly in the fields of constitutional or international law, supreme or constitutional court judges or members of national parliaments.

20 Jonathan Freedland, 'No, international law doesn't have to be dumped because of Al Qaeda', The Guardian, 5 April 2006.

21 See for example the 2001 Report of the International Commission on Intervention and State Sovereignty, http://www.iciss.ca/menu-en.asp; the 2004 report of the UN Secretary General's High-level Panel on Threats, Challenges and Change entitled 'A More Secure World, Our Shared Responsibility', www.un.org/secureworld/; and Kofi Annan's response entitled 'In Larger Freedom: Towards Development, Security and Human Rights for All', May 2005, www.un.org/largerfreedom.

22 The Security Council first made reference to the 'Responsibility to Protect' in

Security Council Resolution 1674 on the Protection of Civilians in Armed Conflict which was unanimously adopted on 28 April 2006. It reaffirms the provisions of paragraphs 138 and 139 of the World Summit Outcome Document regarding the responsibility to protect populations from genocide, war crimes, ethnic cleansing and crimes against humanity.

23 Corfu Channel Case, 1949, ICJ Reports 4.

Chapter 4: Stablisation (pp. 67–95)

1 Testimony to the Senate Armed Services Committee, 25 February 2003.

2 Thomas E. Ricks, *Fiasco – The American Military Adventure in Iraq*, pp. 84, & 183.

3 Prof Philip Bobbitt, *Terror and Consent*, Chapter 3.

4 US Department of Defense, Defense Science Bound, 2004 *Summer Study on Transition to and from Hostilities*, December 2004, p. 42. If the goals are less ambitious, 10 soldiers per 1,000 population may be sufficient and, where the international community have been invited in and there is full domestic co-operation, 1 per 1,000 can be adequate. See also Dobbins et al., 'A Beginner's Guide to Nation Building', Rand Corporation.

5 This force was redesignated as Kosovo Force (KFOR) and was quickly boosted to 50,000 to keep the peace in Kosovo.

6 See Toby Dodge, 'Trying to reconstitute Iraq – What Role for Europe?' p. 128.

7 Brady Kiesling, 'Iraq: A Letter of Resignation', *The New York Review*, 10 April 2003.

8 Bob Woodward, *State of Denial*.

9 Retired French Lt Col David Galula in his book *Counterinsurgency warfare: theory and practice*, Praeger, 1964. Quoted in Thomas E. Ricks, *Fiasco – The American Military Adventure in Iraq*, p.266.

10 See Thomas E. Ricks, *Fiasco – The American Military Adventure in Iraq*, pp. 322–4 for a graphic illustration of this.

11 Maj General David Leakey CBE.

12 Other nations with these 'constabulary' forces include Spain and the Netherlands.

13 Dobbins et al,'A Beginner's Guide to Nation Building', Rand Corporation.

14 Richard Caplan, *Neo Trusteeships: a Solution for Precarious Statehood*.

15 For a fuller discussion of the importance of making economic reform a priority, see the joint report by the World Bank and UNDP 'Rebuilding Post-Conflict Societies; Lessons from a Decade of Global Experience', workshop report, New York, 19–21 September 2005.

16 JCS Directive 1067. Quoted in Killick (1997) p. 60 and in 'America's role in Nation Building – from Germany to Iraq', Rand Corporation, p. 17.

17 'America's role in Nation Building – from Germany to Iraq', Rand Corporation, p. 20.

18 Paul Collier and Anke Hoeffler, 'Civil War'. Chapter 23 (pp. 711–39) in

Sandler, Todd and Keith Hartley (eds) *Handbook of Defense Economics, Vol. 2, Defense in a Globalized World*, Amsterdam: Elsevier, 2007.

19 Abraham Maslow, born in the US in 1908. His most famous work was *Hierarchy of Human Needs*, expressing the needs of individuals as a pyramid, first published in 1954.

20 Milton Friedman – right-wing economist.

21 Keith Mines, as quoted in Thomas E. Ricks, *Fiasco – The American Adventure in Iraq*, pp. 165 &181, 2006.

22 Paul Collier and Anke Hoeffler. 2007. 'Civil War', Chapter 23 (pp. 711–39) in Sandler, Todd and Keith Hartley (eds) *Handbook of Defense Economics, Vol. 2, Defense in a Globalized World*, Amsterdam: Elsevier.

23 *Ibid.*

24 George Packer, 'Knowing the Enemy', *The New Yorker* 12 December 2006

25 For an alternative view in support of early elections, see Rory Stewart, 'Occupational Hazards – my time governing Iraq', p. 322.

26 Paul Collier, Anke Hoeffler and Måns Söderbom, 'Post-Conflict Risks,' Centre for the Study of African Economies WPS 2006/12, 2006.

27 Although local elections were held before this date. In Japan, by contrast, national elections took place less than a year after the surrender.

28 See 'Humanitarian and Reconstruction Assistance to Afghanistan 2001–5. A Joint Evaluation from Denmark, Ireland, The Netherlands, Sweden and the United Kingdom.' Published by the Ministry of Foreign Affairs of Denmark, 2005.

29 For a full list of these see Dobbins et al, 'A Beginner's Guide to Nation Building', Rand Corporation, p 111.

30 Paul Collier and Anke Hoeffler, 'Civil War', Chapter 23 (pp. 711–39) in Todd Sandler and Keith Hartley (eds) *Handbook of Defense Economics, Vol. 2, Defense in a Globalized World*, Amsterdam: Elsevier.

31 See Ian King and Whit Mason, *Peace at Any Price*, p. 253.

32 'America's role in nation building', Rand Corporation, p. 14.

33 Keisinger had been in Germany's wartime Ministry of Propaganda.

Chapter 5: State-building (pp. 96–113)

1 See Dobbins et al, 'A Beginners Guide to Nation Building', Rand Corporation.

2 *No Man's Land*, written and directed by Danis Tanovic, 2001. Awarded an Oscar for Best Foreign Film (2002) and a Golden Globe (2001) for Best Foreign Language Film and Best Screenplay award at Cannes Film Festival (2001).

3 Ad hoc war crimes tribunals have been set up after the conflicts in Yugoslavia, Rwanda, East Timor, Sierra Leone and Iraq.

4 There have been in all, some twenty-seven of these established since 1974: in Uganda (1974), Bolivia, Argentina, Uruguay, Zimbabwe, Uganda (1986–95), the Philippines, Nepal, Chile, Chad, Germany (1992–4), El Salvador, Rwanda, Sri Lanka, Haiti, Burundi, South Africa, Ecuador, Guatemala,

Nigeria, Peru, Uruguay, Panama, Yugoslavia, East Timor, Sierra Leone and Ghana – source 'A Beginner's Guide to Nation Building'.
5 Lord Ralf Dahrendorf.
6 Humanitarian and Reconstruction Assistance to Afghanistan 2001–5 – A Joint Evaluation from Denmark, Ireland, The Netherlands, Sweden and the United Kingdom. Published by the Ministry of Foreign Affairs of Denmark, 2005.
7 For an example of this and its effects see Mark Etherington, 'Revolt on the Tigris – The Al Sadr Uprising and the Governing of Iraq', p. 35.
8 The World Bank does a lot of excellent work in this field.

Chapter 6: Right analysis – wrong solution (pp. 117–19)

1 For an excellent account of the post-Vietnam reshaping of the US Army in order to win battles while ignoring the longer wars and the disastrous effects this had on the US plan for Iraq in 2003, see Thomas E. Ricks, *Fiasco – The American Military Adventure in Iraq*, pp. 130–33.
2 Although the S/CRS was established in 2004, it was not formally mandated by the President until more than a year later (see President Bush's National Security Policy Directive 44 of 7 December 2005).
3 Report of the Secretary General's High-Level Panel on Threats, Challenges and Change.

Chapter 7: The seamless garment (pp. 120–148)

1 Georgina Howell, *Daughter of the Desert; the remarkable life of Gertrude Bell*, Macmillan, p. 310.
2 See Appendix B for details.
3 Conrad C. Crane and W. Andrew Terrill, 'Reconstructing Iraq: Insights, Challenges, and Missions for Military Forces in a Post-Conflict Scenario', US Army War College Monograph, February 2003, pp. vi, 1, 32, 42. This paper drew and reflected on the conclusions of an earlier US Army War College seminar on Afghanistan held in August 2002. See Thomas E. Ricks, *Fiasco – The American Military Adventure in Iraq*, pp. 72 & 444.
4 ORHA was established after the failure of the post-war planning unit, known as Joint Task Force IV (JTF-IV), which was charged with the post-war planning and located within the US Military's Central Command.
5 The previous commander of US troops in the Middle East, retired Marine General Anthony Zinni, was later to point out in clear and pungent terms his criticism of this decision, saying, 'Why the hell should the Department of Defense be the organisation in our government that deals with the reconstruction in Iraq? Doesn't make sense', Thomas E. Ricks, *Fiasco – The American Military Adventure in Iraq*, p. 242.
6 'Preparing for War, Stumbling to Peace: US Is Paying the Price for Missteps on Iraq', *Los Angeles Times*, 18 July 2003, p. A1, Mark Fineman, Robin Wright, and Doyle McManus.

7 See also House of Commons Defence Committee's Sixth Report: 'Iraq: An Initial Assessment of Post-Conflict Operations', 24 March 2005, which details similar planning failures by the British government before the Iraq operation.

8 George Packer, 'The Assassin's Gate', Faber and Faber, p. 122.

9 Karen Guttieri and Jessica Piombo, Interim Governments: Institutional Bridges to Peace and Democracy?, forthcoming, USIP Press.

10 'Coalition Forces Land Component Command (CFLCC) OPLAN COBRA II, 13 January 2003.

11 Thomas E. Ricks, Fiasco – The American Military Adventure in Iraq, p. 116.

12 Karl Bildt, Peace Journey, The Struggle For Peace in Bosnia, p. 172–4.

13 The Utility of Force, the Art of War in the Modern World, Rupert Smith, p. 17, 2005.

14 David Kilcullen quoted in George Packer, 'Knowing the Enemy', The New Yorker 18 December 2006.

15 Ashraf Ghani and Clare Lockhart, 'An Agenda for State Building in Twenty-First Century', The Fletcher Forum for World Affairs – Vol. 30:1, p.120 Winter 2006.

16 National Security Research Division, Rand Corporation, Report on Conference Proceedings 'Integrating Instruments of Power and Influence in National Security – starting the dialogues', 21 March 2006, the American Academy for Diplomacy and the American School of International Science.

17 Francis Fukuyama, State-Building: Governance and World Order in the 21st Century, p. 99, Ithaca, New York: Cornell University Press, 2004.

18 From Professor Philip Bobbitt's forthcoming book Terror and Consent.

19 Full membership today is Turkey, Iraq, Iran, Syria, Egypt, Jordan and Saudi Arabia.

20 An association of some fifty-six Islamic states which promotes Muslim solidarity in economic, social and political affairs.

21 Zalmay Khalilzad, 'How to Nation-Build', National Interest, no. 80, 26 – 2005

22 US General Accounting Office, 'Peace Operations', p. 11 and US General Accounting Office, Strategic Plan 2002–2007, p. 37, June 2002.

23 For details see Thomas E. Ricks, Fiasco – The American Military Adventure in Iraq, pp. 208–209.

Chapter 8: Who's in charge? (pp. 149–178)

1 Although it was NATO bombing which was the decisive act in ending the Bosnian war, NATO forces did not enter Bosnia under the NATO flag until 21 December. In the interim period, forces in Bosnia remained technically under the command of UNPROFOR, which was, however, now taken seriously by the combatants, because they understood that the guns and tanks of NATO were on their way.

2 One case where sanctions do appear to have worked was Libya. Some also

claim that in Iraq sanctions had an effect in persuading Saddam Hussein to disarm after the first Gulf War.

3 'What would military security look like through a human security lens?', Oxford Research Group, January 2007.

4 Paul Collier and Anke Hoeffler, 'Civil War', Chapter 23 (pp. 711–39) in Sandler, Todd and Keith Hartley (eds), *Handbook of Defense Economics, Vol. 2, Defense in a Globalised World*. Amsterdam: Elsevier, 2007

5 'A Beginner's Guide to Nation Building', Rand Corporation.

6 Thomas E. Ricks, *Fiasco – The American Military Adventure in Iraq* p.346 Penguin Press, 2006.

7 Report by Tobias Ellwood MP, June 2006.

8 For a graphic account of how damaging this has been in Iraq, read Thomas E. Ricks, *Fiasco – The American Military Adventure in Iraq*, pp. 174–5 and 209–12, Penguin Press, 2006.

9 'Root's Rules – Lessons from America's Colonial Office', Nadia Schadlow, *The American Interest*, Vol. II, No. 3, Winter (January/February) 2007.

10 Report of the panel on United Nations Peace Operation, 21 August 2000, Paras 198–245.

11 See 'A Review of Peace Operations: A Case for Change', King's College London, March 2003.

12 See Ian King and Whit Mason, '*Peace at any Price – How the World Failed Kosovo*', pp. 239 and 249.

13 *The Iraq Study Group Report*, James A. Baker III, and others, Vintage Books, p. 88, New York, December 2006.

14 Report by Tobias Ellwood MP – June 2006.

15 *International Herald Tribune* 2 September 2006.

16 Figures from United Nations Office on Drugs and Crime, quoted by Baroness Shirley Williams, House of Lords, Hansard, 5 December 2006, Column 1084.

17 At the time of writing, the international community is considering a similar 'Board of Principals' structure for the new International Community Representative's Office in Kosovo.

18 *Washington Post* 31 January 2006.

19 The UN is currently in the process of putting together, at the African Union's request, a ten-year capacity building programme for the AU.

20 'Darfur: Civilian Destruction Accelerates, International Failure Keeps Pace' by Eric Reeves, *Sudan Tribune*, 14 December 2006.

21 Richard Caplan, *International Governance of War Torn Territories*, p. 9. This excellent book argues the case for neo-trusteeship in much greater detail than is possible here.

22 UN Charter Article 78: '*The trusteeship system shall not apply to territories which have become Members of the United Nations, relationship among which shall be based on respect for the principle of sovereign equality*'.

23 Richard Caplan, 'Neo trusteeship; a solution for precarious statehood?' .

24 See for example Henry Richardson, *Failed States, Self-Determination and Preventative Diplomacy; Colonialist Nostalgia and Democratic Expectations*

and Ruth Gordon, *Saving Failed States – Sometimes a Neo Colonialist Notion*.

25 See Chapter 9 for more details of the PBC.

Chapter 9: New structures – new thinking (pp. 179–210)

1 Memorandum submitted (to Parliament) by the Department for International Development, with contributions from the Post-Conflict Reconstruction Unit and the Foreign and Commonwealth Office, March 2005.

2 HC Debate 424 C 173–4WS, 16 September 2004.

3 'Mission Not Accomplished: What Went Wrong with Iraqi Reconstruction' Nora Bensahel, Rand Corporation.

4 Will Anderson, 'Wiring up Whitehall: Ensuring Effective Cross-Departmental Activity', *Journal of Security Sector Management*, Vol. 3, No. 3, June 2005.

5 Paul Collier and Anke Hoeffler, *Handbook of Defense Economics*, Chapter 4 'Civil War', Department of Economics, University of Oxford, April 2006.

6 Jim Dobbins, 'NATO's Role in Nation Building', *NATO review*, Summer 2005.

7 See Chapter 3 on the importance of legitimacy for the interveners.

8 See Chapter 8, for more details.

9 Jim Dobbins, 'NATO's Role in Nation Building', *NATO review*, Summer 2005.

10 'Delivering as One' – Report of the Secretary General's High-Level Panel. United Nations, New York, 9 November 2006.

11 The Afghanistan Compact was negotiated between the government of Afghanistan, the United Nations and the international community, and represents a framework for co-operation for the next five years. The agreement affirms the commitment of the government of Afghanistan and the international community to work towards conditions where the Afghan people can live in peace and security under the rule of law, with good governance and human rights protection for all, and can enjoy sustainable economic and social development.

12 For a more detailed discussion of the role of the PBC, see Report on the Wilton Park Conference, 9–10 February 2006, WPS06/2.

13 The OSCE and the EU are already doing this in a European context – but the UN has the capacity to create a worldwide register of experts. In addition, the package of UN reforms agreed in 2005 includes the creation of a new dedicated Mediation Support Unit (MSU), within the DPA which will serve as a central repository and clearing house for lessons learned and best practice. A new UN Peacemaker Website aimed at professionals working in areas relating to conflict prevention and management is also being developed – for more information see *http://www.unpeacemaker.org*.

14 World Bank Working Paper No. 80, 'The German-Serbia Remittance Corridor', May 2006.

15 See also Federal Reserve Bank of Boston Discussion Paper, 'International Remittances: Information for New England Financial Institutions', 2005-1.

16 'Afghanistan and the Future of the Alliance', 068 PC 06 E-,Bert Koenders (The Netherlands) General Raporteur.

17 See also Chapter 4 on 'Tough Love'.

18 Chaillot Paper No. 90, June 2006.

19 Dr Sarah Percy, 'Regulating the Private Security Industry', Adelphi Paper 384, Routledge & IISS, 2006.

20 *Ibid.*

21 Dawn Kopecki, 'When Outsourcing Turns Outrageous: Contractors May Be Saving the Army Money but Fraud Changes the Equation', *Business Week*, 31 July 2006.

22 Steven L. Schooner, 'Contractor Atrocities at Abu Ghraib: Compromised Accountability in a Streamlined, Outsourced Government', *Stanford Law and Policy Review* 16, No. 2 (2005), p. 556 and Dr Sarah Percy, 'Regulating the Private Security Industry', Adelphi Paper 384, Routledge & IISS, 2006.

23 Deborah Avant, *The Market for Force: The Consequences of Privatizing Security* (Cambridge: Cambridge University Press, 2005), p. 234, P.W. Singer, *Corporate Warriors: The Rise and Fall of the Privatized Military Industry* (Ithaca and London: Cornell University Press, 2003), p. 222.

24 Derek Adgey, jailed in 1995 for passing information to 'Mad Dog' Adair's Ulster Freedom Fighters.

25 For a fuller discussion of these issues, including the complexities of regulating this sector, see Dr Sarah Percy, 'Regulating the Private Security Industry', Adelphi Paper 384, Routledge & IISS, 2006.

Conclusion (pp. 211–215)

1 Heidelberg University Centre for the Study of Conflicts annual report, quoted in *Pravda*, 22 May 2006.

Index